EMBROIDERED TEXTILES

SHEILA PAINE

EMBROIDERED TEXTILES

A World Guide to Traditional Patterns

LINE DRAWINGS BY IMOGEN PAINE

Thames & Hudson

with 508 illustrations, 362 in colour

For Denzil, Rosamund, Morwenna and Imogen

p. 1: Bag of Matyó work, Mezőkövesd, Hungary.
p. 2: Woman's blouse front, *choli*, Sind, Pakistan.
p. 3: Cloth, *suzani*, Uzbekistan.
This page: Bedding cover, *saye gosha*, Afghanistan.
Opposite: Woman's shawl, *trokhoat*, Siwa oasis, Egypt.
Overleaf (background): Boy's robe, *kurta*, Lucknow, India.

Special photography by Dudley Moss

First published in the United Kingdom in 1990 as *Embroidered Textiles: Traditional Patterns from Five Continents, with a Worldwide Guide to Identification* by Thames & Hudson Ltd, 181A High Holborn, London WC1V 7QX

thamesandhudson.com

Revised and expanded 2008

Embroidered Textiles: A World Guide to Traditional Patterns © 1990 and 2008 Thames & Hudson Ltd, London

British Library Cataloguing-in-Publication Data
A catalogue record for this book is available from the British Library

ISBN 978-0-500-51394-1

Printed and bound in Singapore by CS Graphics

Embroidery is the embellishment of an existing fabric with accessory threads and sometimes
with other materials. Such decorative elements as fishskin, teeth, bones, feathers, horn,
shells, beetle wings, tassels, beads, coins, buttons, metal and mirror have all at some time
or place been used in this way. Most embroidery, however, is straightforward stitchery.
The designs are freely drawn, or worked by counting threads, and are applied with a needle,
but occasionally with a hook. The thread used is silk, cotton, linen, wool, gold or silver, but
also whatever comes to hand, including sometimes even human hair, moosehair, sinew
and quills. A separate technique exists for metal or other precious threads, for non-pliable
material such as quills, and for narrow decorative trims, usually cords and braids.
These are laid on the fabric and couched down by stitching with another thread,
so that none of the decorative material is hidden underneath the cloth.

CONTENTS

INTRODUCTION: TECHNIQUES AND TRADITIONS

'Lonely people, delicate people, people without occupation, perhaps, beyond shelling peas, have found embroidery a distraction', declared an article written in the 1920s. It reflected the generally accepted view, which still persists, of embroidery as a pastime for idle ladies – a pastime which, though much modern work can be considered creative art, is more usually relegated by popular opinion to the homely level of a sentimental sampler on the wall, a needlepoint cushion on the fireside armchair, or a linen teacosy worked with crinoline ladies.

These familiar embroideries belong to the domestic tradition of most of western Europe and of America, where a few elements remain of the original function of embroidery; but here, in the main, the craft has been transformed by fashion, trade and individual choice. Outside the West, on the other hand, embroidery has remained close to its origins.

ABOVE *Tattooing decorates and transforms the body. The same patterns are transferred to embroidery, as can be seen, for example, on the textiles of the Kuba people of the Democratic Republic of the Congo (see* OPPOSITE ABOVE*).*

LEFT *Woman's dress, aba, Kutch, India. The sexual area was often protected by embroidery, in Europe usually by a decorative apron. The Seyhud of Kutch choose an extremely finely worked five-petalled pendant.*

THE FUNCTION OF EMBROIDERY

The primary function of embroidery was to decorate, to embellish textiles already created to meet man's basic needs, and the purpose of such decoration was rooted in ancient beliefs and superstitions. In primitive societies the mysteries of cosmic creation and the human life-cycle were harnessed by mythology: disease and disaster, the causes of which were not understood, were explained by a mythical otherworld of pagan gods, of the evil eye, of good and bad spirits to be praised or appeased. Man could emulate them or protect himself from them by tattooing his body or decorating his clothing with symbols of their powers. Tattooed patterns of peoples as diverse as the Bulgarians, the Tunisians and the Kuba of the Democratic Republic of the Congo (formerly Zaire) are transferred from the body to costume in the form of embroidery. Marco Polo called tattooing 'flesh embroiderie' and indeed embroidery is much more closely related to tattooing than to weaving, felting or knitting. Both employed symbolism expressed in pattern. Both had magical associations.

ABOVE AND RIGHT *The traditional disposition of embroidery on Romanian blouses recalls the tattooing of a man found in one of the frozen tombs of Siberia at Pazyryk.*

SYMBOLISM IN EMBROIDERY

The shamanistic world of animals and the hunt was one primitive cult at the source of symbolic pattern, as was the earth goddess. Worship of the sun and of trees was also part of the mythology of many pagan societies. The belief in spirits, both evil and benevolent, dwelling in such places as streams and wells, doors and caves, rocks and trees was universal, and in some societies the power of the evil eye is still feared today.

Most patterns, and the selection of many materials, such as red fabrics and blue beads, derive from the superstitions and symbolism of such cults. The linen towels of Russia are not embroidered with designs of local wildlife – the wolves, wild boars and bears of the region – but with the ancient griffins and peacocks of Iranian art, or with human-headed birds from pre-Christian legend; the blouses of Salamanca in Spain do not depict the domestic animals familiar in everyday life, but the hunted beasts with twisted heads found in palaeolithic rock paintings and in the art of the Scythians, steppeland horsemen who rose into eminence in the seventh century BC. In Japan the appliqué work of the ancient Caucasoid Ainu people, which the Chilkat woven blankets of Alaska vividly recall, is strongly symbolic and a potent protection against the evil eye. It bears no relation to the subtle artistry of commercial Japanese silk and goldwork. Chinese embroidery is generally appreciated for its exquisite workmanship and silken delicacy, but it is riddled with symbolism and played a central role in social hierarchy.

ABOVE LEFT *The patterns on the blanket capes of the Chilkat band of Tlingit Native Americans living in Alaska have the same totemic quality as those on the clothing of the Ainu, aboriginal hunters of Japan. The Ainu garments (as* ABOVE*) are of fabric woven from tree fibres, with the patterns appliquéd and embroidered by couching and chain stitch. The Chilkat garments (as* BELOW*) are fingerwoven in goatshair.*

ABOVE *Woman's jacket, Moknine, Tunisia. In the Islamic world the hand of Fatima,* khomsa, *and the fish are considered powerful talismans against the evil eye. Gold plate, tall, with touches of floss silk on red and green velvet is typical of Tunisian work.*

MOTIFS IN EMBROIDERY

Just as pagan festivals were taken over by formal religions and assimilated into their calendar, so pagan symbolism was often similarly absorbed. Anthropomorphic figures, triangles, pomegranates, carnations and tulips; circles, squares, whorls, swastikas, spirals, 8-pointed stars and birds; diamonds, hooks, dots and waves, zigzags and indentations, columns, plants and crosses, hands and fish – all stem originally from primitive symbolism; and in addition, Buddhism, Hinduism, Islam and Christianity imposed their own symbols from more sophisticated concepts. But it is the common fate of patterns over centuries to be simplified and then abstracted and the symbolism lost. The magic power of horned animals is now concealed in a line of hooks, cockscombs become a row of crests and the sun a simple circle.

The embroideress is normally unaware of their origins: she claims they are just the patterns her mother taught her or that she found in her head. Sometimes, indeed, they are. She also gives them names, such as 'wheels' or 'railway lines', but it is important to remember that these are the names of what the patterns resemble, not what they represent.

This ancient repertoire of pattern is not confined only to embroidery but permeates also all decorative arts, in particular carpets, pottery, woodcarving and what is generally termed 'folk art'; and, most of all, jewelry, which played a magic and religious role as well. There is a certain rigidity in patterns deriving from a cult source, as they are traditionally only used in certain places and in a certain way. Once some freedom in design is apparent, the object is already moving towards the individual interpretation that is an element of personalized art.

ABOVE Stylization of pattern was already apparent in the textiles of Pazyryk, dating from about the seventh to the second century BC.

FAR LEFT Woman's headdress, kakoshnik, Russia. Hair, particularly women's, was universally regarded as magical and covered with a headdress at marriage. These were handed down from mother to daughter. Pearls are typical of Russian embroidery and come from the rivers of the north.

BELOW Modern embroidery, by Jacky Russell, based on the rusting hulks of the fishing boats marooned in the dried-up Aral Sea in northern Uzbekistan.

LEFT Detail of a marriage canopy, Saurashtra, Gujarat, India. The lotus is both a Buddhist and a sun symbol. It forms the centre medallion of canopies hung in courtyards at marriages. Other astrological patterns are added, some quilted in blue thread.

SOCIAL INDICATORS OF EMBROIDERY

Pattern was not only rooted in belief, but also in the part it played in people's lives and social traditions. The Western concept of embroidery as an individual decorative art or leisure occupation was entirely absent: the item itself, its pattern and colour, were evolved communally. Embroidery therefore came to serve, amongst other things, as a means of identification. On a woman's dress it indicates to an informed observer the village from which she comes, and the colour and disposition of the patterns announce her status as a young girl, married woman or widow. Conventions of decoration establish place in the hierarchy, as in the Chinese court, where embroidered insignia of animals identify the rank of military courtiers and birds that of civil courtiers.

Special occasions are celebrated with embroidery. At all rites of passage, when people are considered most vulnerable to spirits, embroidery plays a symbolic role. In ancient societies death was the most important; more recently, marriage. In Romania embroideries are hung outside the house of a marriageable girl; in Turkey the fineness of embroidery on the towels a young girl takes to the public baths announces her quality as a prospective daughter-in-law. Dowry and trousseau embroideries are placed on display in most countries as wedding presents are in the West. At childbirth the passage of forty days is marked with protective embroidery for mother and baby, and at death the embroideries worn at marriage serve as a shroud.

BELOW LEFT Man's 'killing shawl', Nagaland, north-eastern India. Headhunting was a deeply symbolic practice to the Naga people, which even the British during the Raj were unable to stamp out. To go on headhunting expeditions the men wore these shawls decorated with moon and anthropomorphic motifs in cowrie shells, with squares of red dog's hair.

BELOW RIGHT Woman's sarong, tapis, Abung people, southern Sumatra. The ceremonial sarongs of the women of southern Sumatra are worn at all rites of passage and are often among the textiles buried with the dead. Embroidery is an unusual technique in the textiles of Indonesia and may have been brought by early Chinese traders. Many of the patterns resemble those on Bronze Age gongs.

ABOVE Married woman's shawl for 'day of the belt', tahzim, El Jem, Tunisia. In North Africa after consummation of the marriage, usually on the seventh day, the ceremony of putting on the belt symbolizes the bride's return to normal life. She wears an enormous woollen shawl, into which the symbolic fish is also woven and which is half henna dyed and half indigo with an embroidered centre panel. This is tied round with a belt in the presence of small boys to ensure she will have sons.

RIGHT Marriage robe, qmajja, Hammamet, Tunisia. Many ritual embroideries are associated with marriage, among which the shift or robe is the most significant, often also serving as a shroud at death. This robe is heavily embroidered with the talismanic fish and hand and various sexual symbols in couched silver thread, areas of tall, sequins and coral on alternated bands of silk damask and brocaded silk ribbons.

THE PLACEMENT OF EMBROIDERY

If some occasions have spiritual and symbolic potency, so also have certain places. Embroideries are hung where primitive peoples believed spirits to dwell, as at sources of light and water. In eastern Europe and Morocco they are draped around mirrors and windows, in Germany and Scandinavia near washbasins and doorways. As the hub of the palaeolithic home was the hearth, guarded by figurines of the earth goddess, so today's hub, too, is hung with embroideries. This is usually a holy corner with precious icon or perhaps a lurid fairground print of Madonna and Child, augmented with painted plates, with diplomas and photographs and with the family TV. Though the cult object may change over the centuries, the role of embroidery does not.

GUIDE TO IDENTIFICATION

OPPOSITE *Small cloth from the Pamir mountain region of Tajikistan, worked in Bokharan couching. Embroidery of Surkhandaria, the southern region of Uzbekistan, is very similar.*

ABOVE *Purse, Pashtun, Ghazni, Afghanistan. Silk chain stitch on cotton and blue bead edgings are typical of the work of Ghazni.*

GUIDE TO IDENTIFICATION

The embroidery of most countries is finite: only certain things are embroidered and only in a certain way. The exception is the modern embroidery of the West, where total freedom of artistic expression allows an embroidery to be identified as the work of a particular person rather than that of a society.

DATING AND PROVENANCE

There is a schism in Western embroidery between the creative work of the individual and the groundswell of commercially designed canvaswork and kits that give pleasure to thousands of people. All these can be dated with reasonable certainty: no one today embroiders the crinoline ladies of the 1930s, nor the cross-sections of green peppers of the 1960s. Western embroidery can thus be assigned to an era but rarely to any particular place. Embroidery that is closely linked to the customs and beliefs of a society, however, can be very precisely located in place and less easily, less appropriately, located in time. Changes introduced by fashion or the availability of new materials, or else determined by various social factors, were normally minimal, though – as a general guideline – over time, patterns become more abstract, decoration more profuse and workmanship less skilled.

REGIONAL CHARACTERISTICS

Basic elements to consider when identifying the embroidery of different regions of the world are: the items that are embroidered; their cut and fabric; and the decorating materials, stitches, motifs and styles, especially when one or more of these is unique. There will always be the maverick impossible to locate, but large groups of embroidery do have easily observed characteristics.

THE FAR EAST

CHINA

Chinese embroidery is fine, delicate and based on silk and symbolism. It can be divided into professional work, mostly of court gowns and accessories, and the work of women at home and of minority groups.

Silk is the essence of Chinese embroidery. Silk fabrics – plain, satin, damask or gauze – are worked with floss or twist silk and with threads of gold wrapped round a silk core. The repertoire of stitches commonly used is small. Satin stitch, with its variant long and short stitch to provide shading, is by far the most frequent. Counted thread techniques, such as brick, petit point and cross stitch, are worked only on gauze fabrics. Meticulous rows of small knots – Pekin knot stitch – often fill motifs, and stem and split stitch are used for details. The motifs can be outlined or space is left between areas of stitchery, a technique known as 'voiding'. Most depict flowers, birds, dragons, figures, phoenixes, butterflies and bats, all of which have symbolic significance: other patterns relate to Chinese mythology, as the attributes of the Eight Taoist Immortals. The embroidery is often done on paper or gauze and then applied to the fabric, as the *slips* of seventeenth-century English work.

The articles embroidered – formal robes and insignia, informal dress, hangings and pictures – were required by court ritual, formalities of costume and demands of trade. Chinese court costume was rigidly controlled and hierarchical: it combined the ancient silk embroidered robe of the indigenous Han Chinese with the close-cut skin coat worn for horse-riding in the steppes by the nomadic warriors who invaded from Manchuria in 1644, conquered China and imposed a statutory costume that distinguished them as rulers.

The so-called dragon robes, *ch'i-fu*, decorated with a depiction of the universe, were worn by every official for all but the most formal occasions. Their cut is distinctive, with a wrapover side-fastening front and slit flared skirt. The sleeves are long and narrow with a mid-length insertion of plain fabric and with horseshoe cuffs. The sleeves of women's informal wear are wide and straight.

A simple dark coat called a *p'u-fu*, worn over the dragon robe, carries a badge of rank at centre back and front. These insignia are normally square, with the front one split in two for the opening: they depict – in a setting of clouds and sea – an animal, mythical or real, for each of the nine degrees of military rank, and a bird for each of the civil ranks.

Embroidered shoes on raised platform soles were part of Manchu women's costume, while the tiny shoes for bound feet were Han Chinese. Upper-class Han women also wore kilt-like skirts embroidered on the panels and in strips between the pleats. Jacket cuffs of particularly fine

embroidery, usually depicting birds and butterflies, or scenes from history and literature, are frequently now sold in the West framed as pictures, as are insignia and skirt panels. Banners for special occasions, exotic theatrical robes, priests' robes and temple hangings were made commercially, or professionally in imperial and monastic workshops. Such embroidered hangings are still to be seen in Chinese temples.

Professional Chinese embroidery was always exported: by the thirteenth century it was used in Europe for church vestments. From 1578 the Portuguese were allowed to trade from Canton, and by the nineteenth century it had become a very important centre for export embroidery of hangings, tablecovers, shawls and firescreens. This work has a more luxuriant, glossy quality than

ABOVE The cut of the Chinese court robe, with its wrapover side fastening and slit skirt, was based on the early skin garments of the nomadic Manchu rulers. The dragon robe has sleeves extended by a panel of plain fabric ending in horsehoof cuffs; the women's informal robes have wide straight sleeves.

OPPOSITE Panel from a woman's kilt. The large flower is in Pekin knot stitch in silk twist and the rest of the embroidery in satin stitch with voiding, worked in floss silks on satin. Wraparound kilts derive from the double apron worn by the nomadic Manchu before they conquered China. They have two embroidered panels front and back and some motifs in a vertical line in each section of the skirt.

ABOVE RIGHT This ancestor portrait of an unknown aristocratic Manchu shows typical woman's court attire of the mid-nineteenth century.

RIGHT Court insignia of couched gold thread with silk on silk fabric, showing the mandarin duck that indicates a seventh-degree civil official. Embroidered badges on the plain coats of Chinese court officials marked their rank by birds for civil and animals for military.

ABOVE *Detail of woman's summer jacket, made with silk thread on silk gauze, using the counted thread technique of petit point and brick stitch; the faces, hair and hands are in satin stitch. The jacket depicts scenes from the opera 'The West Chamber', a boy-meets-girl love story. In this medallion the boy is dreaming of the girl as he writes to her. Narrative scenes are rare in Chinese embroidery.*

traditional Chinese, with full-blown flowers and exotic birds. The shawls flooded the Spanish market where they were eventually copied and known as 'Spanish shawls'.

In contrast to professional work, small accessories, such as purses and cases for fans, or for chopsticks, knives and spectacles worn hanging from a belt, were usually domestic work. For children, collars, bibs, baby carriers and especially hats were made, the hats intended to disguise the child as a flower or animal to scare away the evil spirits that might attack it. The motifs were flowers, animals and figures and the embroideries have a lively charm lacking in professional work. Many were the work of minority ethnic groups, such as the Bai and Miao.

A group apart are the indigo and white embroideries of rural China. These are mainly bed sheets and clothing made of cotton, with symbols, small figures and animals worked in cross stitch and often set in medallions.

BELOW *Hanging of satin stitch in silk twist and floss on silk, Canton. The ordered disposition of Chinese embroidery is absent from articles made for export, which tend to be luxuriant and free-flowing in style, though still with symbolic meaning. In this hanging, phoenixes, symbol of the empress, are perched on boughs surrounded by chrysanthemums, symbol of autumn.*

KOREA

The professional embroidery of Korea, *koong-soo*, is close to Chinese, but the colours are more daring, blocked rather than shaded, with less gold thread and with outlining rather than voiding. Silk damask is a favourite fabric. The designs comprise similar flowers, birds and animals, but chequerboard rocks are also an important motif. Items usually embroidered are screens, wedding coats, small accessories, and rank badges of dark blue or green damask. As coats were side-fastening, the front rank badge is not split in two as the Chinese is.

The amateur embroidery of women, *min-soo*, decorates small covers and wrappers for domestic and ritual use. This bears no relation to the professional tradition of Korea – or for that matter of China or Japan – but has designs of tree and bird spirits emanating from shamanistic beliefs.

BACKGROUND *Wearing a richly embroidered red and blue court dress, the Korean bride is crowned by sorcerers to bring her luck.*

JAPAN

Most Japanese embroidery is lavished on the kimono. It is easily distinguished from the Chinese robe by its cut of straight strips joined vertically to form both the body and the dangling sleeves, which are of varying length. Exquisitely and precisely tied round the waist is a wide sash, an *obi*, also often embroidered. The same perfection of tying and wrapping extends to gift-giving, and small cloths for presents, *fukusa*, were traditionally embroidered.

The classic Japanese home consisted of austere yet aesthetically pleasing areas of space divided by screens. These were usually painted but could be embroidered. Hangings made for the home are of sombre colouring and feature landscapes or gracefully posed men and women.

Work is usually in floss silk satin stitch and gold couching and is normally combined with other types of textile decoration: tie-dye, stencil dye, resist dye, painting, glued gold and silver foil.

It often highlights rather than forms the main pattern. Background fabrics are silks and sometimes crêpe. Indigo is of particular importance.

Japanese embroidery shows a fine sense of space and of balance: a kimono is often treated as an artist's canvas. Trellis, tartan, geometric repeat and linear patterning in subdued colours – brown, grey and plum – are balanced by curving branches of plum blossom and pine, by reeds and grasses, irises and wisteria. A kimono may also be embroidered with a clan symbol, with fans or books in strict repetition, or with a flowing asymmetric landscape of streams, flowers and birds. In spite of such artistry little heed is paid to whether the design meets exactly at the seams. Where patterns have symbolic meaning – cranes and pine for longevity, the Buddhist treasures – such symbolism is subservient to artistic value.

The Ainu of the northern island of Hokkaido wore straight robes of elm or linden fibres, decorated with appliqué and embroidery in couching and chain stitch at hem and cuffs and particularly at the front yoke and centre back. The designs are typically of continuous patterning of spirals and hooks.

Quilting *sashiko* was an important needlework technique in Japan, especially on indigo clothing for peasant workers. The stitches are of white cotton and the background fabric is often of patched recycled pieces.

Today Japan is in the forefront of individual artists using embroidery as a medium of personal expression, as in the West, with *sashiko* popular.

ABOVE *Door curtain in* sashiko *with design of fans and hemp leaves. On the clothing of babies and children the hemp leaf plays a talismanic role.*

RIGHT *Woman dressed for the ceremony of* Miyamairi, *when a baby is purified and blessed at a local shrine (this is at thirty-two days old for a boy and thirty-three for a girl).*

FAR RIGHT *Bride in traditional wedding costume. Kimonos are now often hired for the occasion. Orange silk is a favourite for the lining.*

ABOVE *Japanese girls arranging flowers, showing from front and back the obi that fastens the kimono. There are many types of obi, and designs differ for winter and summer.*

BELOW *Kimono. Birds in satin and long and short stitch are worked in floss silk onto a design already resist dyed into the crêpe fabric with a rice paste. Couched gold flowers and leaves are added. The entire kimono is a landscape of resist-dyed waterfalls, rivers and rushes, with embroidered flowers and birds. This mixture of techniques would not be found in Chinese embroidery.*

ABOVE *The Japanese kimono is constructed of straight strips of fabric embroidered and then seamed together. Sleeve shapes vary from short (kosode) to very long-hanging (furisode), or are large (osode) or wide (hirosode). The garment is held by the wide sash known as the obi.*

INDO-CHINA

The embroidery of the tribal groups that straddle the borders of south-west China, Vietnam, Laos, Thailand and Myanmar exemplifies the immense variety of all tribal and peasant work throughout the world, where costume differs with each group and village, with the age and status of each woman and with the occasion on which garments are worn. In spite of such diversity, however, certain general characteristics of each group within this region can be singled out.

The women are skilled weavers and produce the clothing for all their family, garments, rather than household textiles, being embroidered for everyday and for festive use. The fabric is normally indigo or black cotton, sometimes hemp or ramie, upon which the embroidery is worked principally in reds and pinks, usually in cross stitch. Patterns are geometric – solid diamonds, 'snowflakes', zigzag, interlaced, serrated, grids in squares, swastikas – and also spirals, horns, trees and, especially in appliquéd fabrics, vaguely anthropomorphic

and zoomorphic shapes. The costumes are weighed down with decorative appendages: silver discs and tapered pendants, cowries, Job's tear seeds, red seeds, buttons, tassels, pompoms, strips or squares of red flannel and, on singing shawls for funerals, green beetles' wings.

Costume varies with each tribe but embroidery can usually be seen on jackets, skirts, leggings, shoulder bags, belts, small back collars, back slings for carrying babies and elaborate headdresses. A combination of techniques on one garment, such as stitchery, batik and appliqué, is common. Distinctive, for example, are the full, short, pleated skirts of the Miao or Hmong, combining bands of wax-resist, appliqué and stitchery in cross and satin. The Miao also use tiny triangles of fabric or of satin stitch to decorate their clothing. Jackets are generally made of straight sections, those of the Akha being decorated with rows of small appliquéd triangles in soft colouring, outlined in couching. The straight trousers of the Yao or Mien are worked in Holbein stitch in horizontal bands of intricate geometric patterns.

Westward into Myanmar and the hills of north-eastern India, embroidery on tribal costume is less significant and simple stitchery supplements brocaded pattern. Professional embroideries of Myanmar are heavily sequined padded cloths called *kalaga*, worked mostly in metal threads and depicting mythological figures.

ABOVE *Cloth,* kalaga, *Myanmar. Padded and appliquéd dancing figure with couched metal threads, sequins and beads. Such cloths, often depicting figures from Buddhist mythology, hung in temples or on bullock carts at festivals.*

LEFT *Woman's hood, Akha tribe, Thailand. Appliquéd triangles of cotton fabric edged with couched thread and with satin stitch, fishbone and back stitch patterns, all in alternating colours. Cotton thread, additional white buttons and beads on indigo cotton. Other hill tribes of Thailand embroider in a different style, but predominantly on indigo in cross stitch, mainly in pinks.*

LEFT *Cloth, Myanmar. Bands of strongly linear patterning in chain stitch alternate with applications of red fabric strips.*

BELOW *A Blue Hmong woman with her children wears the typical short, pleated skirt of her tribe. It consists of heavy cotton dyed in indigo with small geometric patterns of batik, insertions of narrow ribbon and a deep band of bright cross-stitch embroidery at the hem.*

BELOW *A Karen woman of northern Thailand weaving on her balcony. Vivid pink features often in weaving and embroidery, though indigo is the defining dye of all tribal clothing of the region.*

BOTTOM *Wearing beautifully embroidered robes, the emperor of ancient Vietnam sits on his throne, flanked on the left by the courtiers responsible for the treasury and public works and on the right by those for justice and education.*

OCEANIA

Fine weaving and the decorative techniques of brocading, batik and ikat, rather than embroidery, characterize the textiles of this vast region. Patterning is geometric, or depicts stylized animals, men at prayer, or spirits and ancestors, also with raised arms, which can sometimes be worked in couched metal thread. Otherwise, additional decoration is usually made with beads, feathers, cowries and other shells.

The disposition of patterning is often in stripes or bands. On the ritual skirts, *tapis*, of Lampung, southern Sumatra, stripes of ikat are alternated with embroidered ship motifs and touches of tinfoil, mica or spangles.

In east Sonde and central Flores, an intricately woven cloth, wrapping a child to be presented to the community, is decorated with bead and shell embroidery, while sarongs from there and Timor have a border of geometrical pattern and ritual figures embroidered in floss silks of neutral colours.

In the Philippines, European-inspired whitework is done on *piña*, a cloth made from the leaf fibres of the pineapple plant. Delicate blouses, usually in this fabric, have deep edgings in openwork embroidery. Clothing from Mindanao is covered in mother-of-pearl discs.

ABOVE *Two musicians of the Bagolos tribe of Mindanao in the Philippines play a duet. Beautifully decorated shirts are worn by all tribes of the island of Mindanao. These were traditionally made of* abaca, *a type of wild banana, but this has since been replaced by bright traded cloth. Decoration is in vivid embroidery and white beads.*

OPPOSITE *Woman's sarong,* tapis, *Kauer people, southern Sumatra. Striped weave with bands of pattern embroidered in couched gold and sequins. Designs varied with the tribe and are of couched metal in fluid shapes, or of ships carrying people and trees in cream, brown and blue silks, alternated with bands of ikat. Small pieces of mica or mirror,* cermuk, *are normally added.*

INDIA

The embroidery tradition of the Indian subcontinent is one of the most richly diverse and masterly in the world. By the sixteenth century Indian quilts embroidered in chain stitch were already being exported to Europe, those from Gujarat depicting flowers, animals and birds, while those from Bengal, intended for the Portuguese market, were pictorial, worked in wild yellow silk. Today, politics and religion have fractured the subcontinent into India, Bangladesh and Pakistan, some areas sharing an embroidery tradition while the work of most is unique.

Indian embroidery, both domestic and professional, is regional. Most domestic work comes from the north-west, from Kutch and Saurashtra in Gujarat, extending into Rajasthan, and is based on caste. This is a region of cut, as opposed to draped, clothing, where the women made skirts, bare-backed blouses and headcloths for themselves, coats and caps for their children, and also bags, quilts, wrapping cloths, small covers for food, animal trappings and hangings for festivities and marriage.

Techniques and styles vary with each caste, though most common is the use of mirror glass, known as *shisha* by the Hindus and *abla* by the Muslims. One stitch usually predominates, the most usual being open chain, though there are variations with each caste, such as satin, interlacing, herringbone and chain. Cotton is the most common fabric for all articles, with cotton appliqué a favoured technique, for it uses up old clothing. Patterning is mainly floral or circular, allying well with mirror work, though the Kanebi farming caste have peacocks, elephants and mangoes as motifs, embroidered in yellow, white, pink and green on red cotton, while the wall friezes of the Kathi landowner caste are pictorial, incorporating animals and figures. The Joghi snakecharmer caste makes quilts

and bags with straight and fly stitch in subtle colours.

The mirror work of the Muslim traders of Kutch is very fine. Dresses of dark blue or red satin are embroidered on the sleeves, over the front bodice and in a star-shaped pendant over the stomach in floral designs of alternating colour. These are worked in minuscule silk buttonhole, interlacing and chain stitch with tiny pieces of mirror.

Satin skirts with peacocks and flower clusters in chain stitch are the professional work of the Mochi caste, who also undertook commissions for temple hangings. They were mentioned by Marco Polo as embroiderers of leather, working with a hook, an *ari*. Another, entirely different, type of embroidery from this region are the long narrow sari edgings like ribbons, with Chinese figures or birds. They are either worked in pastel floss or in a twist thread, with cream predominating, on a black self-spotted silk. Shawls of this fabric were

BELOW *Chain-stitch work of the Kanebi caste of Kutch is in heavy cotton thread of predominantly yellow, white, pink and green on red cotton.*

OPPOSITE LEFT Phulkari, *East Punjab. Back stitch and darning in floss silk on brick red, hand-woven cotton, khaddar. While the phulkaris of West Punjab are covered by geometric patterning, those of East Punjab are worked with figures and animals, often with shisha. Khaddar can also be indigo.*

RIGHT *Chain-stitch work of the professional Mochi is in fine silk thread on silk and is done with an ari hook.*

embroidered all over in the same style in black thread. Known as *chinai* work, these ribbons and shawls originate in Surat, where many Chinese settled.

From the Punjab come the *phulkari* cloths, dowry textiles made to be worn draped around the body and over the head. They are of coarse reddish or indigo cotton embroidered in a long darn stitch worked from the back, mainly in yellow floss silk. This tradition straddles the border between India and Pakistan, the elegant all-over diapered patterning of the Muslim work enlivened only with touches of puce, purple or green, while the *phulkari* from east Punjab picture people, animal motifs and added *shisha*.

Pictorial embroideries from India also include the small white cotton cloths called *rumal* from Chamba in the Himalayan foothills recounting legends and hunting episodes. These professional courtly cloths, mostly from the eighteenth and nineteenth centuries, were used to cover gifts at weddings and festivities. On domestic work Hindu deities are popular motifs, in particular Krishna with the *gopis*, and Ganesh as an auspicious symbol on a door hanging.

In professional work, the skilled weaving of shawls in Kashmir was emulated more cheaply by embroidery.

The same paisley-type patterns of the shawls, *boteh*, were worked on woollen coats in tiny straight isolated stitches. Today woollen shawls are still embroidered but with simpler motifs. Beige shawls worked with beige couched braids also came from Kashmir, and were fashionable in Europe in the 1850s. Shawls from Delhi are of net or wool worked with floral motifs in satin stitch in vivid floss silks.

The whitework of India, known as *chikankari*, made by Muslims, is still an important produce of Lucknow. Clothing and tablelinen are worked in chunky stitchery in patterns of trailing stems and small petals combined with larger flowerheads in fine pulledwork.

Virtually no indigenous embroidery comes from southern India, except for the work of the Toda tribe and the wandering Banjara. Toda women of the Nilgiri hills embroider their draped costume in geometric stripes of red, black and royal blue.

As the Banjara have settled, their embroidery has evolved into the dense stitchery of the south and the more sparse work of central India, though both groups commonly use cowrie shells.

ABOVE *Motif at back neck of coat, Kashmir. Exceptionally fine straight and chain stitch in silk thread on heavy silk. Kashmiri shawls were similarly embroidered, imitating cheaply the woven ones. The curving motif known as* boteh *is a hallmark of Kashmiri work.*

RIGHT *Sari edging of* chinai *work, Surat. Satin stitch in twist silk with floss for faces and hands on silk satin. These can also be worked in floss silk and the fabric can be a fine black silk woven with an allover spot design. Birds are a common motif.*

They embroider mainly bags and belts for men, and also patchwork skirts with waistbands embroidered with solid chevrons and squares in heavy cotton thread.

Commercial goldwork is not localized. Heavy work on velvets or satins was used for elephant trappings and prayer mats, and finer work on silks for saris or tablemats. This usually incorporates some floss silks, purl, spangles or beetles' wing-cases. Patterns are floral or of Mughal inspiration.

In north-eastern India, it is in Orissa that umbrellas, banners and canopies are made for religious processions and marriages, with simple bright flowers and animals appliquéd with white chain stitch, while Bengal is well known for *kanthas*. These are covers, hangings and wraps for precious objects made out of old white saris and quilted in white. Symbolic patterns grouped round a central medallion are embroidered in red and blue running and darning stitch. This work has died out in Bengal but is enjoying a strong revival in Bangladesh.

In the far north-east, the woven body cloths of the Naga were decorated with small squares of red, stitched with dogs' hair using porcupine needles, and circles of cowrie shells. The men's shawls of Manipur are worked in bands of rough stitchery depicting elephants, peacocks and large plant motifs in a limited range of colours, such as beige and cream or yellow and red.

ABOVE *Man's shawl, Manipur. This cloth, mainly with complex animal designs including elephants, was worn by the southern Nagas of Manipur and men in neighbouring Nagaland.*

ABOVE *The Toda of the Nilgiri hills, Tamil Nadu – ethnically different from the Indian – are the only indigenous embroiderers of southern India.*

ABOVE *Rabari woman in the village of Sumerasa working on a tie-dye cloth.*

BELOW *A married woman of the Rabari people stands outside her decorated home in the village of Bhiren Daria, Kutch.*

BELOW *Girls embroidering in Barmer, Rajasthan. The Bishnoi people of the villages of Barmer embroider marriage shawls with stylized goddess figures among their motifs. Like the Jain, they harm no living creatures.*

ABOVE *Young woman from Ludia, Kutch, in her best sari, embroidering triangles, probably to make an amulet. It is very common for girls and women in India to sit on the ground while they work.*

PAKISTAN

The tradition of north-western India – domestic work using *shisha* and clothing of bodice fronts, skirts and shawls – continues into Sind, though hangings and coverings here are distinguished by circles worked in a radiating stitch, usually in shades of red silk. The straight, stiff women's tunics of the Hindu enclave of Thano Bula Khan are densely embroidered in *shisha* and buttonhole stitch in separate sections on both back and front.

Further west, the cotton or silk dresses of the Baluch have very fine embroidery, particularly on the front bodice and on the deep pocket *pudo* running from hem to waist. A feature of their work is exquisite interlacing, usually in yellow. Underarm gussets are frequently in a bright contrasting colour to the dress, a tradition that spreads across north-west India and Central Asia.

A group of Baluch apart are those in Makran, straddling the border into Iran.

BELOW Hanging, Sind. Radiating stitch with ridged edge, floss silk thread on silk. This stitch is typical of northern Sind, as is the use of shades of pink and red.

LEFT AND BELOW Embroidery of southern Pakistan includes the triangular patterns in satin stitch of the Baluch and mirror work from Thano Bula Khan.

The embroidery on their dresses is always in vertical lines in an established sequence and only in red and burgundy as main colours and royal blue, green, black and white as subsidiary.

Embroidery in north Pakistan is defined by the three north/south valleys of Chitral, Swat and the Indus. The non-Muslim Kalash of Chitral use machine embroidery in linear patterning on their dresses and wear headdresses decorated with cowries. The embroidery of Swat and Hazara is of geometric motifs on shifts and household items such as cushions. Its distinctive characteristic is the vivid pink of the silk thread used, with a more varied palette that includes mauve in the southerly area of Swat Hazara. The basic fabric is black cotton and sometimes white.

In the isolated high valleys of Indus Kohistan, the decoration of garments is distinctly amuletic, a plethora of buttons, red seeds, white beads, useless zips and silver gewgaws being added to fine embroidery in red silk on black cotton. Children's helmets have pointed crowns and a triangular shawl at the back, to protect from the bitter winds. Women used to wear a very full-skirted dress *jumlò*, solidly embroidered over bodice and sleeves, that has now been replaced by a short shift. Designs – as on their shawls – show Swati influence in the use of the shocking pink and the technique of voiding, but now also have patterns of plant derivation worked in chain stitch.

LEFT Woman's shift, Swat Hazara. Embroideries of the Hazara region of the Swat valley are delicately patterned and worked in shades of pinks, reds and mauves, whereas those of Swat Kohistan, the higher mountainous region further north, are much cruder and always in a bright Schiaparelli pink.

BELOW LEFT Woman from the village of Sunsar in Makran, a region of southern Pakistan closed to outsiders. Traditional dress is worn every day by both women and girls.

BELOW CENTRE Kalash woman of the Chitral region making the traditional headdress covered in cowrie shells. Girls wear a simpler version with a back pendant to cover their plaited hair.

LEFT Embroidery of the tribal peoples, living in the remote mountain valleys of Indus Kohistan in northern Pakistan, features red stitchery in geometric patterns edged with white beads and with added white buttons.

BELOW RIGHT Man from the remote Palas valley of Indus Kohistan, northern Pakistan, wearing the heavy woollen coat also worn by the shepherds of Nuristan in northern Afghanistan.

CENTRAL ASIA

UZBEKISTAN

The textile traditions of Uzbekistan are urban: ikat, which is rarely embroidered but more often used to line or form part of embroidered clothing; the goldwork of Bukhara; and *suzanis*, the most valued embroideries of Central Asia.

Suzanis are dowry hangings, covers and bedspreads made of strips of bleached cotton or linen, embroidered mainly with floral motifs in shades of pinkish-red silk. The strips are stitched together for the design to be drawn on them and then separated for various women to embroider, so that joining them again always leaves a slight discrepancy in the patterns. *Suzanis* are ascribed to various towns according to their style, though their origin is not always certain. Those of Bukhara style have the field divided

by a lattice of green leaves and stems, enclosing pink flowerheads; those of Nurata have floral *butah*, those of Tashkent large red circles and those of Pskent stylized solar symbols. The principal stitch is couching, *basma*, except on those of Shakhrisabz which are worked in tent stitch, *iroqi*.

Goldwork of Bukhara was made for the court of the Emir – clothing and horse trappings – and is still an active craft today. The main products are hangings and festive clothing.

An exception to urban tradition is the work of the Karakalpak people living in the north around the Aral Sea. Their distinctive garment is the *kyzil kemeshek*, a bridal headdress covering the head

ABOVE *Suzani, Tashkent. This* suzani *has the large red solar disc of those of Tashkent and Pskent, combined with the more floral work of Bukhara.*

LEFT *Though* suzanis *are generally ascribed to specific towns, it is not always possible to be precise. This one has elements of those of Nuristan, with its central medallion and* boteh *motifs in each corner.*

and front bodice in red fulled wool, embroidered mainly in open chain with motifs of horns, S's, hooked and star patterns. A separate part, often in ikat, covers the woman's entire back from hood to hem. Their wedding dresses are of indigo embroidered in dark red cross stitch with patterns symbolizing mothers and daughters. They are extremely rare.

In the south, the embroideries of Surkhandaria and of Tajikistan can resemble each other. Most common are hangings of cross-stitch horn patterns on background sections of black, white, red and yellow.

Throughout Central Asia caps are a very important item of embroidery and variations are numerous. One of the most common is the *tiboteki*, the Uzbek man's

cap of dark blue or green cotton made in four sections and embroidered in white with a curved motif variously called almond or chili.

RIGHT *Brides in a carpet factory, Samarkand, greeting visitors. They modestly raise embroidered cloths to cover their faces.*

BELOW *This* suzani *is of the Bukhara type with flower heads held in a lattice pattern of leaves. The stitch is chain,* yurma, *whereas most are worked in* basma, *Bokharan couching. Here the holding stitch is small, while in Romanian couching it is longer. In both techniques the holding and laid stitches are in the same thread.*

ABOVE LEFT AND RIGHT *Details from the unique marriage hood, kyzil kemeshek, of Karakalpakstan, the region around the dried-out Aral Sea. These headdresses have a bib front attached to a hood, while the back extends to the ankles in a deep V-shape with an embroidered edging.*

The back is usually of ikat and the front of red fulled wool, embroidered with small motifs of hooks, crosses, S's and zigzags. The kyzil kemeshek is made by the bride and worn until the birth of her first child.

RIGHT *Women in Margilan market, Ferghana Valley, selling ikat fabrics.*

KIRGHIZSTAN

The Kirghiz are semi-nomadic herders famed for their felts rather than their embroideries, though they do have embroidered fur coats. Ubiquitous are the men's four-sectional white felt hats with a small linear plant-like motif worked in each section in brown or black. The women's white cotton caps with heavily embroidered plait and ear covers are often also hung with coins. A distinctive feature is their roughly twisted crown which in wear is covered by a voluminous white turban. Until the mid-nineteenth century, wealthy brides would wear a very high conical hat, *cheukuleu*, of velvet and jewels. Women also wore a festive apron-skirt, *beldemtchi*, edged in fur. Neither of these is to be seen today.

BELOW *Of the three men sitting on a wall in Dzalalabad in southern Kirghizstan, the two on the left are wearing the typical cap of the Uzbeks, while the one on the right wears the white felted cap of the Kirghiz.*

OPPOSITE BELOW LEFT *This Kirghiz man in an Uzbek market is wearing the version of the cap that has a black velvet brim. He carries a traditional bag of bright flower motifs embroidered in cross stitch.*

OPPOSITE ABOVE CENTRE *Woman wearing the traditional headdress of southern Kirghizstan. The cap is embroidered around the front and over the ears with one design, while another decorates the plait cover. The plain crown, of rough white cotton, is covered by a large white turban.*

OPPOSITE FAR RIGHT *Man's triangular marriage shawl worn tied round the waist. Flower heads are worked in satin stitch, and the edging is of needleweaving and tassels.*

TURKMENISTAN

The glory of Turkmen embroidery is the *chyrpy* of the Tekke tribe, a densely worked short cloak worn over the head. Most motifs are of stylized horns and tulips in *kesdi* stitch, a type of double chain stitch, with finer work on the neck edging and on the vestigial sleeves. This garment is still worn for marriage, while a plainer version is chosen for market days. Most are of dark blue or green silk, though mature women wore yellow and older women white, both now rare though crude modern copies appear on the market. Older *chyrpys* are embroidered in yellow, red and white silk, but in modern work orange has replaced the yellow, and rosettes have become a popular motif.

The fabric used for most clothing is a stiff silk, *keteni*, in red and white stripe for men's or women's clothing. Vivid pink with its yellow selvedge featured on dress seams is for girls, and greens and mauves for older women. Most clothing has a tablet woven edging, *dzjiyak*, worked directly on the garment. Trouser cuffs are also embroidered.

The Turkmen are very superstitious and much of their clothing, especially that of children, is covered in amulets and black and white striped cording that symbolizes a snake. Children used to wear short unhemmed shifts, small round caps and bibs, *kerlik*. In Soviet times, men wore embroidered ties depicting the Kremlin with its clock.

ABOVE *Tekke Turkmen woman's cloak,* chyrpy. *Interlaced stitch* kesdi, *in twist silk on silk. The main motif is the tulip.*

ABOVE *Woman sitting by the holy site of the Nadjmaddin Kubra mausoleum in Kunya Urgench, northern Turkmenistan. She is dressed in her best for this visit.*

OPPOSITE ABOVE *The women dealers in Ashgabad market sit on the ground with their goods lying on the desert sand. This woman is selling ready-made embroidered dress fronts and behind her is a camel cover for marriage.*

OPPOSITE BELOW *A carpet dealer in Ashgabad market shows her embroidered trouser cuffs and dress front.*

RIGHT *The only colours used in the embroidery of Tekke Turkmen dresses and chyrpys are orange, yellow, red and white, and dealers sell little else. The thread is now rayon instead of silk.*

AFGHANISTAN

The peoples of Afghanistan also live in the surrounding countries and their embroideries resemble those of their neighbours, such as the Turkmen, Uzbek, Tajik and Baluch. An exception are the Hazara, a Mongol race of Shi-ite faith, who live in the central regions and embroider small prayer cloths, *mohr posh*, mainly in satin stitch.

The biggest group are the Pashtun, whose embroidery varies with tribe and region. The women's dresses are either of a straight embroidered bodice joined at the waist to a very full skirt, or a wide, straight shift. Sleeves are long and wide, with underarm gussets of a contrasting fabric. They are often decorated with beaded discs or with *shisha* mirrors. A distinctive fabric is purple silk, produced in Herat.

The most common embroidered item of men's clothing is the shirt from Kandahar. These are usually in white and have a front neck placket embroidered in white counted thread work in small diamond shapes of varied patterning.

Similar ones are made in Herat with elongated motifs.

Innumerable small articles are embroidered: tent hangings, purses, bags for kohl or tobacco, small cloths, covers for bicycle saddles, telephones and guns, and especially caps in a great variety of styles for men and children.

The Lakai Uzbek subgroup embroider mainly yurt decorations in powerful shamanistic motifs worked either in blanket or cross stitch.

The Pashai and Nuristani of the wild north-east wear shifts of crude white cotton, the men's short and embroidered with intricate sections of black linear patterning and a touch of the bright pink floss silk of the Swat valley at the neck, while the women's long shifts have simpler black linear embroidery and a front neck placket of red with small geometric patterns in green and yellow.

ABOVE *Bicycle saddle cover, Ghazni. Couched silver thread,* shisha, *open chain.*

BELOW *Pashai woman, with her daughter. She is wearing the* čar gul, *the nose ornament of a married woman. Though her dress is of extremely poor fabric, it is still finely embroidered.*

ABOVE *Detail of a Lakai Uzbek V-shaped bedding cover,* saye gosha, *used to decorate stacked bedding during the day, embroidered with solar motifs.*

ABOVE *Small Hazara cloth used to cover food.*
The teapot is a symbol of hospitality. Bold flower
heads and buds in strong colours are typical of
Tajik work.

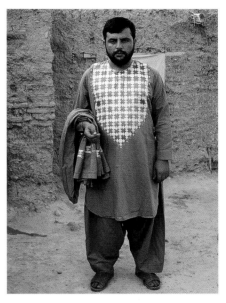

ABOVE *A Mujahedin fighter from Kandahar.*
The men's shirts and shawls are finely
embroidered in varied geometric patterns.
Their counted thread work is extremely difficult
for the women to do on the crude Japanese
polyester available to them.

RIGHT *A Koochi gypsy girl in Jalalabad fetches*
water from a stream to sell. The bodice of her
dress is covered in cross-stitch embroidery.

THE MIDDLE EAST

IRAN

Most embroidery is imitative of the country's superlative carpets, velvets, brocades and printed cottons, with the garden as the major source of inspiration. Most familiar are probably those popular in Europe since the nineteenth century and known as *gilets persans*, a euphemism for women's trouser legs. These consist of solid diagonal bands of flower heads in silk twist mainly in pinks and beiges. They are frequently cut up into bags, cushions and upholstery fragments.

Couched goldwork flowers with fillings of floss silk decorated court cushions, rugs and covers, and goldwork is still popular in the south around Bandar Abbas. Bands of gold plate work decorate women's trouser cuffs and caps.

From Resht in the north come hangings and prayer mats of patchwork, or appliqué of flannel or felt, depicting vases, bouquets of flowers, or trees with birds. Decorative stitchery accentuates all the joins.

Fine whitework cloths displaying a wide variety of techniques used together in one article, each area separated by needleweaving, were also made in Iran.

ABOVE LEFT *A dress from the Bandar Abbas region, southern Iran. It is in very much the same style as the dresses of Bajil in the Tihama coastal area of Yemen in its cut and applied braids of silver plate. It has long been considered old-fashioned and worn only by old women.*

ABOVE RIGHT *A young bride on Qeshm island, off the southern coast of Iran, embroidering a goldwork scarf. She uses the same technique of inserting metal plate into net as the shawls from Azute in Egypt, popular in Europe in the 1920s (see pp. 61 and 200).*

RIGHT *Woman's trouser legs,* nakshe. *Dense cross stitch and petit point in diagonal lines, silk twist on cotton. The embroidery of Persia, like the much more important carpets and brocades, celebrated the garden, though it is one of the few in the Islamic world also to depict figures.*

GULF STATES

Though there are tribal and regional differences in this area, there are overriding common features. In Saudi Arabia these are the frequency of brightly coloured appliqué patches and strips on women's loose dresses, which can be of black twill or a commercial patterned fabric. These patches are combined with linear embroidery of close geometric patterning, often in red and yellow, especially on edges, seams and front neck plackets. Gussets, both side and underarm, are also a feature and some dresses have deep wing sleeves. The addition of white buttons, silver beads, sequins, coins and metal embroidery is common, particularly on face veils and headdresses.

Silver plate work is found in the whole Gulf and Red Sea area, not only in Saudi Arabia but also in Oman, southern Iran, Yemen and with the Rashaida people of Eritrea. Women's dresses have deep cuffs of such work in southern Iran and Oman particularly.

Urban embroidery is mainly goldwork on loose dresses and caps, much of it imported from India. Small caps for men, usually white, are common throughout the Islamic world: many are quilted with superimposed coloured stitchery, or are in eyelet work, such as those from Oman.

ABOVE *Girls from the wadi at Sudd, near Taif, just inland from Mecca. Appliqué is a more frequent technique than embroidery in Saudi Arabia.*

RIGHT *European woman wearing the costume of the Harb tribe in the Hijaz region, close to the northern border of Yemen.*

YEMEN

Yemeni embroidery is found mainly on women's dress, though the belts in which the men wear their curved daggers are decorated with the traditional pattern of a cursive line in gold thread. The garments vary in style from region to region.

In the southern mountains, dresses are embroidered in solid lines in a deep V at the front neck and over almost the entire dress, in white cotton thread with touches of red, green and yellow. Dresses of the coastal plain are of black cotton, cut narrow in Bayt al-Faqih and wide in Bajil, appliquéd in grid patterns in white and silver braid, with areas of silver plate and red and green cotton embroidery.

In Sa'ada in the north, wide wedding dresses of yellow striped Aleppo silk have triangles appliquéd over the breasts and small vertical lines of silver embroidery, culminating in a white button and a tassel. Bright patchwork squares, to protect against evil spirits, are sometimes hidden under the cuff of the deep sleeves or inside the back hem. Around Sana'a in the central highlands, short indigo dresses are decorated with brass sequins, augmented by red and white cotton linear embroidery. Others are covered with complex patterns in chain and running stitch in evenly balanced red, green, yellow and white cotton and silver thread. Many dress patterns are the same as those of the adobe buildings of Yemeni towns and villages. Urban dresses, worn under black shrouds, are often adorned with silver amulets and coins. Trousers embroidered at the cuff with couched silver thread in

ABOVE LEFT AND RIGHT *Women's trouser cuffs. Like the silver jewelry of Yemen, these metalwork cuffs were made by Jewish workers. They are always in the same series of bands of circles and diamond motifs.*

LEFT *Woman's dress, Bayt al-Faqih, Tihama coastal plain. Shaped dress decorated with appliquéd white and silver braid and sections in red and green cotton and silver plate at neck, cuffs and hips. Black cotton fabric with acrylic print insertion. The dresses of nearby Bajil are the same but in a loose, wide cut.*

1

LEFT *The women's straight shifts in black cotton of the Jebel Sabir region, south of Taiz, are entirely covered in lines of white embroidery, with touches of vivid yellow, red, green and blue, differing with each village.*

bands of diamonds and circles were Jewish work.

Hadhramaut in the east, famous for its mud skyscrapers, was an important transit valley for incense. Old dresses are decorated with couched silver thread circles and diamonds over front and back bodice, with neck edgings of silver plate, as in the Tihama. New ones of black velvet are almost covered with a jazzy array of silver and coloured sequins, bright appliqué patches and cowries.

The Jewish population of Sharaf in the north-west, now all resettled in Israel, embroidered indigo dresses with deep zigzag patterning on the front chest. Two symmetric panels are worked each side of the front neck placket, and two asymmetric below, especially over the left pocket. The patterns have a close affinity with the Hausa robes of Nigeria.

LEFT *Motif that appears on each side of the front of a woman's indigo chintz dress of the highlands around Sana'a. The embroidery is linear in threads of yellow, green, red and silver (see also p. 148).*

ABOVE LEFT A woman makes the white cotton and silver braid used on the dresses of Bajil and Bayt al-Faqih in the Tihama coastal plain. The silver threads are imported from India and France. They are also used on the men's belts that hold their daggers. The French DMC threads are more highly esteemed by the men.

ABOVE RIGHT The more recent examples of dresses of the Jebel Sabir only have white linear embroidery on the centre front, rather than all over. This woman is selling such dresses.

LEFT In Jebel Sabir it is the women who cultivate the mild narcotic qat which makes them very wealthy. Here, wearing their finely embroidered dresses, they bring firewood back to the village.

LEFT *The black velvet dress a woman from Jihana, in the highlands near Sana'a, wears for* qat *parties has her dowry silver sewn down the front. She refused to be photographed in it but made her son take her place.*

BELOW LEFT *For everyday trips to the market or to the baths, women in the Sana'a region – here in Rayda – always cover their dress with the same cloth* sitara *originally imported from India but now made in a factory in Sana'a built by the Chinese in 1967.*

BELOW *Small girls in Sa'ada in the north of Yemen wear pixie hoods,* gargush, *of indigo chintz with simple embroidered edges.*

PALESTINE

Palestinian embroidery varies
considerably with each region, but
identifying characteristics include
embroidery disposed in a square front
chest panel – sometimes enclosing a
V-shape – and on the sleeves and around
the skirt hem to varying degrees of depth.
Geometric patterns are worked in rigid
vertical blocks, mainly in cross stitch in
reddish-brown silks, with special
emphasis on the back hem.

Dresses are long shifts with straight
or wing sleeves. Fabrics are mainly
indigo, black, undyed or striped cotton, or
sometimes linen or silk. In the Jerusalem
area a strong yellow and black striped silk,
or of white cotton tamboured with yellow
silk, is used, both fabrics imported from
Syria. In the Gaza area, the chest panel is
a simple V-shape and the indigo fabric
has a purple or green striped selvedge.

The embroidery of Bethlehem is of
circles and flowers of couched threads
enclosing bright floss silks. Touches of
this technique are in evidence on dresses
of other areas, and also chevrons and
patches of appliquéd cottons or striped
silks, usually accentuating edges. These
often help identify Palestinian embroidery.

Headdresses and cushions were also
important embroidered items, cushions
often now made to support aid schemes.

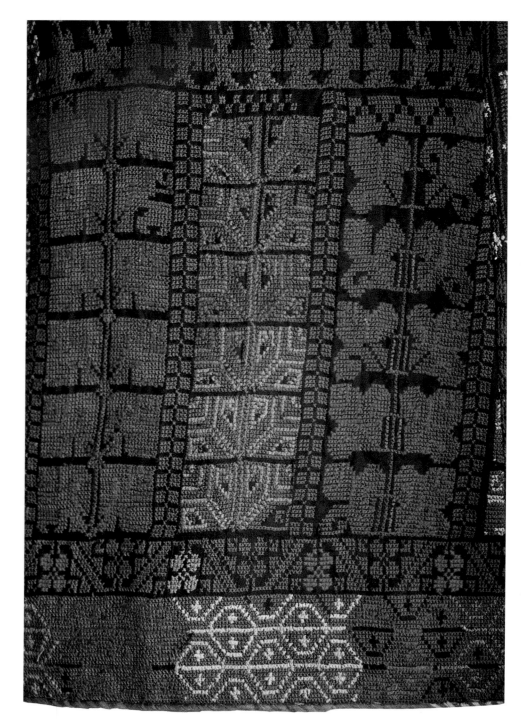

RIGHT *Bedouin dress of Sinai desert, Palestine.
Cross stitch in blue cotton on black cotton fabric.
Skirt embroidery is predominantly blue for
unmarried girls and widows and red for married
women. Unlike Palestinian village embroidery,
Bedouin work often has small birds and
anthropomorphic shapes as part of the pattern.*

LEFT *Women embroidering in the 1920s or earlier, probably in Ramallah. That women embroider together is one factor in the uniformity of the dress style of a particular village.*

ABOVE *On Palestinian dresses the embroidery is usually in a square neck placket and in blocks on the sleeves and skirt.*

FAR LEFT *A Palestinian woman shopping in Syria wears a dress still of a traditional style but no longer attributable to a specific village. The square chest panel remains but the skirt is here embroidered in six vertical bands from hem to waist.*

LEFT *The modern Palestinian dress retains elements of its original decoration but these are now minimal, often due to disruption and poverty caused by war. Fabrics are synthetic and red dominates the colours chosen for embroidery.*

JORDAN

The dresses of northern Jordan and surrounding areas are of black cotton sateen with long, narrow sleeves and V-shaped neck placket. They are decorated with inserts of indigo or white fabric as well as strips of multicoloured satin stitch combined with bands of alternating coloured squares with stitches leaving the pattern in reserve. These are edged with lace-like white triangles.

The festive dresses of as-Salt are extremely dramatic. Of black cotton they are about ten metres long, worn hitched up over a belt under the arms, so that most of the dress is tripled. The sleeves are also immense, and both they and the hem are decorated with inserts of indigo cotton and minimal red stitchery.

BELOW *Dresses of Bedouin girls and women have no regional connections. If they are embroidered, they have merely a front plastron and a braided hem.*

BELOW *Bedouin – wearing simple clothing with minimal embroidery – have long lived in the ruins of Petra, though life is changing with the increase in tourism. Selling tea to tourists is one means of livelihood.*

BELOW *Detail of a sleeve. Typical of costume of the region of northern Jordan, southern Syria and Galilee is the insertion of bands of indigo cotton, and embroidery of triangular patterns in bands of diagonal stitch, mainly in white.*

SYRIA

Embroidery on dresses and coats of northern Syria extends mainly in a V-shape over front and back neck and shoulders like a cape, on the skirt sides in asymmetric form and on the sleeves. In Saraqib this work is of dense red silk cross stitch on black sateen, while in the region of Aleppo and in es-Suchne coats, dresses and skirts are embroidered in diagonal lines of carnations stylized into hexagons, in red, mauve, pink and orange. Around Damascus white or red cotton dresses are embroidered on long sleeves with added wings for dancing and on risers from the hem. These are delicately worked in satin or cross stitch with small flowers and cypress trees, often in pastel colours. Cloths, mirror-hangings and purses were also embroidered in similar styles to clothing.

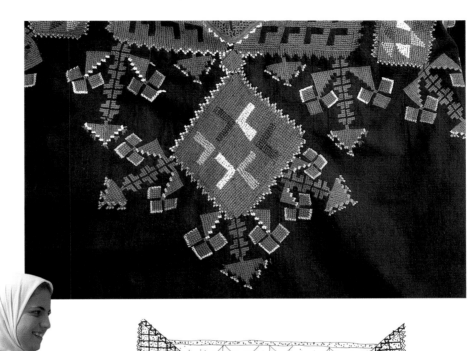

TOP RIGHT AND FAR RIGHT *Woman's dress front, Saraqib. Cotton thread on black cotton sateen. The deep V-shaped embroidery of the front of shifts of this village always finishes in a pendant called 'waterwheels' (see* FAR RIGHT*). The work is done by eye and not counted thread and is consequently never geometrically accurate.*

RIGHT *Heavily embroidered coats are a feature of Syrian, Palestinian and Jordanian costume. The one worn by this woman from Idlib has dense cross-stitch work on the plastron, sleeves and pockets and the vertical lines on the skirt. The coat is edged with tassels and picot work.*

FAR RIGHT AND BELOW RIGHT *The disposition of embroidery on Syrian dresses is in V-shapes at neck and sides of skirt, and on indoor dresses on the centre skirt front and winged sleeves.*

TURKEY

The quality of most Turkish embroidery is extremely fine. The small domestic articles and dress accessories – napkins, towels, wrappers, handkerchiefs and sashes – are made of a white to pale beige slightly crinkly cotton, and their floral motifs, with pink and green as favourite colours combined with goldwork, are worked by women. Outlining is a typical feature of Turkish embroidery and the motifs – of individual flower sprays, or a flowerhead below a serrated curved leaf or hyacinth stem – are normally repeated two, three or four times. Apart from flowers, the symbolic kiosk appears, as also the tents and summer houses along the Bosphorus. Napkins are sometimes worked with fruit, but animals or figures are never found. Decorative edges, usually of alternating colours or small lace flowers, *oya*, worked with a needle or crochet hook, are another distinctive feature.

Turkish embroidery can be divided specifically by technique. On these small domestic pieces stitches are normally reversible, with a few exceptions, such as women's trouser legs which have vertical

RIGHT *Women in Konya. Their almost identical costume shows they are from the same village.*

BELOW *Street scene with pedlar in Diyarbakir, eastern Turkey. Decorative edgings, often of* oya *work, are common on Turkish women's headscarves.*

bands of non-reversible floral embroidery divided by needleweaving. Professional work includes appliqué (mainly for court items) and tamboured chain stitch on silk for hangings and the barbers' aprons in vogue in the eighteenth century. Diagonal darning imitating a twill weave was used in hangings of the sixteenth to eighteenth centuries and straight darning on fine wrapping cloths, headscarves and turban covers of the seventeenth and eighteenth centuries. On embroideries of this period, motifs of artichokes and tulips, of flowers enclosing smaller unworked floral patterns and the symbolic three balls and wavy lines, *çintemani*, are usually in main colours of red and blue.

Goldwork, *dival*, was an important Turkish technique, most commonly worked over card: the thread is couched in whirls and *boteh* on jackets and coats. Velvet dresses for marriage were also worked in gold. Goldwork clothing was made all over the Ottoman empire, and almost all Turkish patterns and techniques are found throughout the countries they subjugated: the same pomegranate design decorates Hungarian leather jackets and Moroccan mirror-cloths.

ABOVE LEFT *Woman in Harran. Wearing a long embroidered dress and plain draped headscarf, she is standing outside one of the linked domed houses unique to that town – a style of architecture that brings cool interiors.*

RIGHT *The flowerhead encircled by a curving leaf, known as the saz motif, is typical of Turkish embroidery and spread throughout the Ottoman empire.*

ABOVE *Napkin border, Turkey. Repeat floral motif in Turkish reversible stitch, similar to stem stitch, in shades of green and pink, combined with metal threads on fine cotton fabric. Outlining, gözeme, is another frequent technique of Turkish embroidery, as is the netted stitch musabak.*

AFRICA
SOUTH OF THE SAHARA

In Islamic West Africa there is a strong tradition of skilled strip weaving, tie-dye, indigo dyeing and – in some areas such as Nigeria, Liberia, Mali and Cameroon – embroidery, especially on men's robes. These are cut extremely wide with no separate sleeves and are embroidered in bold asymmetric patterning of interlacing, spirals, squares, triangles and circles at the neck. Those of the Hausa of Nigeria have distinctive long triangles worked in monochrome cotton thread, mainly in open chain, diagonal satin and eyelet stitch, while those of Mali have patterns on indented risers worked in back stitch. Excessively wide trousers are worn under them, with deep embroidery on the cuffs or curvilinear patterning all over, sometimes in brightly coloured wools.

The Hausa women's straight-cut indigo cotton wraps are worked with zigzag appliqué strips and riser motifs in open chain, predominantly in white and yellow. Women's robes of the Bornu of Nigeria and the Kotoko of Chad are of white cotton lined with indigo and cut with straight, deep sleeves. They have a deep oval of zigzag patterning surrounded by interlacing at the neck, while the rest of the robe is covered with grid patterns, solidly stitched in blanket stitch in floss silk in red, green and yellow. They were worn by female members of the royal court.

The indigo cotton tunics and shawls of the Wodaabe or Boromo people of Niger are embroidered with motifs symbolizing their family history and property. They are worked in eyelet and chain stitch in yellow, red, green and orange. The Fon of Dahomey and the Fante of Ghana work appliqué on ceremonial items such as banners

ABOVE *Man emerging from the high thatched royal palace of Ngaoundéré, Cameroon, after Friday prayers, wearing a strip cloth robe.*

ABOVE *Patchwork banner of military company, Fanti people, Ghana. Cotton fabric joined with run and fell seams, with appliqué and chain-stitch embroidery in cotton. Appliqué is a common African technique, while patchwork was also used for quilted horse armour by the Fulani of northern Cameroon.*

LEFT *Man's robe, West Africa (precise origin not known). Chain stitch and buttonhole in red, pale blue and cream cotton on beige cotton with red felt outlining neck. The snake is attacking a toad. Other motifs include an anthropomorphic figure with raised arms, two more snakes and further linear geometric patterns. The robe is of a very wide cut.*

ABOVE *Courtiers attending their ruler, the Fon of Bafut, in Cameroon, at the annual festival commemorating the female king Mafu, beheaded when she became too powerful. Favoured patterns on the vivid robes are a twisted rope motif and the twinned bells rung to frighten away evil spirits.*

LEFT *Men's trousers, Hausa people, Nigeria. Chain stitch and couching in wool on fabric of joined strips of indigo cotton. The trousers are of extremely wide cut. The anthropomorphic figure is reminiscent of the earth goddess. Hausa women's robes, but not men's, are often embroidered with similar patterns and technique.*

RIGHT *The King of the Yarawa tribe in Nigeria, dancing in honour of a visiting Englishman, wears the traditional 8-knives robe of the Hausa.*

BELOW *Skirt wrap for man or woman, Wodaabe people, Niger. The patterns symbolize such objects as the tribal encampment or aeroplanes, as well as snakes and winding roads.*

where religious, hunting and war scenes are depicted with naïve animals and figures, and often the Union Jack.

In Cameroon, the men's robes are embroidered in a deep curved yoke both front and back and are covered with symbolic motifs, including the double bell, believed to chase away evil spirits.

The Kuba of the Democratic Republic of the Congo make dance skirts, aprons and mats of raffia, decorating them with minimal embroidery in eyelet stitch and small areas of cut and drawn threadwork. The Shoona sub-group work cut-pile raffia in sophisticated maze-like patterns of all-over interconnecting lines and squares in natural beiges and browns.

In East Africa, shifts of the Christian Ethiopians and Eritreans are long and straight and of coarse white cotton, embroidered around neck, cuffs and hem and in a strip down the centre front, ending in a Coptic cross. In contrast, the Muslim women of Harar in Ethiopia wear a very long dress hooked up with a belt below the underarm and doubled over. The top fabric is lined over a deep V at the neck which is reversed for marriage or funerals. Small floral motifs, usually machine-embroidered, define its outline. The Jimma people of Ethiopia wore capes of wool with appliquéd bands of triangles in alternating red and yellow with outlining stitchery and chain-stitch

ABOVE *Woman's dress, Logone Birni, Chad. Satin, chain and blanket stitch in floss silk on cotton. The dress is knee-length, cut wide with side skirt insertions and deep straight short sleeves. The patterns are believed to symbolize myths of the origins of the royal town and the fishing nets that are the source of its wealth.*

RIGHT *Priests of the Ethiopian Christian church prepare for a procession. They are wearing their richest vestments, the central one decorated with a red edging and metal discs forming solar patterns.*

borders of these colours. Silver discs were also applied.

In Sudan, the followers of the Mahdi wore patchwork tunics of red and white with curved motifs embroidered under the arms, at the side pockets and front.

The decorative technique of Southern Africa is beadwork.

ABOVE LEFT *Young Raishada woman of the coastal region of Eritrea near Massawa. This tribe wander over this area and eastern Sudan. Decoration on their clothing is mostly appliquéd fabrics and cording, while their face masks are of heavy silver beads.*

ABOVE RIGHT *Woman in Axum, Ethiopia, spinning outside her home. She wears the traditional robe of the highland women of both Ethiopia and Eritrea. This is in white muslin with a vertical line of vivid wool embroidery down the centre front.*

RIGHT *Woman waiting with her baby for the flimsy reed boat to take her across the Blue Nile just above the falls at Tissasat, Ethiopia. The pattern embroidered on her dress resembles the silver Coptic crosses of the region.*

NORTH AFRICA

EGYPT

Best known of Egyptian embroideries are the appliqué panels copying tomb wall-paintings, still made by men in the Cairo markets, and the net scarves of Azute with geometric patterns of silver plate, which were fashionable in Europe in the 1920s.

Bedouin dresses of the eastern desert are in the Palestinian style of a loose long shift with embroidery mainly on a square front panel and around the skirt hem, but of cruder workmanship than the townswomen's. Motifs can include small stylized figures and birds, but are mainly geometric in form.

In the oases of the western desert, such as Dakhla and Bahariya, black cotton dresses are embroidered in vertical bands down the bodice and front skirt, often with added coins. In the Berber oasis of Siwa, embroidery is of considerable importance. Marriage dresses – white for the third day, black for the seventh – are very wide and embroidered over the front in a sunburst pattern, mainly in orange and with added buttons. White trousers for both dresses have squares of solid chain stitch at the cuffs. Women wear shawls, *trokhoat*, of clear and opaque striped black fabric embroidered with lines of solar motifs

in orange, red and green floss silk. A shawl for special occasions will have fifty-one stripes. Married women never leave the house without an all-enveloping shawl, *milayah*, of blue and white striped cotton embroidered in the same way across the centre back seam and forehead.

LEFT *The positioning and patterns of embroidery on the wing-sleeved dresses of the Bedouin of Sinai emulate those of Palestinian village women* *(see p. 51).*

BELOW *Carpet-makers in the tent-makers' bazaar, Cairo. Awnings, tent linings, cushions and cloths are still made in cotton appliqué, both for the local market and for tourists.*

ABOVE *Appliqué cotton panel based on a tomb painting. Such textiles became popular following the discovery of Tutankhamun's tomb in 1922.*

ABOVE RIGHT *An Egyptian girl wearing an Azute shawl of silver plate on net, over a jewelled turban. Such an opulent costume would probably have been for marriage.*

RIGHT *Cotton dress from Aswan which, though made for the tourist market, is embroidered with many old traditional solar motifs (see also p. 201).*

BELOW LEFT AND RIGHT *Women embroidering in the village of Bashandi in the Egyptian Western Desert. They are copying old dresses to be sold to women in Cairo, who like to wear them for parties.*

TUNISIA

Goldwork on clothing is the principal embroidery of Tunisia, distinguished by the use of flat metal plate worked over thick cotton so that it looks like gilded leather, with touches of bright floss silk. Ottoman-style waistcoats, embroidered in gold cord and sequins and with gold ball buttons, often have epaulettes. Marriage garments include coiffs, shawls, jackets and robes. Shawls for the 'day of the belt', the seventh day of marriage, are immensely long, half of indigo wool and half madder with the centre part from forehead to back hem densely embroidered in goldwork.

Robes are often made of strips of silk ribbon, as those of Hammamet, while jackets are frequently of red and green velvet used together and representing the colours of holy men. Patterns often repeat those of tattoos or are talismanic, the hand of Fatima and the fish being especially popular.

ABOVE *Marriage undershift, Moknine. Tall, silk details and floss silk tassels, on cotton. The black motifs are the same as those tattooed on the woman, while the figures represent the fertility goddess.*

ABOVE *Women at the market in Djerba. Their shawls are made of two loom widths joined by an embroidered seam.*

ABOVE *Woman waiting at the railway station of Gabès. Her skirt has simple linear embroidery and her shawl is held by a silver fibula.*

TOP LEFT AND RIGHT *Young woman from Ksour Essaf. The traditional clothing of the women in the household is kept in a store under the bed, together with the family's supply of grain. The young woman put on the traditional wedding outfit to be photographed but hopes herself to wear a white nylon confection.*

ABOVE *Man in the souk of Kairouan making face flannels of coarse white canvas embroidered in bright wools.*

ALGERIA

Political upheaval has destroyed any embroidery tradition in Algeria, as it has in Libya, though fine cotton curtains, scarves and bonnets were made in Algiers in the seventeenth and eighteenth centuries in the contemporary Turkish style of darning, but with greater stylization. Large floral-derived motifs in red and blue silk are contrasted with small flowers in pastels and some goldwork.

RIGHT *Woman's bonnet, beniqa, Algiers. Eyelet stitch in floss silk, couched metal threads on cotton. The design is Turkish-influenced. These bonnets were worn at the hammam with the lappets wound round the hair as a towel.*

MOROCCO

The indigenous Berbers of Morocco are weavers: refugees from Andalucia brought embroidery to the Moroccan cities where they settled, each of which has its own individual style.

Fez is the most prolific. Cushions and covers of poor quality cotton are worked with monochrome floss silk, usually red though earlier work was sometimes in violet, blue or green, in a stepped running stitch which is reversible. Patterns are disciplined geometric borders enclosing diamond shapes and flanked by small stylized floral risers. An earlier type of Fez embroidery, known as *aleuj*, consisted of small bands of drawn floral motifs worked in soft colours. Henna cloths of Fez were worked in metal plate.

Embroideries of the old pirates' haunt of Salé are in the same stitch as those of Fez but loosely worked, giving a bouclé effect. Newer work is in long-armed cross stitch and not reversible. The embroidery of neighbouring Rabat is drawn and not counted. Curtains of fine white cotton, often tamboured in white, are worked with dense floral motifs in satin stitch in brilliantly coloured floss silks.

In the royal city of Meknès scarves and cloths in fine étamine are edged with massed floral patterning and scattered with small flowers, worked in stepped running stitch in polychrome silks.

Borders in Italian Renaissance style from the small port of Azemmour resemble those of Sicily, Parga in Greece and Avila in Spain. The background is filled with long-armed cross stitch in red, or occasionally blue, floss silk. Motifs of a plant or figure flanked by birds are outlined in black or beige, with small details in the same colour.

Tetouan was settled after the reconquest of Andalucia and embroidered mirror-hangings and cushions were made for display at marriage in the European tradition, not for Arab-style use on the floor. Fine quality cotton, or frequently yellow silk, is worked with drawn floral motifs in soft coloured silks in brick stitch.

The embroidery of nearby Chechaouen, linked to Tetouan by the movement of people, was Hispano-Mauresque in style. Chest covers and hangings of heavy undyed cotton were worked at each end in solid embroidery enclosing a tent-shaped motif. The central area of embroidery was decorated by appliquéd goldwork discs made by Jewish women.

Jewish women were also responsible for the embroidery of the southern oasis of Tafilalet. This was of simple small geometric motifs worked in red, yellow and green on insertions for clothing.

ABOVE *Girl embroidering in a tourist shop in Fez. The girls make mostly tablecloths and mats using the traditional technique and patterns of Fez.*

RIGHT *Old woman of Fez, keeper of the sultan's harem. She wears the extraordinary wide belt of Fez woven in four sections so that it can be turned to complement the gown she is wearing. The ends always feature the motif of the hand of Fatima.*

ABOVE *Cushion cover, Fez. Reversible stepped running stitch* point de trait, *or* Holbein, *in floss silk on cotton. This stitch worked in monochrome – usually red – is characteristic of Fez. Patterns are a triple border of diamond motifs with small floral risers at one edge and large at the other.*

OPPOSITE TOP LEFT AND CENTRE *Women in the market of Tetouan in the traditional costume of the Rif mountains. They wear the* fouta, *a piece of striped material wrapped as a skirt, together with face and head veils and a distinctive straw hat tied with cords and pompoms of navy wool.*

OPPOSITE TOP RIGHT *Indigo dyers in the souk of Marrakech. They work in a narrow alleyway stained with blue. Marrakech has no tradition of embroidery but carpets were made there and in the surrounding area.*

OPPOSITE BELOW *Mirror-hanging, Tetouan. Reversible brick and satin stitch with black outlining, needleweaving at edge. Floss silk on finé cotton. These cloths were hung over a mirror opposite the marital bed for forty days after the wedding.*

SOUTHEAST EUROPE

MAINLAND GREECE

The costume of mainland Greece shows two main influences: Balkan and Ottoman. In the Balkan tradition, layers of clothing are worn, embroidered mainly on the edges and at the neck. Shifts are of linen, indigo cotton or wool with chunky embroidery in geometric patterns principally on hem and cuffs. The linen shifts of Attica have a deep embroidered hem featuring goddess figures. Aprons are an important part of costume in this region but can be woven rather than embroidered. The Ottoman tradition is evident in the goldwork boleros and jackets, which were also worn by men, and in the *bibila* needlelace edgings, as well as in the towels with floral ends.

The nomads of northern Greece, the Sarakatsani, had a distinctive costume of tabard-like garments mainly in black wool, decorated with zigzags of embroidery in gold and silver and with large geometric patterns, repeated on their knitted leggings. Their trapezoidal

aprons of black wool were of great social significance, embroidered with motifs based on magic. A woman would make about twenty-five for her dowry, each to be worn on a specific occasion.

The semi-nomadic Vlachs also wore clothing of black wool, but embroidered with multicoloured floral motifs.

ABOVE *Hem of woman's shift, Attica. Petit point in floss silk on cotton. The shift hems of Attica are distinguished by a top edging of scallops, usually enclosing a fertility goddess motif. Narrow hems were worn by older women and in some villages, while deeper ones were for festive or bridal wear and then usually incorporated gold threads.*

ABOVE *Marriage pillow from Epirus with figure (probably a goddess), birds and animals. The restricted palette of red, blue and green is typical of these embroideries.*

ABOVE *Front of woman's shift, Macedonia/ northern Greece. Cross stitch in wool on linen. Dense geometric patterns, especially based on the* diamond, with hooked edges and worked in wool in dark colours or in red, are typical of much of the Balkans.

LEFT *Sarakatsani bridal couple in the late 1940s, she in traditional costume, he in a European suit. He had probably left home to find work and returned to seek a bride.*

BELOW LEFT *Sarakatsani woman from Attica. Costume of the Sarakatsani people varied with the locality in which they lived or through which they passed. Predominant features are the prevalence of strong pattern and of black and white.*

BELOW RIGHT *Peasant woman in the costume of Attica which is distinguished by arch-shaped risers on the shift hem and jacket cuffs, enclosing a goddess motif.*

THE GREEK ISLANDS

While mainland Greek embroidery, excepting that from the prosperous and mountainous former Turkish province of Epirus, is in the main Balkan tradition, the work from the islands – footholds for all who plied the eastern Mediterranean between Asia, Europe and North Africa – is a hybrid, influenced by both Venice and Turkey. Not all island peoples embroidered, perhaps because of poverty or a very small population, and the tradition of some is much richer than others, especially where they produced their own linen, silk and cotton. Most distinctive of the embroideries are the bed-tents or hangings, the form of which depended on the architecture of the island, while costume was of lesser significance.

The work attributed to Naxos was of bedspreads and wall hangings of red silk, shaded by a change in direction of stitch, in all-over repeat motifs of four leaves forming a circle around a central pattern, with areas in reserve. The bed-tents of Rhodes are in red and green thick floss in long-armed cross stitch, with a variety of motifs on the field, the most common derived from a flower vase and edged with a repeat pattern of slanting leaves. Birds figure at the top of the door opening. The bed-tents of Kos are finer, in pattern darning with more varied pictorial motifs – birds, ships, figures – over the door.

Many embroideries are difficult to ascribe to a precise island. Distinct, however, are the lively pictorial designs of Skyros, mainly of figures and ships, and the marriage processions featuring costumed figures, birds, flowers and animals on the festive hangings and cushions of mainland Epirus. Bedlinen of the Ionian islands is Venetian in style and has confronting birds around a floral motif, or stylized birds and animals often on a drawn threadwork background.

ABOVE *Fragment, Rhodes. Cross stitch in floss silk on cotton. Both the motif, known as* glastra, *vase, and the technique are characteristic of the bed-tents, valances and cushions of Rhodes. A raised chunky effect is achieved by using very thick loosely twisted silk in a slack cross stitch, normally alternating in red and green and with a border of slanting leaves in a yellow shade.*

RIGHT *Cushion cover, Skyros. Double darning in silk on fine linen. Typical figurative motifs of Sporades embroidery, usually attributed to Skyros, include ships, birds, figures and human-headed birds and animals.*

OPPOSITE The pictorial embroideries of Skyros include motifs, half animal or bird, holding branches in their hands, as does the goddess depicted on the great felt of Pazyryk (see p. 133).

A striking feature of Greek island embroidery is that the colour range is limited to red, green and blue with some yellow and beige, the tonal quality varying with the island. Mostly it is soft and muted, but bright and clear in Crete and with added pastel shades in Skyros. Work is either counted thread or freely drawn.

Costume is of varied cut and material. Italian influence is visible in fine drawn threadwork and Turkish in goldwork and in the needleweaving edgings known as *bibila* in Greece and *oya* in Turkey. Such edgings in the islands and in Epirus contrast with tassels and fringes in Balkan tradition in the rest of the mainland. Dresses are made in velvets and silks as frequently as in cottons and linens. One style is that of a simple straight petticoat gathered into a band above the bust: those of Skopelos are black with repeat motifs of green and yellow vases with red flowers, while those of Crete are particularly fine. Polychrome, mainly in Cretan feather stitch, they have a narrow band of repeat pattern in scrolls, topped by a wide frieze of flowing design based on a recurring motif of flower vases linked by patterns of flowers, double-headed eagles and mermaids. They show a strong affinity with the Renaissance designs in Italian pattern books.

A second style is the straight shift, more closely resembling dresses of the mainland. Those of Karpathos are embroidered in solid squares and rectangles over most of the garment, and are worn looped up to form a double skirt, as the dresses of Salt in Jordan and Harar in Ethiopia. This style is depicted in Egyptian tombs.

TOP Two women in the port of Diafani, northern Karpathos, sitting in the street embroidering, wearing the black clothing typical of older peasant women, though their shifts are embroidered.

ABOVE LEFT Woman in the hillside village of Olymbos, Karpathos, working a cloth in modern floral patterns.

ABOVE RIGHT Woman in Olymbos by one of the village fountains. She wears the traditional everyday dress of a heavy white linen shift with floral embroidery on cuffs and neck and whitework at the hem. Over this she has a printed apron and indigo cotton coat.

CYPRUS

Cyprus is known for the whitework of
the village of Lefkara near Nicosia. Mats,
cloths and bags of natural linen are
worked with thick white linen or cotton
threads in alternating squares of
buttonholed pulledwork and satin stitch
8-pointed stars. Articles are usually
finished with a picot edge.

BELOW *Purse of the traditional heavy linen
whitework of Lefkara, combining needleweaving,
pulledwork and satin stitch. Cruder work is still
done on small mats to sell to tourists.*

THE BALKANS

Embroidery is on peasant costume of linen and wool, and on bedlinens for display at marriage, childbirth and death. There is immense diversity from village to village and twentieth-century political boundaries are largely irrelevant.

Linen blouses and shifts, worked in counted thread, are of two types of cut – Dinaric (cut straight with a fold at the shoulder, slit front placket, and straight sleeves with underarm gusset) and Pannonian (having the sleeve and body gathered together into a narrow neckband, with slit front placket and underarm gusset; the sleeves are drawn into a frilled or straight cuff and sometimes have a separate gathered shoulder seam). Purchased white cotton later replaced hard-won home-produced linen, but the cut of the garments, which wasted not a square inch of precious fabric, remained unchanged. Patterns are usually geometric, though Turkish-influenced floral motifs extend as far west as Hungary, and aprons and headscarves are usually decorated with floral designs in silk. Linen shirts for men are mostly worked in drawn threadwork techniques.

Jackets and coats of wool are boldly decorated with freely drawn archaic patterns, and those of sheepskin have floral motifs. Everywhere in the Balkans jackets and coats of Turkish-style goldwork were professionally made.

Wars since the breakup of the former Yugoslavia have highlighted the ethnic complexity of this region. A common theme is that red is the predominant colour and that costume is layered, comprising a shift, apron, bolero, jacket and headscarf, each with uncoordinated embroidery. This is usually geometric patterning in counted thread, often in wool and combined with drawn threadwork. It is worked on the neck placket and hem, often with risers. Shifts can be sleeveless or have wide, loose sleeves which usually have a narrow band of embroidery on the cuffs with a larger motif above. In the mountains of the west, the embroidery is in cross or darning stitch in copper, blue and green wool. Officer collars are common throughout the region.

LEFT *Sleeve from a woman's shift, Galicnik, Macedonia, worked in applied strong wool twist and needleweaving with deep fringing. It was usual throughout eastern Europe for sleeves to be made separately from the shift (see an example of the complete outfit on p. 75).*

ABOVE *Bodice front of a woman's shift from Konavle, near Dubrovnik. The large floss silk pompoms are typical and are often just in yellow.*

LEFT *Detail of men's socks from Bosansko Grahovo, western Bosnia. Strips of fulled wool are embroidered in fine chain stitch.*

Distinctive local styles are the red fringes of Macedonia on chest and sleeves, effective against the evil eye; the dramatic red circles and large stylized flowers of Serbia; the whitework of Bosnia and Herzegovina; in Croatia the hooked crosses of Zadar worked in chain stitch mainly in white, and the square neck plackets of the Dubrovnik area decorated with solid diamond patterns predominantly in red and with large yellow tassels. Further north, patterns are more floral and Pannonian blouses and skirts of white linen or waisted shifts replace straight ones. Whitework features on sleeves and headscarves, though these, or hanging headdresses, are also embroidered with flowers in multicoloured silks or in geometric cross stitch.

Throughout the region knitted socks and gloves embroidered and decorated with beadwork are ubiquitous, as are felted woollen jackets and coats with sun discs, spirals, the tree of life and braidwork. Sheepskin boleros and cloaks herald the embroidery of central Europe, as do the back aprons of northern Croatia.

ABOVE LEFT AND RIGHT *The cut of the linen clothing of eastern Europe is either in straight sections (Dinaric) or gathered into the neck (Pannonian). Both use every scrap of precious linen fabric.*

RIGHT *The finely embroidered white muslin blouse and goldwork bolero of Montenegrin costume is very Turkish in style.*

RIGHT *The heavy linen costume of Macedonia with its dense embroidery on sleeve and hem and its woven apron is in the Balkan tradition. Here the embroidery is combined with sequins, beads, buttons and coins.*

LEFT *Dance troupe from Crna Trava in Serbia. Under Soviet rule, distinctive village costumes were amalgamated into uniform 'national costume'.*

BELOW LEFT *'National costume' was mainly used in folk festivals and for set dances, as this group in Travnik, Bosnia.*

RIGHT *This Serbian bride wears a costume heavily hung with coins and with sober embroidery of geometric patterns in blue and black on the skirt and sleeves. An embroidered scarf hangs on each side of the skirt.*

FAR RIGHT *Woman's costume from Macedonia. Long fringes of twisted red wool are typical of this costume. Embroidery is in the same thread in couched bands alternated with needleweaving.*

ALBANIA

In Albania the layered linen shift, apron, bolero and jacket tradition continues. The Ottoman influence is strong, especially in Kosovo, and delicate muslin blouses, edged in *oya*, are worn with boleros of black or white fulled wool, with vestigial sleeves and decorated with goldwork or braiding. Black braiding is also common on men's trousers.

Christian Orthodox women wore shifts with neck plackets and sleeves that were separate from the garment. Sleeves were flared and densely embroidered and sometimes had an undersleeve with a deep embroidered cuff. The decoration of hems was of less importance.

Three items of embroidered clothing unique to Albania are the *giubbia* and the *japangi*, both from Scutari (now Shkoder), and the *xhubleta*, also from northern Albania. The *giubbia* is a sleeveless indoor coat of dark facecloth, cut with an immensely flared skirt and covered in gold cording. The *japangi* was worn by Catholic women. It is a scarlet cloak, its back yoke and two front sides embroidered with a dove and serpent amid floral motifs, worked in chain stitch and made by men. At widowhood, the embroidered yoke was replaced by black stripes. The *xhubleta* is an archaic skirt of black or white fulled wool, flared into the shape of a bell.

BACKGROUND *The population of southern Albania is mostly Greek from Epirus, though these women wear Albanian costume of their adopted region. Men's shirts had the same wide sleeves but without the whitework edging.*

ABOVE *Woman in Prizren market making the needlelace edgings known as oya in Turkish and bibila in Greek, and found throughout Ottoman lands. They were also sometimes crocheted.*

TOP LEFT AND RIGHT *On market day in Prizren women from the mountain village of Haas come into town wearing their unique aprons. Clamped onto wooden frames, they enable the women to climb steep slopes carrying water, firewood and babies.*

ABOVE LEFT *Women travelling by train to market at Mjede wear their white embroidered linen shifts and trousers with black aprons and headscarves. Almost everywhere market day was an occasion to wear best clothes.*

ABOVE *Shoulder and bodice front panel from a japangi, the cloak of a married Catholic woman of Scutari. When the woman was widowed, the panels were taken out and replaced with black and red strips of fulled wool.*

THERE IS A UNITY in the embroidered costume and household furnishings of peasant Europe in spite of the widest diversity. Each village is unique and then fractured into social status, religious belief, age, wealth. The unifying ethos is the home origin of most materials, with touches of exotic traded goods. The result is normally a white linen shift or blouse, woollen or cotton aprons – often both at front and back – felted or sheepskin overgarments and an ornate headdress.

Throughout the countries that came under Soviet dominance – from the Baltic States westward – the immense diversity of clothing was channelled into 'national costume' for folk dances, a tendency that in some places was already occurring by the late nineteenth century.

BULGARIA

As elsewhere in eastern Europe, embroidery varies with village and ceremony. A basic item is the white shift, normally of linen. This is distinguished by the discreetly patterned embroidery on its hem, front bodice and sleeves each being in a different design and material: a dense geometric counted thread on the sleeve in cotton, for example, may accompany more open stylized plant patterns in wool at the hem. The cut is usually Dinaric with a small officer collar, and with embroidery on the bodice front, shoulder and in a vertical panel on the sleeve. Another style has a side-buttoning neck opening and smocked bodice centre front and back, with straight sleeves embroidered in one band at the hem and another halfway up. Colours are sombre, ranging from soft red to black: stitches are cross or diagonal, with double running for the small hook patterns common around motifs. Hems can be of pulled threadwork, and crochet and *oya* edgings are frequent.

The motifs of Samokov and Stanke Dimitrov are unlike the small geometric patterns found elsewhere: large stylized solar motifs decorate the lower sleeve of shifts and cover the back pendant of headdresses.

Shifts were worn with a double apron or with an overdress and apron. Though the apron was an important item of costume, it was rarely embroidered but more often woven.

Woollen coats with archaic patterning are also to be found, as in northern Greece, but in spite of five hundred years of Ottoman rule, there is little Turkish influence beyond a few goldwork jackets.

Men's clothing was in white or black wool, often with braiding round trouser pockets and with embroidery on the neck opening and lower sleeves of the shirt.

BELOW LEFT *Front of woman's shirt, Sofia. Cross stitch in cotton thread on cotton fabric. Red with black outlining and small hooks is typical of Bulgaria.*

BELOW *Folk costume from the village of Govedartsi, south-east of Sofia. Decorative aprons, heavy metal buckles and embroidery on shifts that differs on hem, sleeves and collar are also typical of Bulgaria.*

ABOVE Woman's shift sleeve from Samokov. Sleeves of the small towns of Samokov and Stanke Dimitrov are embroidered with a solar motif combined with spirals. They also always feature a comb-like pattern: such a pattern on early Paracas textiles (see p. 126) denoted rain.

TOP RIGHT Young mothers from the village of Kamenez, northern Bulgaria. Their front aprons are made of one or two straight lengths of fabric. The back aprons are made of several pieces of fabric that are joined either vertically or horizontally and then pleated or gathered.

ABOVE Woman, also from Govedartsi (see OPPOSITE RIGHT), wearing a costume she made herself. It includes the soukman, a rough oval-necked, short-sleeved pinafore of home-spun, handwoven wool with simple white cross-stitch embroidery round the neck and hem.

ROMANIA

In Romania, and in Moldavia, it is still possible in the early twenty-first century to see both men and women attending a village church on a Sunday dressed in their local traditional dress, whereas in many countries of eastern Europe all that remains is the hybrid costume of the folk festival.

Characteristic of Romanian embroidery is a fine sense of balance: a full-sleeved richly embroidered blouse is worn with a straight dark woven skirt and apron, areas of dense stitchery alternate with fine open linear patterning, dark colours with light, cross stitch in silk with chain stitch in metal, depending on the region.

Patterns everywhere are geometric or occasionally stylized floral, and the colouring restrained, frequently black. Black is chosen particularly by the people of Saxon origin living around Sibiu.

From the northern region of Bukovina comes the Romanian blouse of Pannonian cut in crinkly white fabric – originally homegrown, handspun linen, but from the nineteenth century cotton – with its distinctive sleeves. The disposition of the embroidery is particular: the most solid work is over the shoulder, the bottom part of the sleeve is lightly embroidered in diagonal or vertical lines of isolated motifs and the two areas are separated by a narrow contrasting band usually of drawn threadwork or pale quilting. Cuffs are narrow.

Sleeves in other regions can have a simple vertical band of embroidery and a flared decorative cuff, often incorporating crochet, or, as in Hunedoara, they will have a dense band of red cross-stitch embroidery covering most of the sleeve. Others, as in the region of Huedin, are flared below an embroidered upper arm band.

ABOVE *Old woman from Bukovina. Her blouse has the typical sleeves, with three sections of embroidery:* altita *at the shoulder, then the horizontal band called* incret, *and below that the diagonal lines of pattern known as* râuri.

LEFT *A group of Romanian women from different villages in festive dress. The decoration on their aprons is woven, while woollen coats and blouses are embroidered, with emphasis on the sleeve.*

OPPOSITE *Old man from the Reterat region on the river Jiu, southern Romania. He wears an embroidered sheepskin jerkin. Throughout the Carpathian region embroidered sheepskin jerkins, boleros and jackets were an important item of men's and women's clothing, and were professionally made.*

Aprons are mainly of wool, which is embroidered in horizontal bands of floral motifs, those of Nasaud being particularly long and narrow. Back and front aprons are common, as also in Slovakia. In Banat and Wallachia, metal threadwork is common on both apron and shift. It is often the apron that identifies the village the costume comes from.

Headgear can be an embroidered cap or a fine muslin scarf worked in white or gold thread and of Ottoman inspiration.

Whitework is mostly on men's shirts, though an unusual pleated technique is used on women's shifts at shoulder and neck in the Maramures village of Budesti.

Embroidery is different in the western region of Transylvania with its Magyar population, resembling the style of Hungary. Here embroidery is mostly red on white with motifs of tulips or rosettes, and including whitework. Unusual are the men's shoulder bags of Oaş, worked in cross-stitch flowers in wool, with a vivid multicoloured pompom edging.

Men's trousers, as in Poland, are decorated around the pockets by appliquéd cording.

Outer garments for both men and women are professionally embroidered by men. Boleros, jerkins, jackets and coats are worked with exuberant floral designs on sheepskin or fulled wool. It is still possible to see wool being fulled, as in pre-Industrial Revolution western Europe, by being hammered in a fast-flowing stream.

Towels embroidered in red, principally with goddess motifs, the tree of life and birds, are hung around windows, wall display plates and over icons both in home and church. Cushions to be displayed and pillow ends are more often woven than embroidered and looms are still to be seen in many homes.

LEFT *The Romanian girl on the right wears the typical costume of Bukovina with its sleeves embroidered in three distinct sections.*

BELOW LEFT *Woman in Magyar dress in the village of Sincraiu, in the region of Romania that was formerly part of Hungary. Here Magyar traditions have survived longer than in Hungary itself.*

BELOW *A woman from Transylvania wears a typical richly embroidered sheepskin coat of the Carpathian region.*

LEFT People leaving church in the village of
Budesti in Maramures. The men in the
background are wearing the small straw hats
typical of the village, while the women wear the
dark headscarves suitable for special days.

BELOW LEFT Man attending church in the village
of Gaura Râului in Transylvania. Men usually
abandon traditional costume before women
do, as they leave their villages for seasonal
work or military service, but in the remote
villages of Romania both men and women are still
wearing it on Sundays at the beginning of the
twenty-first century.

BELOW Woman in winter clothing in the village
of Budesti. At the beginning of the twenty-first
century she is wearing opinci, the ancient Dacian
shoes made of a rectangular piece of pig or cow
skin, together with obiele, the strips of thick white
wool wrapped round the lower leg.

UKRAINE

The embroidery of Ukraine is concentrated on the full gathered sleeves of women's shifts of linen or hemp and is predominantly in black or red. The two colours are combined in the costume of the Kiev area, while in other areas each is used alone. Black can also be worked with yellow. The embroidery, principally in cross stitch, is almost always combined with intricate drawn threadwork. Minor embroidery on hem, officer collar and front neck will relate to that on the sleeves. Patterns are symbolic, usually representing blood, the sun and fertility: the berry of the guelder rose, the poppy, rose, hop, oak leaf and strawberry.

Floral, multicoloured work in wool is found in the Lviv area, particularly on men's shirts, and also on felted coats in the Carpathian region.

Ritual towels, *rushnyk*, are of major importance in Ukrainian life. Their embroidery is completely different, depicting goddess figures, flowers or birds, and is predominantly red. As in other parts of eastern Europe, these towels are hung around plates and windows, but also wrapped around the body of a person in a position of rite, such as a bridegroom or a shaman. Still today, as in Russia, a guest will be greeted with bread and salt proferred on a *rushnyk*.

TOP LEFT *Hutsul woman from Kosmach, a village in the Carpathians. Her blouse shows Romanian influence from the nearby region of Bukovina. The apron is a ubiquitous item of eastern European dress.*

TOP RIGHT *A poet from the small town of Kolymiya in the Carpathians. Under his winter coat he wears a traditional embroidered linen shirt.*

RIGHT *While brightly printed and woven fabrics are typical of much of Ukrainian costume, the blouse sleeves remain the most important embroidered part.*

ABOVE *Detail of a rushnyk, the ritual cloths used at all rites of passage, in religious ceremonies and also to greet strangers, when bread and salt are presented to them on such a cloth. The same custom exists in other countries, such as Russia and Albania.*

RIGHT *Oil painting of Ukrainian women land workers by S. M. Prokhorov, 1922. As in most Ukrainian costume, the bright floral embroidery is mainly on the sleeves, while the hem has delicate needlework.*

OPPOSITE *Bright red isolated flowers, or even strawberries, feature particularly on the sleeves of shifts from Kiev.*

RUSSIA

Russia is one of the places where the clash of the two traditions of embroidery, cited at the beginning of this book, occurs. There was a ruling aristocratic elite, directed under Peter the Great towards western Europe, as well as established ecclesiastical workshops of the Orthodox church, while the local peasantry, mainly serfs, retained their traditions rooted in archaic pattern and in the amuletic role of embroidery. This dichotomy has never been better expressed than by James Laver: 'For the greater part of human history, if you stayed where you were, your clothes never altered. But if you went into the next village, everything was different. This was to be subject to the tyranny of Place. But the whole meaning of the Renaissance, the whole meaning of Modernity, the whole meaning of Fashion, is that we have substituted for the tyranny of Place, the tyranny of Time.'

This dichotomy filters through to western Europe, the tyranny of Place becoming weaker ever westward, so that in Slovakia the tradition of Place dominates, whereas by the Czech Republic and the old Hapsburg empire it has diminished, occurring then in Germany, Austria, Italy, France, Spain and Portugal in a few pockets and in England not at all.

In Russia from the time of Peter the Great professional workshops were established following the same styles as the West. For example, the men's silk floral waistcoats fashionable in England and France in the eighteenth century were also made in Russia. These workshops continued the early tradition of

RIGHT *Marriage handkerchief, Russia. Gold thread on fine linen. Handkerchiefs were traditionally embroidered in most of northern and eastern Europe by the bride, to give to special wedding guests.*

ecclesiastical embroidery, showing Byzantine influence and distinguished by the ubiquitous use of the seed pearls found in the rivers of northern Russia. Pearls and goldwork also adorned the clothing of the aristocracy and merchant classes.

Particular to Russian costume is the *sarafan*, a pinafore on narrow shoulder straps over which a short flared bolero was worn. The blouse underneath was of white linen with drawn threadwork and bands of red brocading and bobbin lace. The headdresses worn with this, *kokoshnik*, varied with each region but were mostly decorated with goldwork and seed pearls.

As everywhere in eastern Europe peasant clothing identified the place the woman came from. For those from the north and the Volga bend, such as the

OPPOSITE TOP LEFT *Woman in the St Petersburg region, spinning. The embroidered aprons of Russia are often in horizontal bands and the embroidery is almost always red.*

OPPOSITE TOP RIGHT *The headdress,* kokoshnik, *worn by merchants' wives and wealthier peasant women of northern Russia varied in shape and style with each village. Pearls that came from the local rivers were commonly used to decorate both* kokoshnik *and also ecclesiastical embroideries.*

ABOVE RIGHT *Detail of a bed valance. Lively pictorial scenes of whitework on a drawn threadwork background were a feature of Russian embroidery of the eighteenth and nineteenth centuries.*

RIGHT *Group of women in festive costume in the village of Podgornoye Konakovo, Temnikov district. The uniformity of the costume of one village and its role in identification is clear.*

Mari and Chuvash, embroidery was predominantly red with heavy cross-stitch embroidery on the sleeves and hem, and in vertical panels down the front of the dress, as well as inserts of red calico. The fabric was white linen and embroidery was commonly combined with drawn threadwork and bobbin lace incorporating an added thread of colour. Aprons were worked in the same technique.

In Siberia, ceremonial dresses of fishskin were decorated with protective motifs of butterflies, bats, dragon scales and bears' heads, outlined by small stitches. Clothing was also embroidered in moose and reindeer hair, as it was in North America.

In the south of Russia, multicoloured chain stitch was more common, especially used on towels and bedlinen. These everywhere had a pulled threadwork border forming a squared grid, over-embroidered with motifs in red or multicoloured thread. These depicted contemporary figures, goddesses, horse-riders, stylized peacocks, the double eagle, hunting scenes, buildings, the tree of life, or the mythological bird with a human face, Sirine.

Such towels, as in Ukraine, were hung at crossroads, from birch trees and in the home around icons, mirrors, plates and windows, and also in the 'holy corner' of the room.

OPPOSITE ABOVE *The coin headdresses of Chuvash women are of ancient origin and are also found among Finno-Ugric peoples. The Chuvash are a Bulgar people living among Finno-Ugric peoples at the bend of the Volga.*

OPPOSITE BELOW *Chuvash people in modern costume greeting visitors with bread and salt. Strong, isolated motifs in red are typical of their costume.*

BACKGROUND *Hunter from the Khabarovsk region, south-east Siberia. The materials used for clothing in Siberia differed with the people's trade — reindeer herding, fishing, hunting — and so were fur, skin, sinew and also wool. Mosaic and appliquéd patterns were embellished by embroidery.*

RIGHT *The loose pinafore dress, sarafan, of Russia is not always embroidered but can be of heavy brocade. The white filet work on one of the aprons resembles that of the bed valances (see p. 87).*

CAUCASUS

This region is ethnically diverse, but has much shared tradition. Embroidery is mainly in goldwork or as simple cross-stitch patterns edging costume, such as the neck and trouser cuffs of both men's and women's costume in Armenia. There is also Turkish-influenced work such as floral borders of reversible coloured pulledwork on towels.

Armenian lace is particularly skilled and crocheted or needlewoven floral edges were made, as the Turkish *oya*, while a

special feature of embroidery was the *marash* stitch. This four-stage interlacing stitch was introduced by the Armenians into Sind and Baluchistan, in southern Pakistan, where it is known as *chenuk*.

The gem of Caucasian embroidery is the work of the Kaitag, a small multi-ethnic group of Daghestan. These are ritual cloths used to cover the head of a baby's cradle, or to wrap wedding gifts or as cushions to be used in mourning ceremonies. They are worked in multi-

coloured silk on a cotton ground, mainly in laid stitch held by straight lines of small couching stitches, giving a flat surface. Some details and outlining are in other stitches, such as chevron or stem. The designs are an extraordinary medley of archaic symbols and patterns from many sources – amuletic, zoomorphic, solar, religious, mythical. Executed with a strong freedom of movement, they are among the greatest works of art in embroidery.

RIGHT *A pattern of dragons and* simurgh, *a mythological Persian bird, on a silk embroidered cloth made by the Kaitag people of Daghestan.*

OPPOSITE *Women of the Kumyk ethnic group – one of the many in Daghestan – working in a local textile workshop of the Soviet period. Felt mosaics with curly vegetal patterning, not unlike those of Kirghizstan, are still made, as are very long tapestry carpets,* dums *and* davaghins. *Natural dyes are being reintroduced.*

THE BALTIC STATES

A DOMINANT DECORATIVE ELEMENT of the costume of the Baltic States is the use of striped and tartan textiles, particularly for aprons and shawls.

BELOW *Girl from Piekarski Lowiczanka, a village in the Warsaw region. The only embroidery on her costume is the red floral decoration on her sleeves. The striped woollen apron is typical of Polish costume.*

RIGHT *Bridal couple from the south of Poland. Both the man's and woman's costume are decorated with simple red and blue cross stitch.*

POLAND

As in neighbouring countries, the embroidered costume of Poland changes with each region and village as well as with status and occasion. Distinctive is the frequent combination of bright natural flower motifs with whitework, usually broderie anglaise but also embroidery on net and Dresden work. Many of the materials were purchased rather than being made at home.

Whitework was used on blouses, bonnets, aprons and boleros, though aprons were also of striped wool. Skirts were usually floral prints, as were shawls, while laced bodices were beaded. Goldwork bonnets of Lower Silesia, neighbouring Bohemia, were professionally made with sequins, spangles and gold cord. Floral embroidered sheepskin jackets with leather trimmings were worn by both men and women.

While women's clothing was more modestly embroidered than in, say, Slovakia, men's was more ornate. Style was influenced by the Austrian military uniforms brought back to Polish villages, and a particular feature of the clothing of Polish mountain men were the trousers of white wool or linen deeply embroidered round the front slit pockets in red, green and black. The patterns of this *parzenice* embroidery depended on the region but were mainly symbolized horns or heart shapes, usually worked by the tailors' sons on the finished garment. Men also wore embroidered white shirts and, for marriage, short white felt coats worked with flowers on the front bodice, hem and cuffs.

Influence from the aristocracy, as well as from urban life and technical progress, meant that much clothing was as in western Europe. Peasant styles had disappeared by the end of the nineteenth century in northern Poland, but survived longer elsewhere, though often only as costume for dance groups. In a few places, such as the Tatra mountains, traditional embroidered clothing is still worn in the early twenty-first century.

ABOVE *A local band plays at a mountain festival. The embroidery round their trouser pockets and the tasselled braiding down the sides are usually in black.*

LEFT *Girl from Lowicz, near Warsaw, whose costume incorporates the skirt and typical apron in vertically striped wool, and brocaded silk ribbons.*

LITHUANIA

Though the terrain of dense forests and peat swamps isolated many villages and thus led to local differences, most embroidery of Lithuania follows that of the peasant work of much of Europe. Whitework decorates linen shirts, both for men and women, and headshawls. Red embroidery of stylized floral and simple isolated geometric motifs is worked in Lithuania Minor, a part of east Prussia free from Russian control. In the rest of Lithuania, embroidery is often merely a copy of the much more important textile technique of brocaded weaving.

As elsewhere in eastern Europe, 'national costume' was an invention based on the earlier, more diverse, peasant costume and functioned in the realm of political statement and folk dancing.

RIGHT *As in the entire Baltic region, Lithuanian costume combines coloured woollen outer garments with finely embroidered whitework blouses and shifts.*

LATVIA

The most important textiles of Latvia were woven belts and knitted mittens, both playing a symbolic as well as a practical role, and the overriding textile technique was weaving. Striped and tartan wool was used for aprons, shawls and most men's clothing; ribbons were the most common decorative element.

Embroidery was on white linen shirts, both men's and women's, on cuffs, officer collars and on separate shoulder pieces. The style was chunky drawn threadwork, often combined with some needleweaving and a picot edge.

Distinctive were the women's white woollen mantles held at the chest by a circular pin brooch. These were embroidered in a wide band along the edges in pattern darning – where the darning stitches follow the weave of the cloth – in green and yellow with a soft red and blue. The old motifs were geometric with the usual symbolism: solar patterns and the tree of life, for example. The zigzag pattern in Latvia was, like the herringbone stitch in Germany, known as the 'witch's pattern', while the triangle represented a gable and was thus a symbol of home.

Women's caps were embroidered, mainly with urban-influenced floral patterns, while girls' headbands were beaded, with white tubular beads predominating. Ribbons hanging from the head were embroidered at the ends with simple natural flowers or traditional solar motifs.

ABOVE *The traditional festive dress of Latvian women includes the distinctive coronet headdress, not unlike the Russian* kokoshnik, *and heavy silver breast buckle or fibula.*

LEFT *Drawing of a woman from Kuldiga, 1895. She is wearing the typical white mantle of Latvian women, edged with geometric embroidery and held by a golden fibula.*

SCANDINAVIA

INSCRIPTIONS such as 'M K ANNO 1680' and 'B J 1756' on Swedish cushions betray the Western influence on Scandinavian embroidery, and thus a motivation that is entirely different from embroidery conforming to social customs and beliefs. It is personal and in the fashion of its time. Pattern books from Italy and Germany were disseminated from the seventeenth century throughout Scandinavia, as in most of Europe. Festive linen – bedcovers, pillowcases, hangings, towels, shirts, aprons, scarves – is embroidered with mainly pattern-book motifs in drawn threadwork and red cross stitch. Aprons are also very often of striped wool.

Localized traditional embroidery is mainly in wool. Bed-hangings, wall-hangings, cushions for the hard wooden benches of peasant homes, and cushions also for sleighs, are roughly worked in shaded wools in long satin stitch; in Sweden sometimes these have added French knots. Motifs depict flower sprays, tulips, roses, carnations, pomegranates and 8-pointed stars with small birds, horses, deer and figures, usually arranged around a central motif and closely resembling the decoration on carved and painted peasant furniture. In Norway such floral embroidery can be seen on headdresses, skirts and bodices, where the flowers are mainly depicted without stems, very much in Hungarian style. In Iceland they are worked in split stitch and decorate the hem of festive dresses of black wool, and also purses hung from belts.

Iceland had a magnificent medieval ecclesiastical tradition of narrative embroidery of animals, saints and scenes enclosed in roundels. Techniques were laid and couched work in wool, and straight and pattern darning.

Pattern darning was an old technique also used on the coffin covers of Telemark in Norway. Hardanger is a Norwegian whitework where blocks of satin stitch are worked before the threads are cut. Appliqué is another technique, and is used on pockets to hang from a belt, and on cushions in Sweden: along with tin thread embroidery, it is a technique also used by the Lapps. They edge their bright blue wool costume in red with touches of white, yellow and green.

In Finland, women's costume in Karelia comprised a white linen shift densely embroidered with hooked motifs in red and black. The summer apron was of whitework on linen or cotton in alternating strips of embroidery and bobbin

ABOVE *Couple from northern Norway. The remoteness and isolation of such regions of Europe led to the survival of ancient patterns rooted in mythology, and also the predominant use of the local wool.*

RIGHT *Swedish woman from Vastergotland in festive dress. This relied more on purchased fabrics than on embroidery, though the bag hanging from her waist is embroidered.*

lace, while the winter one was of wool, mainly red, embroidered with flowers and added braiding. Embroidery on the forehead band of the linen caps of married Orthodox women was in red and black cross stitch with motifs of the swastika, 8-pointed star, heart and cross. Towels to hang round images of saints, or to place on the knees when eating fatty pastries, were of the Russian type with stylized peacocks, 2-headed eagles or human and animal motifs worked in red Holbein or chain stitch, or in white drawn threadwork. A common motif was the horse, often stylized and paired each side of a tree or 'giant'.

In Denmark, pictorial woollen embroidery was found on cushions for home and carriage, but most embroidery was of delicate realistic flowers, such as cowslips and pansies, on small items of household linen. The whitework known as Hedebo originated in Denmark and was used on household items and shirts. A complex technique of soft threads on linen, it went through various changes over time as it became commercialized.

OPPOSITE ABOVE *Two Sami from Lapland in typical horned caps and tunics with short flared skirts. These were made of blue felt, or felted wool, edged in bright primary colours.*

OPPOSITE BELOW *Girl from Kaukola, Finland. Her costume has minimal embroidery on the apron and bolero edges and whitework on the blouse. The unusual headdress, sykero, consists of her hair braided on a circular support with silk ribbons and was worn for festive occasions.*

ABOVE *Bench cushion, Denmark. Chain, stem and satin stitch in wool on wool. The tree of life is in the form of a vase with the flowers of fertility: the tulip, carnation and rose.*

ABOVE RIGHT *Children in a village school in Sweden would not normally have worn their Sunday best bonnet and fichus, and were no doubt specially dressed for the benefit of the artist.*

CENTRAL EUROPE

HUNGARY

Hungarian embroidery is epitomized by repeat chunky flowerheads in heavy cotton or wool thread – tulips, pomegranates, roses, carnations, rosettes – of Turkish inspiration, but small birds may also enliven the work. Satin is the most common stitch, often combined with white drawn threadwork, and monochrome square chain stitch, originating from the region of Kalotaszeg now in Romania, is also popular. On costume, bright colours are worn by the young, and sombre by older people. Best known is the floral work of Mezőkövesd which was commercialized at the beginning of the twentieth century and attracted attention abroad in the wake of the English Crafts Movement.

The glory of Hungarian embroidery is the floral work on sheepskin jackets, *ködmön*, coats and cloaks, *suba*, and on woollen frieze coats, *cifraszür*. Sleeves are always worn hanging loose. These garments were traditionally worked in white and red leather appliqué in patterns of oriental origin, but embroidery in silk and wool gradually overran the old designs.

On linen clothing, the sleeves of shifts and blouses are the most important area of embroidery. They are extremely full and gathered into the shoulder, upon which the embroidery stretches across the upper arm in a band, usually in heavy geometric patterning combined with whitework – a style in which the hems of aprons, skirts and petticoats are also embroidered. Kerchiefs are normally of fine whitework or of white appliqué like a paper cutout. Pillows are often worked in this technique, usually in red, while most bedlinen was embroidered with motifs of flowers and birds.

ABOVE *Woman's sleeveless jerkin. Satin and buttonhole stitch in silk on sheepskin. Sheepskin and leather garments were made by artisans of the Carpathians.*

BACKGROUND *Horseman of the Great Plain in his* cifraszür, *a coat of embroidered frieze. Made by professional tailors, the* cifraszür *varied in style for horsemen and farmers, and was worn particularly for courtship and marriage.*

TOP LEFT *The embroidered sheepskin cloak of the shepherds of eastern Europe 'serves as chair and bed for a man of peasant type. One can eat on its surface and dry meat upon it; and if a growing lad is bundled into it, three days' fever will pass away. Best of all a beautifully embroidered* suba *decorated with chamois is a festive cloak to parade in on Sundays.'*

TOP CENTRE *Mothers of Mezőkövesd wear the local aprons embroidered with flowers, and hold their babies on bolsters of brightly printed or brocaded fabrics.*

TOP RIGHT *Wedding procession in Mezőkövesd. Bride, groom and attendants all wear embroidered aprons. The large flowerheads are worked in thick floss silks in bright colours, mainly in satin and buttonhole stitch.*

ABOVE *Fragment, Mezőkövesd. Satin stitch in cotton on linen. The Matyó rose motif often clearly shows its origin in the Turkish* saz *motif of a flowerhead surrounded by a curving bell-hung stem or leaf.*

SLOVAKIA

Though other effects were, of course, far more important, the political rupture of Czechoslovakia has highlighted the difference in the embroidery traditions of the two regions: the western Czech Republic, including Moravia, having been part of the Hapsburg empire and open to the West, while the eastern territory of Slovakia was under Ottoman rule.

In Slovakia, embroidery is mainly on blouses and aprons and can be identified by the presence of coloured bobbin lace, brocaded floral ribbon and broderie anglaise. The blouses are of Pannonian cut, with or without a shoulder seam, and often reach only just below the bust. The sleeves are very full with a flounced cuff and are often intricately pleated; collars are also embroidered and are usually of officer style with a ruff of ribbon, bobbin lace or needleweaving. Skirts are very wide and short, pleated or plumped out with several petticoats. They were often open at the centre front and usually embroidered in geometric pattern along the back waistband. They were worn with an apron decorated with natural flower patterns and with bonnets worked in the same particular village style as the blouse.

Typical techniques are the flamboyant broderie anglaise in yellow and orange of the Piešťany region: satin-stitch patterns in bright colours combined with drawn threadwork of Čičmany; metal thread stitchery with whitework of Trnava; tamboured cutwork of Detva and Zvolen; bright woolwork of Rybany and cross stitch of the Hron valley. Patterns are geometric and floral, but can also portray confronting birds and the tree of life.

Sheepskin coats are appliquéd in coloured or red leather or have floral embroidery, less colourful than Hungary. The sheepskin boleros of the Hron valley are covered in appliquéd leather circles and discs. Felted wool coats are decorated with archaic motifs, including horn-derived hearts, and braiding and pompoms.

Men's linen shirts have heavily stitched bands of geometric patterning and floral motifs on sleeves and neck placket, while woollen trousers are embroidered on the front pockets with flowers, a style that extends from Poland as far west as south Germany.

The women's traditional costume was replaced by purchased clothing only after the Second World War, while the men's disappeared a generation earlier because of contacts through trade, itinerant work or military service.

LEFT *Bedcurtain,* kutnice, *Trnava. Pulled threadwork with satin stitch. To protect the mother and newborn child from evil spirits both were confined for forty days behind an embroidered curtain. Pulledwork enabled the mother to see into the room and the designs were usually symbolic, here the tulip of fertility.*

LEFT *Detail of a* polka, *the shawl from the village of Cataj, draped across the arms at marriage and then used to wrap round a baby, particularly to take it to church.*

ABOVE *Slovak costume from different villages, all sharing the style of a wide short skirt, apron and full elbow-length sleeves. Decoration is of embroidery and brocaded ribbons.*

BELOW LEFT *Man's sleeveless jacket, Trencianské Teplá. Chain stitch in silk, red zigzag appliquéd edging on black wool. Patterns on the woollen garments of eastern Europe were generally more archaic than those on linen.*

BELOW *Married woman's bonnet, Piešťany. The combination of broderie anglaise, bobbin lace and floral brocaded ribbon – here lining the hem of the bonnet – are typical of Slovakian embroidery.*

LEFT *Young woman from Helpa in the Hron valley. Each village, though only a few miles away from the next, has its distinct costume. Such caps were still being worn at the end of Soviet rule.*

ABOVE *Girl from Piešťany. The broderie anglaise work of the flamboyant costume of this small town is always in yellow or orange, and occasionally in red (see also p. 193). The collar is in needleweaving and the back and front aprons are of indigo chintz with cream silk flowers.*

LEFT *A boy from Dobrá Niva wears a richly embroidered blouse. Slovak children's costume followed closely the exuberant styles of the women's.*

FAR LEFT *Excessive ornamentation and wide, short skirts are hallmarks of most peasant costume of the former Czechoslovakia.*

BELOW *Woman from Abelová. The sleeves of her blouse are of cutwork, which is sometimes machine-made.*

CZECH REPUBLIC

Though again styles differ from village to village, much the same picture as in Slovakia is found in Moravia. A common theme is the short, very wide skirt, decorative apron of floral embroidery and bobbin lace, brocaded ribbons, white blouses with exaggerated puffed sleeves embroidered over the flounced cuffs, and boleros of floral brocade with edgings and rosettes of ribbon. Caps were of whitework or goldwork, while scarves were either floral print cotton or embroidered with flowers in one corner.

An example is the village of Kyov where the embroidery was of black flowers on the sleeves and sailor collars of the women's white blouses and the blue cotton aprons were heavily embroidered with flowers and edged with bobbin lace.

Men's festive white linen shirts were embroidered with naturalistic flowers or, for example, in the village of Vlcnov, front plackets, cuffs, shoulder bands and officer collars were worked in satin stitch in patterns of tulips and 8-pointed stars on a background of Slav knot stitch, usually in orange or white.

In Bohemia, costume was similar but was long ago replaced by purchased ribbons, trimmings and an excessive use of broderie anglaise. Only scarves and aprons of whitework, with white bobbin lace trim, are significant.

BACKGROUND *Women outside a church in Sobeslav, a village south of Prague. A mixture of embroidery, lace, print fabrics and ribbons are used to decorate the ubiquitous headscarf and apron of eastern Europe.*

ABOVE Woman from Kyov in Moravia. Strong black and white embroidery is characteristic of Kyov, as is the large collar, while the puffed, frilled sleeves and waistcoat are found in many villages of the Czech Republic.

LEFT Detail of a man's shirt cuff from Vlcnov in Moravia, worked in cross stitch on a background of Slav knot stitch, with a border of needleweaving. Embroidered cuffs, collars and neck plackets were often worked separately from the garment so they could be used again.

WESTERN EUROPE

THE KEY FACTOR in identifying the embroidery of the West is its date rather than geographical location. It is an ecclesiastical and urban tradition, a professional or leisure occupation subject to fashion and trade, and is not rooted in beliefs and social customs.

As we move into western Europe, the origin of an embroidery becomes much more difficult to identify. The general availability of commercial materials and the pattern books published from 1523 onwards, mainly in Italy and Germany, and sold throughout Europe, impart a certain uniformity to embroidery from Russia to Spain. Urban and court fashions were copied assiduously by the prosperous middle class almost everywhere. But for the peasants of western Europe, subjected to sumptuary laws forbidding the decoration of costume, it was the French Revolution that brought prosperity and freedom. They too then began to copy urban fashions but mainly with materials available commercially – few had to produce their own, as in eastern Europe. Outer clothing was thus usually decorated with ribbons and trimmings, and handwork was lavished on whitework coifs, aprons and fichus, on goldwork bonnets, and on red cross-stitch embroidery on linen. Only in isolated regions – mountain valleys, for example – did embroidery survive with its old purpose.

Most embroidery of western Europe follows commercial trends and could come from almost anywhere, but with some, especially on costume, it is possible to pinpoint its origin with precision. It can be placed within a very small area, if not an individual village, and then by status, age and religion.

However, more significant are the unifying elements. These are above all the role of linen, that hard-won, back-breaking mainstay of all peasant costume and household textiles, that was also the basis of the importance of whitework throughout Europe, both east and west. Then, the simplicity and symbolism of red cross stitch; the articles made – coifs, bonnets, fichus, bodices, aprons and dowry linens; finally, the descent into survival only in so-called 'folk dance' groups. Ecclesiastical embroidery was everywhere an established tradition, but followed a general professional style, rather than being regional.

ABOVE *The home production of linen in Europe was a life-consuming task, each stage of which was imbued with ritual. Trousseau textiles included embroidered shirts and shifts and household linens marked in red cross stitch.*

FAR LEFT *Though the coif of peasant costume lingered in western Europe, women used commercial textiles in preference to embroidery. Cashmere shawls were among those sold by itinerant pedlars in nineteenth-century rural France.*

LEFT *A couple in Vienna. Unlike peasant embroidery which could be located to a precise village, costume and embroideries of the middle and upper classes and townsfolk followed fashion and therefore differed but little from country to country.*

GERMANY AND ALPINE LANDS

Europe has long been a continent in flux – neither Germany nor Italy were countries until the nineteenth century, while Austria was at the heart of a vast empire. Throughout Europe it was in the remoter regions that traditional embroidery survived, even then dying out in some regions by the late nineteenth century and in most after the First World War. It was replaced by commercial materials, especially ribbons.

In the Alpine region, naturalistic flowers, including the edelweiss as almost a local symbol, and hearts, were the most common motifs. These were worked on women's aprons, as well as men's shirts and jackets. Other motifs, especially in cross stitch, were the tree of life with paired birds, the dove, eagle and peacock. Herringbone, known as *Hexenstich* (witch stitch) was deemed by its crossing to keep evil spirits at bay.

Whitework throughout this region, and particularly in Switzerland, was very skilled, often professional, and ranged from pulled threadwork on linen to embroidery on muslin and net. The technique of drawn threadwork on muslin, known as Dresden, was made in Denmark as well as in Germany. Articles were household linens, fichus and coifs, though often the only traditional handwork was devoted to the linen shirt, other decoration being of purchased materials or, in the case of coifs, of lace.

Embroidery of the Black Forest is of restrained floral patterns on aprons, of goldwork on velvet for bonnets and stomachers, while particular to the region are yokes separate from the shirt and worn by both men and women. These are richly embroidered wth flowers and hearts.

In more northern regions of Germany, such as Vierlände and Nord Siebenburg, black counted-thread floral and geometrical motifs were common on linen shifts. Hearts were also embroidered on the smocks of the men of Schwalm.

Berlin woolwork spread from Germany to the whole of Europe in the late nineteenth century, as did Viennese petit-point from Austria, and was often commercially produced.

ABOVE *Purchased fabric replaces embroidery in the festive costume of the Austrian Alps, and it is the headdress that forms the traditional decorative element.*

BELOW LEFT *A newly married couple from the Black Forest wear sober dress, the bride's enlivened by some discreet floral embroidery on her apron and by her bizarre chaplet of glass balls and beads.*

BELOW RIGHT *A Catholic Corpus Christi procession in Appenzell, an occasion on which women wear their old ceremonial costumes and pointed coifs.*

THE NETHERLANDS

Coifs, caps and aprons are the major decorative elements of Dutch costume. Each varied with region, village and also religion. It was on the island of Marken that embroidery was an important form of decoration and survived the longest. Floral motifs, many taken from the Indian chintzes imported from the Coromandel coast, and particularly roses, were worked on caps and on the girls' boleros worn at Whitsun. Similar floral motifs were embroidered on aprons in a frill below the waist, rather like a peplum. This was a fashion also in Volendam, where a matching neck placket was worn. In Zeeland such floral neck plackets were beaded.

Though caps and coifs were the most decorative item of costume throughout the Netherlands, they were more often of handmade lace, though, as well as embroidered, they could also be crocheted, beaded or made of ribbons.

ABOVE *A woman from Volendam in festive dress. The top part of her overskirt or apron is embroidered with brightly coloured flowers. Simpler costume was worn on Sundays and other days, Sunday aprons often embroidered in black and red cross stitch with the wearer's initials.*

ABOVE *A peasant girl from Walchersch. The white fichus and bonnets of the Netherlands could be of lace or whitework.*

ABOVE *In a bonnet of lace, the fisherman's wife embroiders, like Penelope, as she waits on the banks of the Zuiderzee for her husband's boat to return.*

LEFT *Earlier costume from Volendam than appears on the opposite page has a similar decorative top to the apron, a square neck placket and lace bonnet, though with noticeably less embroidery than in the more modern version.*

RIGHT *Peasant woman from Nieuwlansch. Not only were fichus and bonnets different in each locality, but the complicated way the bonnets were draped was also unique.*

FRANCE

In France it is again particularly the coif that survived the longest as a traditional embroidered garment almost everywhere, but especially in Brittany, Normandy and Touraine. Not only was it different in each region but also within each village and within a certain period only. Most mixed whitework with lace and net.

Unique to France were the embroidered jackets made by men from Pont l'Abbé in Brittany and worn by both men and women. Whereas the coifs were made by women, sitting in groups in the open air from April to November, the men worked alone at home. On black or dark blue woollen cloth, they embroidered a solid block of orange and yellow patterning of the old Indo-European motif of the sun and solar barque – often mistakenly named as a peacock's feather – with other symbols such as rams' horns, stars and fishbones.

A blue smock with simple white embroidery round the edges was worn by peasants to protect their clothes while travelling and was also best wear for the shepherds of Provence.

LEFT AND BELOW Norman inhabitants of Cotentin, the peninsula of Cherbourg. The ladies wear the local coif, one of which is shown in more detail below. Ladies wearing such costume would have been fairly wealthy.

BELOW LEFT Breton women from Pont Aven in their distinctive high whitework coifs. Members of the Pont Aven school of painting, of which Paul Gauguin is the best known artist, were attracted by the local peasant costume.

FAR LEFT *Woman from Boulogne-sur-Mer in the local bonnet and fichu.*

LEFT *Embroiderer from Pont l'Abbé in Brittany. Worn by both men and women, these jackets were fastened on different sides for festive wear or for mourning. The women from Pont Aven on the opposite page are wearing them.*

BELOW FAR LEFT *Folk dance musicians wearing the typical blue smock of the French peasant. This usually has narrow white stitchery and cording on edges and seams.*

BELOW *Man's waistcoat, first half of the eighteenth century. Tamboured chain stitch in silk on silk. Such waistcoats were made all over Europe. To protect the English embroidery industry imports were forbidden and were burned. This one from France is stamped: 'Customs House Seized Dover G R II'.*

ITALY

Italy's preeminence in luxury textiles, both produced locally and imported from the east through Venice, left little place for a national tradition of embroidery. Urban clothing of the rich independent city-states was of brocades and silks that needed no further embellishment. Weaving was a more important textile technique than embroidery.

Embroidery was mainly professional and ecclesiastical. Most domestic work was whitework on underdresses, shirts and household linen, cutwork being popular. Peasant costume had far less embroidery on it than in countries further north.

Styles that spread through Europe were Florentine stitch and also Assisi where patterns are left in reserve on a background of long-armed cross stitch. Similarly animal patterns were worked against a background of drawn threadwork in Sardinia and in Sicily which in the twelfth and thirteenth centuries had a reputation for superb embroidery featuring paired animals and birds.

RIGHT *Ecclesiastical embroidery of Italy was formal and followed the luxurious weavings for which Lucca, for example, was famous.*

LEFT *Embroidered band from Sicily. These share the same technique as the embroidery of Assisi in Italy and Azemmour in Morocco, where the background is embroidered and the motifs left unworked. Such designs were taken from pattern books published in the sixteenth century and circulated around Europe from that period on.*

BELOW *Documented as Italian, this woollen apron is embroidered with the ancient Sumerian motif of confronting birds around a plant, fountain or tree, in this case surrounded by the fertility motif of pomegranates.*

SPAIN

With Sicily, Spain was the Arab and Islamic gateway to Europe, and this is reflected in the hallmark of Spanish embroidery: intricate patterning executed in simple stitchery and limited colouring. The background fabric is usually linen and the threads black wool, honey and blue linen, or red and green floss silk, used to make men's shirts and trousers, women's blouses and shifts, offertory and funeral cloths and display linen for the marriage bed. All come from the region to the west and south of Madrid, although there are marked differences in the work of each town or village: examples are the monochrome latticed patterning in darning stitch of Navalcan and the Assisi work in floss silk, especially on the shoulders, neck and cuffs of shirts or blouses of the Sierra Morena. The cut is usually straight with a curved or square neckline and full sleeves, often smocked into neck and cuff. Linen shirts for the bridegroom are beautifully worked over the front bodice with white drawn threadwork and needleweaving, in honey silk or linen threads, and with red cross-stitch initials below the neck opening. The finest come from Lagartera in Toledo province, where the blouses have black wool spirals down each side of the front, surrounded by small repeat motifs of floral derivation. Salamancan women's blouses have full sleeves displaying Asian motifs of animals with reserve pattern worked in black, and on cloths the same motifs appear in pastel colours.

The linen Renaissance bands of Avila, inserted into household and ecclesiastical hangings, can be distinguished from those of Azemmour in Morocco by their stitch and colour. The patterns are the same tree of life or vase flanked by birds left in reserve, but the background is either black wool in darning, or soft green, blue or red silk in cross stitch, pulled thread or reversible tent stitch, where Azemmour bands are in long-armed cross, as is Assisi work. Motifs are outlined in self colour or black.

'Spanish' shawls were originally imported from Manila and then copied in workshops in Andalucia. They are simpler and brighter than the Chinese.

LEFT *Sleeves of the women's shifts of Salamanca depict palaeolithic motifs of the hunted animal and predator, together with flowers, birds and fish. The animals feature body markings and the head separated by a collar.*

ABOVE Cloth, Navalcan. The embroidery of monochrome silk on cotton was of Coptic origin. The villagers believed this labyrinth pattern to have magic powers.

LEFT The town of Murcia was an important centre of the silk industry. In embroidery, it was particularly Chinese shawls that were copied and teamed with floral festive aprons.

ABOVE Women working in an alleyway in Lagartera, Toledo. Embroidery was a general activity in the town and was of geometric patterns and stylized flowers in black, and later red.

PORTUGAL

Portugal is the only country of western Europe where embroidery is still a significant commercial activity. The leitmotif is sentimentality: linen production was suffused with symbolism of love and fidelity, and the main motifs on linen garments are hearts and flowers, coats of arms, the word *amor*, initials and dates, always worked in red. The stitches used are satin, cross and pulledwork, with bullion and eyelet in Guimarães, in colours of red, white and blue. The most common articles so decorated are bridegrooms' shirts, worked over the front bodice in white stitchery, with a red motto below; women's blouses, which have much simpler work, usually blue embroidery and smocking at the shoulder; and linen for display on the marriage bed and washbasin. The sweetheart hankies of Minho have mottoes and vows of love worked in red.

From Portugal's role as a trading nation come the embroidered carpets of Arraiolos still made today, which are copies of imported Persian ones. A border in two colours, usually sludge and blue but occasionally chestnut red, is contrasted with a field in reverse colour order. The Persian designs were later replaced by animals and flowers.

Bedcovers of Castelo Branco are of strips of linen embroidered with patterns derived from Indian palampores in laid couched floss silks. Focus of the design is a central medallion, often enclosing a couple or a tree, surrounded by a riot of flowers and birds. Their source was the Indo-Portuguese quilts of the seventeenth century – works of art depicting scenes from Indian mythology or the Bible.

BELOW *A quilt known as 'Indo-Portuguese'. These were made in India for the Portuguese market in the seventeenth century, and had pictorial and floral motifs worked in chain or back stitch in the wild yellow* muga *silk native to Bengal.*

OPPOSITE *Coverlet for the marriage bed from Castelo Branco, worked in floss silk in laid and couched stitch. These were made until the end of the nineteenth century by both skilled and amateur needlewomen.*

BELOW *Women in the village of Arraiolos embroidering carpets of evenweave linen with thick wool in a double cross stitch known as Arraiolos. Animals and flowers are favourite motifs.*

RIGHT *Purse, Viana do Castelo, Minho. Beads, sequins, satin stitch in silk twist on velvet. The word* amor *is typical of Portuguese embroidery.*

LEFT *A man at the Moncao festival proudly displays his linen shirt, resplendent with motifs of love.*

Quilts, born of the necessity to utilize every scrap of precious fabric, and of the pleasure of social gathering in a frontier society, are the cream of American needlework. Embroidery, in general, followed the fashions of western Europe, with a slight time-lag, interpreting them in a more limited vocabulary of stitches, simpler designs and cruder materials, with a consequent gain in vitality and charm. Samplers and needlepoint are particularly revered.

Embroidery of the Native Americans varied with tribe and geographical environment. Traditional work was in caribou and moose hair, and also porcupine quill. This was gradually replaced by beadwork as from the early 1800s beads from Venice were brought to the Great Plains and elsewhere. As traders came on ponies, these were known as 'pony beads'. After 1840 they were replaced by smaller seed beads in a wider range of colours. Traditional patterns included the thunderbird and hour-glass motifs, as well as the dragonfly symbolizing strength, agility and speed. As beadwork gradually replaced moosehair and porcupine quillwork, most geometric and mythological patterns were dropped in favour of flowers, worked on cloth as well as on the indigenous skin and bark. An enormous range of articles was embroidered, including coats, shirts, moccasins, gloves, saddles, pouches and bags. By the early eighteenth century there was already a market for trinkets, such as boxes, scissor-cases and sundry 'native fancy goods'.

Today, the United States, with western Europe and Japan, is the home of a vibrant culture of embroidery as an individual artistic medium.

BACKGROUND *The shirts of the Native Americans of the Plains are true works of art. The property of warriors, they played an important spiritual role and were often buried with the owner. When they lost this role, they were worn for dancing. Made of the skin of mountain sheep, elk or deer, they were decorated with quill or bead embroidery or were painted.*

LEFT *Triple pouch, Ojibwa or Ottawa tribes. Quillwork on smoked skin. The thunderbird is a mythological creature associated with rain and fertility.*

OPPOSITE ABOVE LEFT *Inuit women wearing inner parkas beaded in the same patterns as in tattoos. Northwest Territories 1903–4.*

OPPOSITE ABOVE RIGHT *A Flathead mother of the Plateau people with beaded cradle and floral bib on her horse's bridle. Motifs of beadwork were mainly floral, but could also be of horses and wagons.*

OPPOSITE BELOW *Randomly patched quilts were popular in North America and England. This crazy patchwork lap quilt was made in England in 1898. Silk and velvet sequins, beads, varied stitchery.*

CENTRAL AMERICA

From Maya, Aztec, Inca and even earlier civilizations comes one of the finest traditions of weaving in the world, still continued by many women of Central and South America. Decoration on their untailored clothing of handwoven cotton or wool – tunics, shawls, wrap-around skirts, and sashes – is usually brocaded and embroidery is only introduced as weaving skill declines.

MEXICO

Embroidery is normally on factory-made cloth and is European-inspired. Thus the traditional tunics, *huipils*, and shawls, *quechquémitls*, of Mexico are brocaded with geometric patterns and with stylized sacred animals and birds, but the white cotton blouses, with square necks and short sleeves of European cut, are embroidered with massed large motifs of flowers, birds, animals combined with 8-pointed stars, all mixed together in a riot of gaudy colours in satin stitch (although crochet edges are commonly in white). Flouncy dresses with brilliant flowers, and gold-embroidered suits, are reminiscent of the bullfights and fiestas of Andalucia.

On some garments more sober negative patterning and cross-stitch designs following the weft recall brocading techniques. Styles vary and, though men's clothing is usually plain, some festive shirts and bags – necessary as clothing has no pockets – are embroidered with geometric motifs and animals.

Left and below Girls in the village of Na Bolom spin and embroider in the street. Mexican blouses are typically short-sleeved.

Right *These girls of Yucatan, of mixed Spanish and Mexican descent, wear embroidered dresses whose floral patterns and lace edgings are very European in style.*

LEFT *The women of Zinacantán all wear shawls of bright pink or mauve with huge pink tassels, embroidered with flowers and touches of sparkly thread. They buy the materials in the market, which is a kaleidoscope of colour, dominated by pink.*

BELOW *Blouse yoke from San Juan Ixtenco. The technique is* pepenado fruncido, *where the running stitches form folds and leave the pattern in reserve.*

GUATEMALA

The great strength of Guatemalan textiles is supplementary weft weaving: stylized birds and animals of sharp diagonal lines, combined with plant forms and zigzags symbolizing the serpent, in sophisticated colourings, embellish clothing of stitched straight loom widths. Embroidery, symbolic or floral on *huipils*, is far less significant, though it is important in the villages around Lake Atitlan, especially on men's clothing. Trousers of Santiago Atitlan are embroidered in squares of motifs derived from local carvings, while the collars and cuffs of men's striped red shifts of San Antonio Palopo are worked in lines of heavy cotton back stitch in bright colours.

BELOW *Detail of man's trouser leg. Some are embroidered with ancient Mayan designs and others with bright birds and flowers. The patterns are always worked over or within a grid of stitchery.*

ABOVE *Trouser legs for sale in Santiago Atitlan. These embroidered trousers are still worn by the men of the village.*

OPPOSITE ABOVE *The stylized animals and geometric motifs embroidered on the shift of this girl from a village near Antigua are in the tradition of brocaded patterns on* huipils.

RIGHT *The market of Chichicastenango is always a riot of colour. The women's huipils are decorated with brocaded weaving as well as embroidery. The designs mix vivid flowers with the local mythical birds and creatures.*

BELOW *A couple waiting for the bus at Sololá, near Lake Atitlan, identify themselves as local by their clothing. The embroidery on the man's trousers is of bands of stylized animals alternating with stripes, while the design on his jacket includes confronting birds.*

PANAMA

Unique in the world are the blouse fronts and backs, known as *molas*, of the Kuna Blas islands off Panama, worked by a complicated technique of layering. Of brightly coloured cotton with red predominating, slit to disclose patching of varied hues, they depict local mythology, birds and animals, and often images derived from the modern world such as cigar boxes and political slogans.

ABOVE *A Kuna girl from Vaguitupu, San Blas, Panama, cutting through layers of fabric to make a mola.*

LEFT *A girl from San Blas working on the first stage of her* mola, *cutting and stitching the outlines of the main motifs. The* mola *forming the lower part of her blouse front is of geometric patterns.*

RIGHT *Kuna Blas woman's* mola *blouse front of layered and cut cotton appliqué. Mola designs are taken from local mythology and contemporary life.*

SOUTH AMERICA

T HE TEXTILES of Bolivia and Peru perpetuate the superb weaving skills of the Incas and earlier peoples: symbols of the sun, the sacred condor, serpent and jaguar are woven and there is also a tradition of fine knitting, but not of embroidery. Yet from the arid desert region on the Peruvian coast come some of the oldest embroideries in the world. They belonged to the Paracas culture, active there from about 600 to 200 BC, and the related Nasca culture of the first millennium. They buried their dead élite, prepared for the next world, in mummy bundles containing often hundreds of textiles, mainly woven but also embroidered in vivid wools in loop and stem stitch. The motifs depict felines, serpents, birds of prey, killer whales and human forms intermingled in a contorted maze of appendages, with weapons and trophy heads – images conveying mythological beliefs and ritual and social obligations that remain mystifying. They resemble some of the huge animals cut in outline in the nearby desert, which are interspersed among giant straight lines visible only from the air: the puzzling Nasca Lines of unknown sacred or astronomical purpose.

This early indication of the link between embroidery motifs and concepts of myth and magic can be followed throughout most of the world.

OPPOSITE AND BELOW *Embroideries from the necropolis of Paracas in Peru bear the same motifs as the mysterious Nasca Lines cut into the desert. The figure with bristly head on a shirt,* unku, *is* *similar to three figures cut into a hillside in the Ingenio valley, and the feline motif on a mantle is echoed in the enormous figure drawn on the desert near the town of Ica.*

BOTTOM *A Nasca single-faced mantle border embroidered in stem stitch, depicting a jumble of supernatural and riverine deities.*

127

THE DECORATIVE POWER OF CULT

OPPOSITE *Cloth, Ottoman, probably Balkan (the origin of these cloths is in some dispute). The tree of life transposed as a vase containing flowers or a plant was a device of Sumerian art. The flowers were usually those associated with fertility, and the tree was still flanked by birds and figures. It is here supplemented with large pomegranates. This piece recalls embroideries of the Middle East in its version of the tree of life, the suzanis of Tashkent, the archaic patterns of Samokov in Bulgaria in its pomegranates and the skirt hems of Crete in the style of its linear embroidery.*

LEFT *Cloth, Ionian Islands, Greece. The goddess figure, with animals and plants arranged in an orderly fashion around her, is found on archaic Greek vases. With wings as well as arms, this goddess resembles votive figurines of the third millennium BC from the Cyclades. The flowers with her are the usual tulip and carnation, symbols of fertility.*

THE GREAT GODDESS

Certain guidelines can be observed in determining when the purpose and pattern of tribal and peasant embroidery are mythological in origin. The patterns are likely to appear on articles associated with some ritual or rite of passage, such as marriage or death, or with something of symbolic significance, such as a woman's hair. The embroideries often come from an isolated or ethnically different area of a country, like the northern wastes of Russia or the 'barbarian' provinces of China.

An embroidered female figure is usually goddess-derived, rather than merely a depiction of a woman, if she is accompanied by other mythological symbols, such as zigzags, birds, chevrons or toads, or by a worshipping figure. She will normally form part of a repeat symmetrical pattern or be one herself, portrayed in a ritual stance, often with the suggestion of a held branch. The deformation of figures – women that are half trees, or birds, or bees, or that have a base like an idol rather than legs – also usually indicates a cult origin. Symbolism is not, however, clear-cut.

IDENTIFICATION OF A CULT SOURCE

Primitive mythology is a complex attempt to grasp the concepts of fertility, life, death and cosmic creation and cannot be categorized into a series of separate cults. So patterns from different sources merge: the fertility goddess can be transfigured into a tree of life or bestowed with horns; the moon is a goddess or is male; the sun is a hunter or a life-giver. Myths overlap or oppose in different cultures, some disseminated through movement of peoples, most generated from the same basic human needs and instincts, surviving for millennia. The mythology of the great goddess persisted to classical Greece and was then absorbed into Greek legend, passing eventually into Christianity as the cult of the Virgin Mary.

BELOW AND ABOVE RIGHT *The goddess figure on an Archaic-Cypriot jug of 700–600 BC and on East Greek metal plaques of 720–520 BC is accompanied by mythological symbols also found on later embroidered examples.*

OPPOSITE BELOW LEFT *Marriage coif, Bekalta, Tunisia. The lozenge shape of the three goddess figures on this marriage coif recalls that of the prehistoric figurine of Venus found at Lespugue. The raised arms are a ritual stance taken by the Tunisian bride at her marriage jelwa (see p. 134) when she is presented to her guests wearing such a coif. The fish and sun are accompanying symbols.*

OPPOSITE BELOW RIGHT *Ritual towel, Russia. Russian towels, ceremoniously hung over birch trees or at crossroads, abound with depictions of the earth goddess, almost always embroidered entirely in red. Most show her in various stages of transmutation into plant form, and with her arms raised. Accompanying birds, 8-pointed stars, swastikas, zigzags and alternating pattern make her identity clear.*

ORIGINS OF THE GODDESS CULT

The concept of the earth as a bearing and nourishing mother is almost universal: in every early society, practically without exception, a myth exists recounting the creation of the universe. Usually it embodies the idea of a static life-producing earth in the form of a goddess, fertilized by an active, stimulating, penetrating manifestation of the male thrust, such as a bird (a link between heaven and earth), or a serpent or toad.

Mankind's earliest sculptures – cult figurines dating from the palaeolithic period of about 30,000 BC and made of mammoth ivory – are of this goddess: earth mother, source of life, symbol of fertility. From the neolithic period of about 5000 BC onwards such figurines are found in quantity in Asia and the Near East, in the pre-Indo-European matriarchal society of Old Europe and in the Cycladic, Minoan and Mycenaean civilizations. The figurines, of terracotta or bronze, come mainly from graves and sanctuaries and their precise purpose is not known. Those at sanctuaries seem mostly to have been votive offerings, left perhaps as substitutes for sacrifices or in place of worshippers. Some were left at domestic shrines where they were placed to guard both hearth and home. All may not be representations of the goddess but rather of a priestess or human worshipper. Often they are decorated with red, symbolizing the mystery of blood.

FAR LEFT AND LEFT *The lozenge shape of the Lespugue ivory Venus of the Aurignacian period (30,000–25,000 BC) is echoed in the embroideries of Bekalta in Tunisia and the wedge-shaped head of the Mycenaean goddess of 1300–1200 BC in the embroidery of Russian ritual towels.*

THE GODDESS IN EMBROIDERY

These figurines were particularly common in Old Europe, which extended from the Adriatic and Aegean to the Ukraine and Poland, and it is especially in the Mediterranean region and in Russia that goddess figures predominate in embroidery. Pagan mythology survived in the Mediterranean to the period of classical Greece when much was absorbed from the earlier Aegean civilizations, and Greece accepted most of the panoply of gods of the Thracians, citizens of the Achaemenid empire that stretched eastward to the Hindu Kush. They worshipped the earth goddess and featured her, riding a lioness, on their silverwork of the fourth century BC. Not surprisingly, Greek embroidery has many examples of figures derived from the earth goddess, such as those holding branches, common on the cushion covers and towels of Skyros in the Cyclades, home of a flourishing civilization in the third millennium BC. Seated figures holding branches are also worked on cushions and bed valances from Epirus in north-western Greece, a region that was Roman, Byzantine and then a prosperous Turkish province. In Attica the hems of the women's shifts are decorated almost entirely with simplified versions of the goddess.

In early figurines the goddess was depicted with extended egg-shaped buttocks giving her a bird-like appearance, which was accentuated by a beak. The association of the goddess with birds was strong and features frequently in embroideries. In Skyros she is half bird in form and in Russia the bird sirens known as Sirine and Alconoste have female faces and exotic plumage. They are the birds of ancient fable who charmed the saints in paradise with their singing.

The oldest surviving textile depicting a manifestation of the goddess is the great felt found in one of the tombs of Pazyryk in the Altai mountains of southern Siberia. Over the centuries rain seeped into these burial chambers, even poured

in where robbers had left open shafts, and then froze solid, preserving in deep freeze objects dating from the seventh to the second century BC, the felt among them. Repeated across its width is the motif of a seated goddess figure holding a sacred branch. She is believed to be Tabiti, deity of the hearth and therefore of fire and fertility, worshipped in Russia in pre-Scythian times. She is approached by a male rider on a horse,

TOP *Picture, England. The motifs of 1930s English embroidery sprang from nostalgia for a vanishing rural life, but the crinoline lady herself was an anachronism. Holding a bunch of flowers, might she not also perhaps derive, through more obvious examples in the peasant embroidery then being copied, from the goddess holding her sacred branch?*

ABOVE AND LEFT *The bird goddess or siren forms an East Greek terracotta perfume bottle of 640 BC and is in the shape of the fabled sirens of Russian pagan mythology, Sirine and Alconoste.*

possibly a worshipper. In later embroidered depictions of the goddess in many countries she is frequently associated with a mounted horseman.

The anthropomorphic figures of Western embroidery are not goddess-derived but normally come from the Bible or from engravings or prints, or are of contemporary scenes. However, in the 1930s a new motif appeared in English embroidery: the crinoline lady. The thatched cottages and hollyhocks that accompanied her sprang from nostalgia for an imagined simple rural life, aroused by the ribbon development and suburban sprawl then taking place. But the lady herself was an anachronism. It was not nineteenth-century fashion plates that were being copied by embroideresses then but peasant work that conveyed the same idyll of security in a changing world. Might the origins of the lady not also perhaps be traced, through more obvious examples in peasant embroidery, to the same fertility myths going back to palaeolithic times?

ABOVE *The seated goddess holding a sacred branch and approached by a rider, depicted on the great felt of Pazyryk, is a motif found in various guises and derivations in the embroideries of many countries.*

RIGHT *Woman's marriage shift, Attica, Greece. Marriage shifts show a more obvious fertility goddess than the everyday ones, repeatedly enclosed in a somewhat phallic shape. The embroidery was usually the work of professional women, with different women having responsibility for coloured silk or goldwork.*

THE GODDESS STANCE: RAISED ARMS

The stance of the goddess was everywhere of ritual significance. Often she is portrayed with arms raised or legs outspread or in a frontal pose with symmetrical excrescences of animal or plant form at her sides.

Raising the arms is an instinctive gesture of self-defence and an imprinted one of surrender. It is also associated with worship and for primitive peoples, such as the pigmies, with supplication to the sun. Mayan gods raised their arms to hold up the sky. It is always an important gesture of dance – bird-headed dancing women, so postured, are in the Aurignacian rock-paintings of Pêch Merle in France. Dancing often implied imitation of animal movements and therefore identity with them.

In embroidery the motif of a female figure with upraised arms is common almost everywhere. She resembles early terracotta goddess figurines, for example those of Neolithic Iberia, Egypt, Old Europe and India. The same form appears in Tunisia as an ancient carving, a modern embroidery motif and a ritual of the marriage ceremony. There the Phoenician carvings on the stelae of Carthage, showing the goddess Tanit with raised or outstretched arms, often simplified and stylized to a circle with linear hands on a triangular base, are matched in embroidery on women's marriage garments. These depict the earth goddess and are also a rendering in embroidery of the modern bride at her *jelwa* – at this presentation ceremony on the fourth day of the wedding the bride is veiled and dressed as an idol in seven tunics, the outer one heavily embroidered and stiff with gold, topped with goldwork boleros, a coif and all the jewelry of her dowry. For this climax of the seven-day marriage ceremony she stands on a platform, her arms raised and the palm of her hand turned to the assembled guests

BELOW *Woman's dress, Saraqib, Syria, depicting the goddess with upraised arms. Ancient Syrian association with goddess worship is evident in Phoenician cult and is reflected in the thirteenth-century pottery of Raqqa and Hama where the goddess is a decorative device.*

to be unveiled in their presence. After this the marriage is consummated. This ritual is understood to originate in a lost fertility rite and is supposed to avert the evil eye – the hands here are raised for protection. It clearly dates back to the Phoenician worship of the goddess, though the embroidery motif is normally described as 'the bride at her *jelwa*' rather than as the goddess Tanit.

The heartland of Russia and the Ukraine retained until early this century ritual embroideries whose pagan origins are clear both in their uses and motifs. The Russian ceremonial towels, hung at crossroads and on birch trees, are decorated with archaic motifs, the most common of which is the goddess, arms raised in supplication and often with huge hands to avert evil. The same motifs are on Ukrainian towels called *rushnyky*, hung around icons and crosses or on the walls of houses to fend off evil.

Western European embroideries have many examples of female figures with raised arms. These are normally interpreted as representing dancing women or the wise and foolish virgins, possibly a Christianized version of the pagan motif.

ABOVE Mola, *Kuna Blas islands, Panama. The theme of many molas is obscure. Lizard-like creatures and upraised arms are associated with the goddess, while the mouth bristling with teeth symbolizes in the art of the Americas the concept of death as part of life. Four strips refer to stages of the eight-layered heaven and underworld of Kuna mythology.*

LEFT *A terracotta figurine of the goddess with raised arms, from Razgrad, Bulgaria, dates from around 4000 BC. Later Minoan and Mycenaean figurines also feature the goddess in this stance. It became a very common embroidery motif.*

THE GODDESS STANCE: OUTSPREAD LEGS

The stance with outspread legs, the body opened like a book exposing the genitals in a birth-giving posture, is found in almost all primitive art and was sifted through Renaissance pattern into the decorative arts of Europe as a two-tailed mermaid creature, sometimes with a masculine face. As such it is common, for example, on the embroidered skirts of Crete.

The same posture of splayed legs denotes the toad, a symbol of fertility. Conception was not understood by primitive man, and as a miscarried foetus resembles a toad these creatures were believed to crawl into the womb to fertilize the woman. They were considered a protection against barrenness and are still votive offerings to Mary in south-eastern Europe.

The addition of an appendage between the legs confuses the imagery still further. It is then usually intended to convey a lizard, worshipped like the snake for its skin-shedding, a symbol of the renewal of life. Shapes with splayed legs and raised arms that are a confused medley of male and female anthropomorphism, toad and lizard are embroidered on coats of the Iban people of Borneo. These probably belonged to medicine men, whose powers would be evident in the motifs on their clothing. Such motifs, surrounded by other lizard-like creatures, are worked in cowrie shells on the skirts of Sumba in Indonesia. These skirts were an important part of the woman's dowry and were also

ABOVE *Roman mosaic, second century AD, Tunisia. The stance of the goddess with outspread legs is found in almost all primitive art and came into European iconography as a two-tailed mermaid, often with a masculine face.*

ABOVE *Minoan seals of 1700–1450 BC are engraved with a lizard-like creature and the fish and axe associated with creation.*

LEFT AND ABOVE *The goddess with outspread legs, flanked by lions, features on a bronze Etruscan chariot and lingers in both female and male form in Italian art of the sixteenth century.*

often used as grave gifts and buried with the woman.

In her role as life-giver the goddess is most frequently shown frontally with animals, plants and insects growing out of or surrounding her body. Her wide skirt, possibly denoting the huge buttocks and stomach of early figurines, is often surrounded by or filled with birds, animals or 'daughter' goddesses. Bronze figurines of Luristan dating from about 1000 BC depict creatures as an integral part of her body, whereas in the depictions on archaic Greek vases they are generally arranged in an orderly fashion around her. In early Iranian art she was also shown as queen of the beasts, holding animals at her sides.

As fertility goddess she projects her powers through plants and animals – their presence with her on embroideries helps identify her, as do added cosmic symbols such as the swastika or the double axe.

RIGHT *Cloth, India. The goddess is still discernible as a two-tailed mermaid and is flanked by birds. The animal life that denoted her fertility became in later art her acolytes.*

OPPOSITE *Skirt hem, Crete. In her European guise as a mermaid the primitive goddess with splayed legs came through Renaissance pattern into the embroidery of Crete, both on women's skirts and ecclesiastical robes. She is flanked by birds.*

GODDESS ACOLYTES

The animals that symbolized the goddess's fertility became in later art her acolytes: she was shown flanked by birds, dogs or lions, or approached by riders offering sacred branches or baskets of fruit, as in Sumerian art of the fourth to third millennium BC. A derivation of this theme is the so-called 'boxer' motif on seventeenth-century English samplers.

The mounted horseman in scenes of the hunt is portrayed in a naturalistic way, but when he is of mythological origin he is stylized, often with arms raised in the votive position. Bent legs are frequently one of the characteristics of the horse; the animal alone with such bent legs appears on Russian towels and Dutch samplers. This distortion cannot be attributed merely to their counted thread technique.

The horse itself – a favourite animal, for example, in Nordic pre-Christian mythology –

ABOVE *Ritual mounted worshippers feature on peasant Chinese embroidery* (TOP) *and as Greek terracotta figurines of 580–550 BC* (ABOVE).

is replaced in many instances by a more exotic creature, such as a bull, dragon, elephant, cock or cat. The Indian mother goddess, Devi, herself rides on an elephant on the embroideries of Kutch and Gujarat and the *kanthas* of Bengal.

In Minoan and Old European mythology a column was an incarnation of the goddess, rather than a cosmogonic symbol forming the axis of the world as in other cultures. As such she was flanked by rampant lions or griffins, to form a motif disseminated through Europe by the Renaissance pattern books. More commonly she is transfigured as a tree rather than a column, with guardian or worshipping animals or birds, forming an axis between the waters of earth and the heavens.

ABOVE *Ritual towel, Russia. The goddess raises her arms and the flat-topped shape of her head is reminiscent of Minoan goddess figurines. The horseman recalls the one approaching the goddess on the great felt of Pazyryk dating from about the fifth century BC* (see p. 133).

BELOW LEFT *The mother goddess in the Indian form, Devi, is depicted riding on an elephant* (ABOVE) *and on a Turkish towel she is transmuted into a column, flanked by a mounted worshipper* (BELOW).

BELOW *Sampler, England, mid-seventeenth century. A derivation of a worshipper offering a sacred branch appears on seventeenth-century English samplers as the 'boxer' motif. The goddess is usually transmuted into a plant of obvious anthropomorphic aspect.*

ASSOCIATED GODDESS SYMBOLS

The associations of the goddess are manifold. Water is a major one, with the mystery of life represented by the waters of birth – and thus of cosmic creation – expressed in chevron and meander patterning. The ship is the sheltering vessel through the sea of life and a common embroidery motif. Mermaids are guardians of the waters, often with mirror in hand, and are a motif of seventeenth-century English samplers. Fish symbolize the waters' power as the origin and preserver of life and are often the emblem of the soul. In Bengal fish are embroidered on *kanthas* as a fertility symbol for a marriageable daughter. A felt hanging dating from about the first century BC, found at Noin Ula in Mongolia, is embroidered with turtles and fish, hardly familiar creatures in the Gobi desert. Crocodiles are also frequently venerated for their association with spirits, who are presumed, like the crocodile, to reside in hidden dark corners of rivers.

Rainwaters bringing life and fertility to animals and crops were associated with the milk of the goddess and symbolized by parallel lines and triangles. The appearance of these patterns on the breasts of goddess figurines made during a prolonged dessication of the earth's atmosphere in the sixth millennium BC suggests such an association. Modern wedding dresses of Sada'a in northern Yemen have such triangles and lines embroidered on the breasts.

ABOVE *Ritual towel, Russia. Water, as part of the birth process and therefore of cosmic creation, is associated with the goddess. The ship of life sailing through the cosmic waters is one of her attributes and a common embroidery motif.*

BELOW *Sampler, England, mid-seventeenth century. Mermaids, as guardians of the cosmic waters, often with mirror in hand, are a motif of seventeenth-century English samplers.*

SYMBOLS OF FERTILITY

Marrows and apples piled for harvest thanksgiving at the altar of an English church, decorated eggs at Easter, the biblical scourge of the barren woman – fecundity of soil and woman has always been a primary concern of mankind. The earliest sacred precinct was where women gave birth and is symbolized by a lozenge, often with a central dot. Figurines of the goddess in Old Europe have this pattern, often divided into four, incised on the stomach or the head. It is a device found also in embroidery.

Symbols that express fruitfulness are almost universal and so commonplace as to have lost their original meaning. Most obvious is the pomegranate with its viscous blood-red seeds. In embroidery it is often transmuted to a rose encircled by a bell-hung or serrated leaf of the *saz* style of Turkish art. Although in the West the tulip is probably embroidered merely as a precious flower, with its shape akin to the female vulva it is another symbol of fertility in other cultures, and is often associated with the pomegranate, as is the carnation. The carnation is the most frequent motif in the embroidery of northern Syria, symbolized into a hexagon and barely recognizable as a flower. This Syrian pattern is matched in a Christian Coptic embroidery of the early Middle Ages. All the motifs on it are religious: crosses, inscriptions, a figure – possibly St George – killing a dragon, and naïve people apparently in positions of adoration. The carnation motif may therefore also have had some religious significance.

Fundamental symbol of female fecundity is of course the pubic triangle, exaggerated in primitive figurines and depicted alone in prehistoric rock-painting.

LEFT, BELOW AND BELOW RIGHT *Symbols of fertility include the pomegranate – a ubiquitous motif which was probably also the apple of the Garden of Eden – and the carnation. The Syrian stylized row of carnations known as 'railway lines' is already found in Coptic embroidery.*

ABOVE *Towel, Russia. Ritual towels showing the goddess were sometimes replaced in the nineteenth century with towels of modern figures but still with the fertility symbols of the pomegranate and carnation and with flanking animals.*

OPPOSITE *Towel border, Turkey. Symbols expressing the fertility of the goddess are commonplace. The tulip, resembling the female vulva, and the pomegranate with its blood-red seeds, are obvious ones. The cypress in Phoenician lore represented the tree of life.*

So commonplace as a geometric pattern it has retained virtually no vestige of symbolic meaning, except when used as a potent talisman. Embroidered triangles, like silver amulets, are frequently hung on children's caps, over the ear. The protective power of the triangle is also invoked in the appliquéd chevrons of striped fabric used to edge embroidered costume in many countries.

2. THE TREE OF LIFE

The tree of life is one of the most common motifs in embroidery almost everywhere. Whereas the great goddess is the unrecognized source of many an anthropomorphic motif, almost every vaguely foliate shape and every pot of flowers is deemed to represent the tree of life. Most in fact do.

IDENTIFICATION OF A CULT SOURCE

The tree is one of the most potent of symbols. Its roots delve into the underworld, its trunk links the earth to the heavens – it transcends all three spheres. Its life-cycle unfurls before our eyes in each season of the year, the symbolism of birth, maturity, death and rebirth embodied in leaf, bud and fruit. Its fruitfulness is matched by the fruitfulness of woman and even sap and milk were equated by primitive man.

Versions of the tree of life are manifold but it is this fertility and consequent embodying of the goddess with attendant worshippers or guardians that is the one most commonly found in embroidery. The tree can, however, also be depicted as a half-goddess, a vase of flowers, a fountain or a symbol from local iconography, such as an eagle or a heart. It may be a simple linear pattern intended to signify a particular tree, such as a palm, or more often to convey the general concept of growth and fertility. When the tree of life is depicted as an actual tree, it is stylized to convey its mythological significance. Consequently foliate patterns or simple branched devices signify the tree of life, rather than a realistic tree with trunk and leafy branches.

The tree of life in the guise of a plant form with every leaf split into different colours is found in the *min-soo* peasant work of Korea, in the embroidery of southern Syria, where sacred trees were worshipped by the Phoenicians, and in Hungary and Portugal. These plant forms are often in the form of a cross, and trees were linked to the magic power of crossroads. The cross is but one aspect of the tree at the centre of the universe, the *axis mundi*, a mythology dating from the fourth or third millennium BC and especially important to Nordic and Central Asiatic races. From the tree as a central pillar the cross radiated to the four corners of the universe. In the Balkans the pre-Slav veneration of tree and pillar was still observed in the early years of the twentieth century. The tree as a pillar is rare in embroidery, though some Renaissance versions of this motif are worked in the monochrome bands of Sicily, Azemmour in Morocco, Parga in Greece and Avila in Spain, used for display around the home, or in the case of Avila incorporated into altar hangings.

ABOVE LEFT *The palm-leaf pattern of a Cretan gold pendant of 1700–1500 BC remains a common form of the tree of life motif.*

ABOVE RIGHT *This version of the tree of life on a dress from Qutayfé in Syria is also found on the peasant embroideries of Korea.*

BACKGROUND *Tcheremiss people of Siberia in festive dress return from a sacrificial grove. Hanging embroideries from trees and sacrificing beads to the gods were common customs in parts of Russia.*

ABOVE *Marriage shawl, El Jem, Tunisia. The archaic patterns on the woollen marriage shawls of El Jem, Sfax and Ksour Esaf in Tunisia depict the tree of life with guardian serpents and with solar symbols, motifs believed to protect the bride from evil spirits.*

RIGHT *Coverlet, Castelo Branco, Portugal. Coverlets were made in this small town from the early seventeenth century, when Portugal was still active in India, until the end of the nineteenth century when a disease of silkworms brought the tradition to an end. Many depict the tree of life, as in Indian palampores, rising out of a hillock, with symbolic pomegranates, carnations and small birds.*

BELOW *Purse, Afghanistan. The tree of life in its various guises is one of the most common motifs in embroidery almost everywhere. Reduced to its simplest form it protects the contents of this purse. One piece of mirror strategically placed, jazzy colours and tassels also play a role.*

THE GODDESS TREE

The most primitive sacred place devised by man was an enclosure with tree, stone and water. The stone held the force of the goddess and the water symbolized her role in cosmic creation. Such enclosures were found in the Indus valley civilization of Mohenjo-daro of the second millennium BC and were still common in Buddha's time. Trees, with stones placed around them, are still venerated in India and will be enclosed even if they grow in the path of a road, which must then be detoured around them.

LEFT The goddess with raised arms, transmuted into a tree or plant form, is evident on the cuffs of a burial shift from Martovce in Slovakia.

The tree symbolizing the goddess was a motif that appeared in the arts of the ancient civilizations of India, Mesopotamia, Egypt and the Aegean. It was often depicted flanked by worshippers or birds or by fabulous beasts in heraldic posture. From thence it found its way into decorative arts everywhere and can be claimed to be, in its several variations, the most common design of all. The animals can vary locally – the horse, for example, was popular as an object of pre-Christian cult – but in general they are fabled creatures such as dragons and griffins rather than familiar animals. In Islamic countries the fish is often added, and already appeared with the sacred tree in Mesopotamian art. Birds occur frequently, usually the symbolic peacock of oriental

ABOVE A tree is left growing from a Calcutta pavement and converted into an altar to be venerated by passers-by.

origin, or the cock, believed to drive away the spirits of the night and a symbol connected with solar mythology. The cosmic tree and goddess are also closely allied with the serpent, guardian of sanctuaries and the underworld and one of the most complex of symbols, associated also with rain and hair.

Ritual that linked the cult of the tree with the goddess survived in Russia and

Ukraine until the Second World War. A birch tree standing alone in a clearing was chosen to personify the goddess. It was then clothed in a woman's dress and the ritual towel was hung on one of its branches. Alternatively the towel would be suspended from a cross at the village crossroads. On these towels the goddess was depicted as such, or transmuted into a tree, but always embroidered in red. This transmutation is common in peasant embroidery, for example on the shift hems of the mountainous area of Stanke Dimitrov in Bulgaria. Similarly ambiguous are the cuffs of women's burial shifts of the village of Martovce in Slovakia, cut in black taffeta around outspread hands and thus known as the 'four-fingered' motif.

Opposite Ritual cloth, Russia. In its fertile fruit-bearing aspect the tree of life often bore a goddess in its branches. Symbolic motifs of two-headed eagles and cocks, carnations and further goddesses surround the tree while at its core is a heart, itself probably derived from horn symbolism.

Above Cushion for marriage sleigh, Sweden. The tree symbolizing the goddess was often flanked by worshippers or by birds or animals, which could vary locally. The horse was an object of pre-Christian cult and was both a solar and lunar symbol.

Below Cloth, Azemmour, Morocco. From a vase of carnations the tree of life is pared down to a simple stylized carnation alternating with another version as a column, both flanked by birds.

SYMBOLS REPLACING THE TREE

THE goddess-tree was also symbolized by flowers and plants and water, as a never-ending process of creation. In Sumerian art the tree itself was replaced by the device of a plant growing from a vase. This version of the tree of life motif, still flanked by worshippers or guardians, is the favourite motif of the folk art of Europe. Significantly the flowers are always those associated with the earth goddess: the carnation, tulip and rose, often with added pomegranates. Sometimes, conveying the symbolism of water, a fountain replaces the vase and flowers.

Not only is the tree substituted by symbols pertaining to water (and therefore still to life and fertility), but in the embroideries of some countries it is also replaced by motifs from local iconography. The eagle, with one or two heads, is an example. This ancient solar symbol, representing the power of the sky gods, later a European heraldic emblem and device of the Habsburgs, can replace the tree in the embroideries of Spain and Russia, for instance, as can the heart in those of central and eastern Europe.

ABOVE *The goddess-tree becomes a plant on the shift hems of Stanke Dimitrov and Samokov in Bulgaria, but can still be recognized.*

ABOVE *Woman's dress, Ramallah, Palestine. The tree of life as a vase of flowers flanked by birds was among patterns from European books introduced in Ramallah from the late nineteenth century when Quakers founded schools there and promoted embroidery. The traditional motifs of Palestinian embroidery were geometric.*

RIGHT *Woman's blouse, Djerba, Tunisia. The motif of the tree transposed as a vase containing a plant or flowers, especially carnations, and still with flanking birds, was disseminated by the pattern books of Europe. It became the favourite motif of the folk art of Europe, spreading from there to the Middle East and North Africa.*

OPPOSITE *Woman's bonnet, Rybany, Slovakia. The heart as part of the tree of life, with the symbolic pomegranate and confronting birds, is worked in wool or heavy silk on the bonnets and blouses of Rybany. A solar rosette sometimes replaces the heart.*

THE INVERTED TREE

The cosmic tree of primitive mythology was sometimes conceived as an inverted image, drawing strength through its roots in heaven and bestowing them on the world. At first glance the upside-down flower vases on a wedding dress of Thano Bula Khan in Sind would seem simply to indicate that the pattern had not been understood, but there are so many examples in embroidery of inverted renderings of the tree of life that it is most unlikely that all are merely mistaken. There are many upside-down versions of the pine or palm with a central trunk or spine and radiating lines. The date palm, venerated as a source of wealth, appears in this guise in many embroideries of the Arab world.

Right   *Woman's dress, Kaulan, Yemen.*
The cosmic tree of primitive mythology is frequently depicted as the inverted central trunk of a pine or palm tree with radiating lines, or an upside-down vase.

THE TREE OF KNOWLEDGE

The birth, life, death and regrowth of the tree symbolized in its fertility also the concept of immortality, an inestimable treasure. In ancient Babylon such treasure was protected by a serpent and the concept of two trees, the one of immortality attained through the heavily guarded one of wisdom, formed part of mythological belief. In biblical terms this is the tree of knowledge with the serpent that deprived Adam and Eve of paradise, and that became the central motif of a great number of nineteenth-century English samplers. In Scandinavia it is also a popular motif on samplers but is almost always disproportionately small in the general medley of patterns.

The regeneration of the tree, with its symbolism of spring, celebrated in Europe in hundreds of folk rites concerning the decoration of bushes or dancing round maypoles, surprisingly appears hardly at all in embroidery; an exception is the maypole motif of Swedish samplers.

As the symbolism of fertility entwines the cult of the tree with that of the goddess, so the tree is also linked with hunting mythology. The palaeolithic hunters placed it at the cosmic centre and the shaman, emissary between the spirits of the animal world and their human hunters, still today ascends the cosmic tree on his journey of suffering and rebirth.

BELOW *Sampler, England, 1826. The biblical tree of knowledge is the central motif of many nineteenth-century English samplers, and is shown in a more natural rendering but still with flanking birds and animals and also carnations.*

THE HUNT

Palaeolithic man was a hunter. He derived his food, clothing and even his shelter from the great herds that roamed shifting land masses between eras of glaciation and warming. As they were crucial to his survival he imbued the animals with souls, taking care as he killed them to ensure by magic rites their regeneration for his future needs. In the deep caves of northern Spain and southern France he drew symbols and abstractions of their shapes and powers. In the art of these sanctuaries of hunting magic animal is superimposed on animal with visible internal organs; a bovine with head turned is attacked by a predator; a shaman with stag's antlers takes on its identity as he dances.

IDENTIFICATION OF A CULT SOURCE

Death for the primitive hunter was usually violent, understood to be the result of magic and not natural causes and therefore to be propitiated by ritual. His hunting terrain extended from Cantabria to Siberia and beyond to the Americas. After some thirty thousand years, evidence of some of his hunting rituals are to be found in the embroidery of the same region from Spain to Siberia: the motif of the predator and hunted animal with body markings, the symbolism of horns representing the magic power of the animal itself, the role of the shaman, and the spiritual aspect of birds.

BACKGROUND *The steppelands, traditional home of the early nomadic hunters, extend from Asia to the Great Plain of Hungary and were always a transit region of eastward and westward migration bringing, for example, conquering peoples such as the Mongols into Europe. Shepherds of the Hungarian Plain wear embroidered skin and woollen coats, often with vestigial sleeves that indicate an Asian origin.*

THE PREDATOR AND HUNTED ANIMAL

The most famous example in embroidery of the palaeolithic motif of a hunted animal attacked by a predator – in this case a camel and a lion – is on the coronation mantle of the Holy Roman Emperors, thought to have been made in Palermo in 1133–34 for Roger II of Sicily. Significantly, Sicily and Spain were the two points of penetration into Europe of Arab and thus oriental culture, and in Spain it is the embroidery of the small university town of Salamanca which features this palaeolithic design of the hunted animal, head half turned and separated from the body by a collar – a device also of Islamic art – with spaces in the body that originally represented the animal's organs. In these spaces the swastika, or symbols also worn as silver amulets such as the trout or heart, are worked. Over the head is normally a crown and in the mouth a curving floral branch. The animal may be either resting or rampant, and around it are flowing lines interspersed with flowers: the usual fertility symbols of carnations, tulips, pomegranates, but also lotus, papyrus and palms.

This motif of the hunted animal with turned head is used on certain Salamancan embroideries of ritual purpose, worked in pastel silks: cloths used as hangings for balconies and windows on the days of religious processions, as festival covers for chests, or as covers of gifts of bread and fruit on wedding days. The sleeves of women's linen bridal shirts, the neck and cuffs of men's, and also offertory cloths for the church, are embroidered with the same motifs but in black wool, with the small designs in the body spaces sometimes in red and blue.

Many of the felt saddle linings (*shabracks*) of Pazyryk, dating from about the fourth century BC, show the same hunted animal, with head turned and spaces in the body, attacked by a predator – usually a lion or eagle. The designs are appliquéd or inserted leather or felt, and the embroidery simply outlines them in cord, emphasizing the details in wool chain stitch. These animals in combat are usually winged and antlered and the spaces in their body are frequently depicted as punctuation marks. This style is typical of the animal art of the Scythians, kindred of the Pazyryk people.

In the embroideries of the Ionian islands of Greece the body spaces of stags and other animals are worked with smaller deer and birds. The same device of smaller versions of the creature within its own body features in the embroideries of the Paracas culture and lingers in the textiles of Guatemala.

Palaeolithic decorative devices of hunted animal and predator, both with body markings, survive in the textiles of Pazyryk and the mantle of Sicily. The head was often separated by a collar – and, on the mantle, by the lion's claws.

The hunted animal with half-turned head is a frequent motif in one group of peasant embroideries of the isolated provinces of rural western China, mainly of Szechnan. Their indigo cotton thread patterning, that follows warp and weft and fills almost all the design areas leaving only a few elements in reserve, is in the tradition of the embroidery of the Miao tribes, spread across south-west China and northern Thailand. Mainly valances for the marriage bed, the embroideries are in cross stitch in indigo cotton thread on coarse white cotton with a pattern of medallions interspersed with small motifs.

RIGHT *Cover, Salamanca, Spain. The palaeolithic design of a hunted animal, head half turned and separated from the body by a collar – a device also of Islamic art – features on the embroideries of the town of Salamanca in Spain. The motif is often combined with trout and with the swastika, both symbols also worn as silver amulets. The designs were worked in black wool on linen shifts and in pastel silks on ritual cloths.*

LEFT *The palaeolithic device of the half-turned head that survives in embroidery is shown in the indigo and white work of peasant China.*

HORNED
AND ANTLERED ANIMALS

To primitive hunting societies the most important animals were horned and antlered. The curved horns of rams and goats had a myriad uses for the mounted nomads of the steppes and these animals were, after the horse, the most important element in their economy. The stag, deer, caribou and reindeer, too, formed the focus of human hunting economies and were worshipped not only for their meat and skins but also because the mystery of rebirth was manifest in the shedding and regrowth of their antlers. Elsewhere the buffalo, bison or bull were revered. Horns are still hung above doorways from Afghanistan to Spain as a protective device.

An early example of a horned animal used as a votive or amulet is the gold plaque of a bovine dating from 4500 BC, found in the tombs of Varna in Bulgaria. The holes in this plaque would indicate that it was stitched onto fabric.

Motifs derived from horns and antlers occur especially on embroidery from Central Asia, where they are also very common on carpets, felts and ikats, and from northern and eastern Europe. Native North American hair embroidery also featured curved horn designs, until about 1860 when European-inspired floral designs took precedence. Though both derive from animals of the hunt, antlers and horns as motifs diverge more and more with stylization, the antlers becoming almost lines of zigzags and the horns a double curve, even possibly a heart.

In Western European embroidery the stag itself as a motif features in depictions of the hunt and, having no particular symbolism, is portrayed naturalistically. Sibmacher's pattern book of 1597 contained a heavily antlered seated deer, which became a favourite motif on samplers.

ANTLERED ANIMALS

There are two aspects of antlered animals that relate to embroidery: the shape of antlers as a design motif and the use of the hair of the animal as thread.

Antlers as a motif are naturally found mainly in the embroidery of Siberia, northern Russia and Finland. Depiction is never realistic but always stylized, even into a pattern of mere interrelated zigzags. The linen shifts of the Siberian Mordu and Tcheremiss peoples bear such patterning over almost the entire surface, with white and blue or red beads, gold braiding, studs and sequins. In addition all the seams and the deep hem are appliquéd with red fabric. They were worn with headdresses which were often decorated with hanging bands of linen similarly appliquéd with red swastikas.

Hair embroidery was common to approximately two thirds of the northern world – the area between Scandinavia eastward to the Atlantic coast of Canada, where the reindeer of Europe and Asia and the caribou of America, both of the same *Rangifer* genus, and also moose, were indigenous. Hair embroidery probably originated during the period when reindeer were hunted rather than domesticated. In North America moose hair was preferred to caribou for embroidery and is often mistaken for quillwork, to which it bears a strong resemblance. In Siberia reindeer hair was most commonly used and is often combined with beadwork and paint. The finest work is that of the Aleuts who combined hair embroidery with fishskin and the gut of sea mammals. Only the Sami have no tradition of hair embroidery, probably because of their early trade contacts with the Scandinavians, but edge their clothing with brightly coloured strips of wool and for embroidery use tin wrapped round sinew.

Much hair embroidery is endowed with magical properties. The hair chosen comes from the animal's throat and is white. The finest were sacred to some Siberian tribes and believed to impart magical force to the clothing of shamans. For the Montagnais people of north-eastern Canada mats of birchbark with caribou hair embroidery recorded the caribou killed by the owner and were reserved for important occasions, in particular for the *macusham*, a men's ceremonial feast associated with hunting magic.

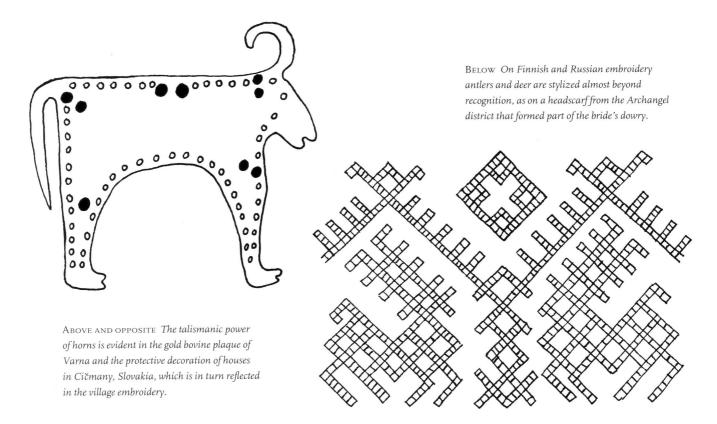

BELOW *On Finnish and Russian embroidery antlers and deer are stylized almost beyond recognition, as on a headscarf from the Archangel district that formed part of the bride's dowry.*

ABOVE AND OPPOSITE *The talismanic power of horns is evident in the gold bovine plaque of Varna and the protective decoration of houses in Čičmany, Slovakia, which is in turn reflected in the village embroidery.*

CURVED HORNS

Bovine horns as a motif, such as those of the ram, goat, buffalo, bison and bull, can be curved inward or outward, and often end in a spiral. The neolithic pots of China, for example, bear this pattern in both forms, combined with lunar and water symbolism. In embroidery, as in felts and carpets, this curved horn features particularly in the work of the peoples of Central Asia. It is also used as an amulet on the high embroidered hoods worn by babies in the remote mountains of Indus Kohistan in Pakistan. While the deep back of the hood forms a shawl to protect the baby from the freezing winds, the horn on the front protects it from disease and misfortune. Similar hoods, but different in shape, are also occasionally worn by women.

The curved horn as a motif extends westward beyond the limits of the steppelands in the embroidery of the nomadic Sarakatsani of Greece. It is also found particularly on the embroidery of the homemade woollen garments of isolated sheep-rearing areas of eastern Europe, where ancient motifs lingered. An example is the archaic rural clothing of Montenegro, which contrasts with the

entirely Turkish style of the costume of its capital Cetinje – before the First World War the town was a dazzling outpost of the Ottoman empire meriting a dozen or more opulent foreign embassies. At its westernmost point in the embroidery of Hungary and Bulgaria, the horn remains as a small hooked motif worked on the edge of patterns, usually in black thread.

When stylized, the curved horn motif with inwardly twisted spirals

ABOVE *Hood for a baby with shawl attached to protect it from the Himalayan weather, Kohistan, Pakistan. The horned amulet and button would protect it from evil spirits and disease.*

on prehistoric Chinese pots could be the basis of the heart pattern of eastern and central Europe. In the embroidery of both the Czech Republic and Slovakia a motif halfway between this design and the Western heart appears frequently. By the Alpine regions the heart as a sentimental motif is established and in folk art is naturalistically portrayed in the Western European manner, but still with the symbolic pomegranate, rose, carnation and tulip. The western-most geographical penetration of Asian peoples would seem to mark the region of transition from stylized inwardly curving horn to conventional heart.

LEFT *Girl's bolero, Luhacovice, Moravia. The curved horn motif with inwardly twisted spirals, found on prehistoric Chinese pots, could be the basis of the heart pattern of eastern and central Europe. It appears frequently in the embroideries of both Slovakia and Moravia in this form, but by the Alpine regions of western Europe the pattern is a conventional heart.*

ABOVE *Shepherd's coat, Nuristan, Afghanistan. The ubiquitous horn motifs of the carpets and felts of Central Asia, as also of the embroideries, decorate in a random fashion the heavy wool coats of the shepherds of Nuristan. The patterns are combined with solar whorls. Horned animals were essential to the economy of the peoples of Asia and horns are still placed above doorways as a protective device.*

LEFT, ABOVE AND RIGHT *Curved and hooked horn shapes decorate neolithic pots of China (ABOVE) and clothing of the rural Balkans – here, on a woollen slipper (LEFT). In a Chinese ritual bronze (RIGHT) of the Zhou dynasty (c. 1050–771 BC) the inwardly curved horns evoke the heart shape.*

HORNED HEADDRESSES

Donning a horned headdress is still part of the shaman's ritual, putting him into contact with the spirit world: the dancing shaman with horned headdress in palaeolithic rock art is an image that has survived to the present day. Human heads with hair arranged in horn shapes, or with horned headdresses, feature on stone idols of the Russian steppelands dating from about 1000 BC; the Egyptian goddess of love, Hathor, is depicted in tomb paintings with a two-horned headdress holding the sundisc between the horns; the Sassanid kings of southern Iran wore single-horned caps which also, in a painting of the third century AD, supported the solar disc; Uygur women in the cave paintings of Chotso in Turfan, dating from the ninth to the tenth century AD, have a two-horned hairstyle; when the Spanish arrived in Mexico they drew pictures of the local women with their hair arranged in two horns; and this ancient concept survives to this day in the embroidered caps of Slovakia.

In the valley of the upper Horn river a string of villages, each with its own dialect though only a few miles apart, has retained its distinctive headdress, although the tradition would now seem to be slowly dying. Each village has a different style of cap, either one- or two-horned, beneath which the hair is first arranged in a complicated system of winding. In many places a ritual was associated with gathering a branch to make the wooden frame which often supplemented the hair. Women working in the fields wear their cap covered with a black scarf, which they remove to go to

church or for special occasions. The old women of the Hron valley expect to be laid to rest in their best embroidered clothes and their cap, but now fear that by the time they die there will be no one left able to dress their hair so that they can be buried in their cap, whose horn symbolism links them to the spirit world.

Horned headdresses were common in Russia and in Bulgaria, Romania, Transylvania and Albania. In Russia they were worn by the poorest peasants. Martha Wilmot, on her travels in the region in the early nineteenth century, comments that the mother of the nine-year-old girl she was given as a serf wore a kerchief and was thus a degree above the lowest peasants, who wore horned headdresses. In Moldavia women always had to wear a horned headdress to go to church and also to grind corn and bake consecrated bread for the sacrament.

ABOVE AND RIGHT *Origins of the single-horned headdress and hair arrangement can be seen in the Sassanid kings and of the double in the goddess Hathor. Double-horned hair arrangements are also found in cave paintings of Uygur women of the tenth century and on stone idols of the steppes dating from around 1000 BC.*

RIGHT *Woman's bonnet, Polomka, Slovakia.* The ancient horned headdress, augmented by dressing the hair in a single or double horn or using a wooden frame to support it, survived in eastern Europe and is still found in the bonnets of the married women of the Hron valley in Slovakia. Some headdresses are of the single horned shape, as those of Polomka, and some double as those of Rousse in Bulgaria.

LEFT *Appliqué cloth, Egypt.* The Egyptian goddess Hathor is depicted in tomb paintings with a two-horned headdress, bearing the sundisc. After the discovery of Tutankhamun's tomb in 1922 it became fashionable to copy such tomb paintings in appliqué pictures to sell to tourists (see also p. 61).

SHAMANISM

The prime example of decoration endowing the wearer with the magical force of the creature it symbolizes is the shaman. Originating in the hunting societies of the palaeolithic era, shamanism lingers in the Arctic north, Korea, pockets of South-East Asia, Aboriginal Australia, Africa, among the Ainu and Native American tribes, and in South America. Everything in the natural world has a spirit which the shaman controls.

The shaman is identified by his costume and its decoration. The wearing of antlers to associate him with the animal world and invest him with its powers and spirits is common, as is the hanging on his vestments of all manner of symbolic accoutrements: amulets which in Islamic countries contain Koranic verses, bells to arouse the soul, trophies of the hunt, towels with stylized antler motifs embroidered in red.

The embroidered decoration on his clothing is in sacred white reindeer thread and is often of skeletal patterning – ribs and bones – symbolizing his figurative death and subsequent rebirth.

Mystical animals found in archaic embroidery are those linked with shamanism such as the jaguar, an animal who hunts at night and who in the Americas was the shaman's familiar. The bear in many northern cultures was believed to be a human ancestor and guardian. It was revered by the Ainu, whose appliqué patterns portray the bear, and by the Ghiliak of Siberia. For their festival, when the men of one clan about to marry into another are invited to kill the bear, clothing is worn with embroidered spiral patterns that symbolize the animal. Stags, like birds, were believed to transport souls between earth and heaven: most shamanistic ritual is accompanied by the use of hallucinogenics, especially magic mushrooms, and a state of transcendence, or trance, was linked to the stag. Creatures believed by some peoples to be incarnations of the soul, such as lizards or toads or bees and particularly birds, were also regarded as mystical.

ABOVE RIGHT *War coat, Asante, Ghana. Talismanic charms sewn on to clothing were used by hunters, warriors and also shamans. The shaman, originating in the hunting societies of the palaeolithic era, also identifies himself with the animal world by decoration. For the hunter the amulets afford protection.*

RIGHT *Hem of leggings, Ainu people, Japan. To the Ainu of Japan the bear was the shaman's familiar and believed to be a human ancestor and guardian. He is stylized into a pattern on the edges of their clothing.*

BIRDS

Birds almost everywhere represent the spirit world. They are messengers from heaven, the sky and the sun gods, and they carry the souls of the departed to the afterlife, where they become birds themselves. The Ugrians of Siberia tattoo birds on their shoulders to keep the soul in the body, carve them on cradles to prevent offspring wandering in the woods during sleep, and embroider them on fishskin bridal robes as symbols of the souls that would lodge in the future children.

In South-East Asia, too, spirits of the dead were believed to take the form of birds. Thus people with birds' heads are a motif found on the ritual sarongs of the women of Lampung in Sumatra, appearing as figures on the ships of the dead patterns that are the main feature of one type of these embroideries. In Borneo the hornbill was venerated and features in simple embroidery on barkcloth coats and festive hangings.

Birds are one of the most common embroidery motifs in the world, often associated with the tree of life, with solar patterns and with floral symbols of fertility. They may range from a simple

BELOW The traditional symbol of the Ghiliak Siberian bride is the tree of life carrying birds that represent the children to be born.

good luck symbol to a statement of spiritual belief that is shared by a clan but remains ultimately private and personal, such as the thunderbird of Native American tribes. The thunderbird, generally accepted as a benign creature of the upper world, bringing rain and fertility, but who also attacked the evil animal life of the underworld with lightning, is decoratively transposed as the thunderbird pattern combined with zigzags.

Birds as an ornamental motif are chosen for their general symbolism, or else for the specific attributes of their species – power, epitomized by the eagle and condor, the regal beauty of the peacock, or such harbingers of daylight as the cock. The latter, believed to chase away the evil spirits of the night, is often associated with solar symbolism and with the tree of life, for the rebirth of the day mirrors the rebirth of the seasons. Most commonly the cock is depicted in confronting pairs with or without a centrally placed related symbol.

In Christianity the symbolic attributes of birds as messengers from heaven are assumed by angels and in many embroideries these are little but birds in disguise.

LEFT Pouch, Ojibwa or Ottowa, North America. Thunderbirds were mythological beings that caused thunder and lightning and brought the spring rains. As air spirits they fought against underwater deities such as panthers. In embroidery they are often depicted with zigzag patterning denoting lightning.

ABOVE Door hangings, sakhyo, toran, Kanebi caste, Kutch, India. Birds are often chosen as symbols of the attributes of their species. The peacock is not only a bird of regal beauty but is also associated with sun worship and is an emblem of Sarasvati, Hindu goddess of wisdom, music and poetry. Hangings such as these decorate doorways in India on special occasions.

THE SUN

In a small quiet garden of ancient Carthage, now an affluent suburb of Tunis, broken stone stelae lie around a sacrificial altar where first-born sons were beheaded to honour the sun god Ba'al Hammon and the fertility goddess Tanit. A sun demanding human blood was also a Mayan cult, whereas for another great sun-worshipping civilization, the ancient Egyptians, it was the beneficent and positive aspects that were venerated: its life-giving rays and daily rebirth. To palaeolithic hunting societies the sun was the greatest hunter of all, nightly slaying the stars but ensuring the survival of their souls so that they would return the next evening.

Primitive veneration of the sun did not always lead to formalized solar cults. It was almost always inextricably linked with that of the moon, which because of its waxing and waning, its control over tides and waters and its mystical relation to the menstrual cycle of women, held a stronger position in pagan mythology. In most societies the sun was regarded as male and the moon as female, though in some this was reversed. European languages, for example, still retain this duality.

Below Of the conventional pictographs for the sun the Bouriate people of Siberia take the crossed disc and combine it with the moon, the tree of life and symbols of shamanism on a cult drawing.

IDENTIFICATION OF A CULT SOURCE

The pictographs that conventionally denote the sun in decorative arts, and that are found in embroidery over most of the world, already appear in palaeolithic art. Concentric circles were originally a lunar symbol and with the addition of a cross became solar; the simple circle with a cross is also solar and conveys the linking of the four corners of the earth. The spiral, as well as expressing creative force, symbolizes the sun and the moon and was especially important in Bronze Age Scandinavia and in Celtic and Viking traditions. The circle with a central dot, the whorl with twisted rays and the circle with straight rays all feature in cave paintings.

The swastika, another accepted solar symbol, but more complex in that it also expresses concepts of movement and change, first appears in the neolithic period around 4000 BC, together with the rosette as a solar emblem. A rosette is also formed by the opened petals of the lotus, a flower associated with the sun, especially in Egyptian and Hindu mythology.

The four-rayed star served as a symbolic representation of Shamash, the Sumerian sun god, and later became the Maltese cross, while the 8-pointed star, one of the most common motifs of all in embroidery, represented his consort Gula.

The axe was a solar emblem of the sky gods and an Egyptian solar symbol. The double axe possibly conveyed the union of the sky gods with the earth goddess and was imbued with magic power by people as diverse as the Yoruba of West Africa and the Minoans of Crete. There are many possible interpretations of its meaning and derivation; it is believed to represent, for example, the wings of the goddess, and the waxing and waning of the moon, but it is always associated with fertility.

Solar worship is manifested in embroidery in varied ways in different regions of the world.

Left Doorway, Benares, India. Many protective devices, such as horns, fish, hands, crosses, diamonds, rosettes and swastikas are carved or painted on buildings in many parts of the world, especially over doorways. Solar mythology is one source of such protection.

THE SUN MOTIF IN NORTH AFRICA
EGYPT

The embroideries of Egypt that seem to be intimately linked with the cult of the sun are those of the Siwa oasis in the Western desert. Amid the date palms and olive groves of this large oasis, once an important staging post on the only route across a waterless desert, are ancient solar temples. The area is populated by the original Berber and Bedouin, who still retain their own languages, and were known as worshippers of the sun god Amon-Ra.

Siwan girls are married at about fourteen and the family of the bride sew all the clothes. For their wedding, and for the only other occasions on which they stepped out of their homes – to go to other marriages and funerals and to

congratulate a new mother on the birth of her child – women wore seven underdresses: white, red, then silk ones of black, yellow, blue, orange and green and on top the embroidered wedding dress, either of white or black.

This overdress is cut wide with deep sleeves and is embroidered with a sunburst pattern over the entire front. Rows of chain stitch around the neck and front opening, often also seven in number, are edged with seven blocks of almost solid embroidery, three on each side and one at the centre front, sometimes finished with multicoloured ties with tassels. From these emanate lines of fine stitchery interspersed with small patterns, mainly also solar symbols: Maltese crosses, small stars, spinning circles, double axes. At each corner of the blocks and down the neck opening are white pearl buttons, though on some the entire front is decorated with buttons, often in groups of three which in other cultures, such as the Naga of Assam, denotes a star. The dominant colours of yellow, orange and red are also solar. Sometimes green, blue and black are added, which with the white pearl buttons make the seven colours of Siwan embroidery. These same colours, with purple instead of black, are the seven colours of joy associated with the sun in Sindhi embroidery. In modern work coloured plastic buttons replace the pearl ones, but the colour range is normally adhered to. Similar embroidery decorates the headscarf and trousers worn with the dresses.

Egyptian appliqué pictures of the goddess Hathor with the sundisc between

LEFT *Marriage dress, Siwa oasis, Egypt. The black and white marriage dresses of the Siwa oasis are embroidered with a sunburst design over the entire front. Lines of chain stitch from seven blocks of pattern at the neck are interspersed with solar symbols and buttons of white pearl or coloured plastic.*

ABOVE *Marriage shawl, Ksour Esaf, Tunisia. Marriage shawls add the sun and crescent moon to the tree of life and strange anthropomorphic patterns, believed to protect the bride from evil spirits.*

her horns are not designs that still remain from ancient sun worship, but are merely copies of tomb paintings that it became fashionable to make and sell to tourists after the discovery of Tutankhamun's tomb.

TUNISIA

The coastal plain of Tunisia is planted with soldierly rows of olive trees from which rises, like the cathedral of Chartres above the cornfields of Beauce, the Roman amphitheatre of the small town of El Jem, sixth biggest of the Roman world. The bride of El Jem, and of the large village of Ksour Esaf not far distant – a poor place of narrow unmade streets and adobe buildings – wears seven white tunics, a jacket and a hood all heavily worked with gold, and with them a headshawl of half indigo and half hennaed wool, embroidered with archaic motifs. The origin of most of these motifs, which can be either plant-like, reptilian or anthropomorphic, is impossible to determine, but there is no ambiguity in the depiction of the sun and moon. The embroidery forms a wide band along the edge worn over the forehead, and is in thick couched threads, beneath which a line of tassels frames the face. These bridal textiles were a present from mother to daughter.

THE SUN MOTIF IN THE AMERICAS

Many North American tribes considered the sun to be the god of creation and made sacrificial offerings to it. Symbols of the sun are a widespread motif in the embroidery and tattooing of the Iroquois and Algonquin.

CENTRAL AND SOUTH AMERICA

The solar worship of the Aztecs, the Incas and Mayans has left little trace in embroidery, though in the brocaded weavings of Guatemala and Bolivia the sun is a common motif, stylized into a diamond shape. In embroidery pre-Conquest cloaks of Mexico were decorated with designs of solar rays but once subject to European influence, the sun motif appears infrequently, and then depicted with the moon and Catholic symbols.

It is particularly in the men's black suits of the Guatemalan town of Santo Tomás Chichicastenango that the ancient sun motifs survive. A flap, usually called an ear, made of light-coloured cotton, is attached to the side of the trouser leg, extending from hip to knee. On it are embroidered solar patterns which indicate the age and virility of the wearer. The most ornate, known as the *Ma Kij* – or *Abuelo Sol*, 'grandfather sun' in Spanish – has a large rayed sun with extra flowers and leaves, and is worn by virile men between twenty-five and sixty. A man who is sterile does not have the right to wear this decoration. From puberty to the age of twenty-five the pattern is of two plainer suns, one below

the other. The upper one represents the elder man who still takes precedence over the younger. From the age of about six a boy has one simple rayed sun, with a cross below it to which rays will be added as he reaches puberty.

The short black woollen jacket worn with these trousers has a sun embroidered in chain stitch at the base of the neck opening. The costume was worn every day until about the 1930s but is now only used for festive occasions. The work is done by men embroiderers of the town and motifs of flowers and birds are gradually supplanting the symbolic suns.

RIGHT *At the procession of All Souls' Night in Chichicastenango, the men wear their solar embroidered costumes and carry images of Santo Tomás and of the sun. Fireworks are let off only after magicians have been consulted.*

RIGHT *Sampler, Mexico. Solar mythology was linked with the moon. In European style embroidery the sun and moon together, especially with the crucifix and Catholic symbols such as IHS, more frequently convey the darkening of the sky at Christ's death, recounted by Luke.*

THE SUN MOTIF IN EUROPE

In European embroidery motifs derived from the sun are mainly in the form of rosettes, though the ritual towels of Russia associated with the goddess depict the sun as a galloping horse, recalling its trajectory across the sky, or as a magnificent firebird, in honour of the marvel of its appearing in spring at the end of a long dark winter. The sunbird was already a solar symbol in the palaeolithic era.

FRANCE

In Brittany the motif known as 'the peacock's feather' on the embroidered jackets of Pont-Aven comes from an Indo-European symbol first found in the rock drawings of Bohusland and in the fibulae and bronze knives of prehistoric Denmark. It represents the sun, or more especially the ship of the sun. These embroideries are always in yellow or orange, colours with obvious solar associations.

BELOW The 'peacock feather' pattern of men's and women's jackets of Finistère, Brittany, derives from prehistoric solar motifs. The bands of patterning never vary, but are more richly embroidered on the side front worn outside for festivities and inside for mourning.

ABOVE The solar motif of a quadruple hook, derived from the swastika, is embroidered in chain stitch on woollen fabric, grada, *and appliquéd at the hip of a Serbian woman's woollen jacket,* sadak.

SPAIN

In Spain the village of Lagartera in the province of Toledo is still the commercial centre for embroidery. Here the women's linen blouses, *gorgueras*, which cover the chest and back and tie under the arms with tape, have a dominant front border of spirals. Instead of the satin and back stitch of the rest of the embroidery the spirals are worked in a double loop stitch known as *punto real*, giving a raised effect. Edging these, and worked round the neck and outer edges, are repeated motifs of the tree of life, confronting birds or animals and stylized carnations. All the embroidery is in black wool and the fabric is homespun handwoven linen. Similar blouses from the nearby village of Navalcan have patterns based on the labyrinth instead of the spiral.

RIGHT Cloth, Buzsák, Hungary. In European embroidery, motifs derived from the sun are mainly in the form of rosettes. In the village of Buzsák, near Lake Balaton, such rosette patterns are combined with hooked spirals. The spiral is an associated solar symbol and also expresses creative force.

EASTERN EUROPE

In eastern Europe solar patterns are mostly Central Asian in origin. They are frequently worked in wool or in leather appliqué and are combined with associated symbols such as hooked spirals and birds. The rosette is the most common form and there are many examples in the embroidery of Hungary and of Slovakia. In Buzsák, close to Lake Balaton in Hungary, for instance, the women embroider cloths in black and red with circles and rosettes combined with hooked spirals, while in the village of Rybany in Slovakia the women work a rosette flanked by birds and tulips on the back of their linen caps and across the sleeves of their shifts.

Solar-derived motifs in the embroidery of Bulgaria and the former Yugoslavia are more obviously pagan. In Bulgaria the sleeves of the linen shifts of Samokov and Stanke Dimitrov, small mountain towns to the south of Sofia, are embroidered with a solar motif with rays ordered into a comb-like row and combined with spirals. The same comb-like pattern on Paracas textiles denoted rain. Spirals and swastikas on the sleeveless woollen coats of Serbia, Croatia and Montenegro evolve into a four-hooked pattern incorporating associated symbols of horns, stars, triangles, zigzags and S-shapes. These patterns are worked in chain stitch on pieces of homespun wool of red, blue or green which are then applied to the garment.

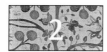

THE SUN MOTIF IN CENTRAL ASIA

Portable wealth in the form of textiles is part of the nomadic way of life of the peoples who wander across the steppelands of Central Asia and who are only now adopting a more settled way of life. Of the greatest importance were felts and carpets, embroideries less so. All have solar motifs, which can be circular, as discs and whorls, or a circle within a circle (a pattern used in felts and believed to ward off the evil eye) or versions of the scroll motif known as 'running dog' or 'wave'. This reversible pattern was presumed mystic as it bears the magical significance of the balance between life and death, light and dark, male and female, sun and moon. It is a pattern also found on neolithic pottery of Old Europe.

The most famous embroideries are the *suzanis* made by the Uzbek, a mixture of peoples who grouped under Uzbek Khan when he conquered the central steppelands in the early fourteenth century. They are large hangings or bedcovers worked as dowry pieces and made in the area from Bokhara and Nurata in the west to Tashkent and Pskent in the east.

They are made of strips of unbleached cotton or linen embroidered predominantly in reds and pinks, with touches of contrasting colour, in Bokhara or Romanian couching, with some chain stitch. Most are floral with the field of flower motifs divided by stems and leaves into latticework. Further east the source of their pattern is more solar than floral. In the *suzanis* of Tashkent the flowers become large plain red discs and cover the field almost entirely, the leaves and stems reduced to small tendrils. In Pskent the designs are overtly solar, with astrological patterns of suns, moons, stars and solar symbols.

LEFT Suzani, *Tashkent, Uzbekistan. Though* suzanis *are regarded as floral embroideries, the 'flower heads' on those of Tashkent, as this one, are large plain red discs of solar aspect, while the* suzanis *of Pskent are overtly solar, with astrological patterns of suns, moons, stars and solar symbols.*

ABOVE *Pazyryk textiles featured the mystic patterns of a row of horns and the 'running dog' scroll motif associated with the sun and moon.*

During the early twentieth century many Uzbeks left Russia for Afghanistan where they could still lead a nomadic life. Among them was a particularly wild and tough group of mounted warriors, the Lakai. The embroidered dresses of their women and the small mats for wrapping presents that girls made for their dowry have solar motifs in the form of whorls, together with rams' horns, hook and wave patterns, spirals and stars. Similar motifs of freewheeling whorls and discs, horns, spirals and circles, and also fish and exotic unrecognizable plant forms, are very common on the embroidery of the Kalmuk, a people who live to the north of the Caucasus mountains.

Another brigandly tribe were the Tekke Turkmen, who were known for their raids into Persia stealing women and even men. Edmund O'Donovan, visiting the Merv oasis in 1880, described these people as ruffianly, irreclaimable scamps who, when they rode into town, were made to leave their swords and guns with the guard at the town gate and allowed only their knives. The embroidery of the women of the tribe features repeat swastikas on the cuffs of the trousers they make for their dowry, in the same interlaced stitch with ridged outline called *kesdi* in which they work the tulip and hook motifs of their cloaks.

ABOVE *Cloth, Lakai Uzbek, Afghanistan. Many tent hangings, bedding covers and dowry cloths of the Lakai Uzbek are embroidered with the solar symbol of a freewheeling whorl. On this cloth this pattern is combined with motifs of heart-shaped aspect which enclose tulips, symbol of fertility.*

THE SUN MOTIF IN INDIA AND PAKISTAN

The high mountain passes through the Hindu Kush, the Pamirs and Karakorum, though in modern times obstructed by national frontiers, were an established route from the deserts traversed by the silk roads to the Indus valley and Indian subcontinent. The recent construction of the Karakorum highway, blasting a path through wild terrain, has disclosed petroglyphs carved on rocks along its way from the fifth millennium BC onwards.

The earliest are of palaeolithic hunting magic. Later animals of the first millennium BC show the same characteristics as the animals of Scythian art. As Buddhism spread through the first and second centuries pictorial Buddhist themes were incised alongside and over the ancient designs. By the ninth and tenth centuries there seems to have been a revolt against Buddhism. Roughly hewn motifs appear of axes, mounted worshippers or deities and especially of sun discs. Not only had sun worship been brought to this area many centuries before by migrating peoples from the west bringing the Phoenician sun god Ba'al, the Greek Helios and the Sumerian Shamash, but also at the period the rock carvings were made there was a flourishing sun cult in Kashmir and at Multan in the steppelands, whose sun temple was the main sanctuary for the whole region.

LEFT *Boulders along the Karakorum highway have been carved through the centuries with solar discs, hunting scenes, horsemen, figures, animals, axes and Buddhist stupas.*

BELOW *Wedding canopy, Rajasthan, India. Canopies erected at weddings in Rajasthan have a solar disc as the central motif. Variations of this are the central lotus, itself also a solar symbol, on the canopies of Gujarat, and also on the kanthas of Bengal.*

KOHISTAN

In Kohistan – the region bordering the valley where the highway passes – embroidery motifs on the women's and children's clothing resemble the solar emblems on the rock carvings, either in the form of eight rays within a squared-off disc, or more usually, a disc divided into sections.

The motifs cover the deep sleeves and bodice fronts of the women's black cotton dresses, their short flared skirts made of hundreds of godets being left plain. Usually a particularly complex disc is set at the shoulders. One also forms the centrepiece of the V-shaped back flap of the babies' hoods. They are also worked on blouses and children's jackets.

The embroidery is in floss silk thread in darning stitch forming narrow diagonal rows with voiding between, with some finely worked detailing in cross stitch, especially on garment edges. The predominant colour is ruby red, with touches of yellow, orange and green. All motifs are outlined with small white beads and accentuated by white buttons, and the garments themselves are lined with floral print or blue cotton and bordered with lead beads or old zips.

ABOVE *Woman's dress, Kohistan, Pakistan. The solar discs embroidered on the women's dresses and blouses and children's jackets of Kohistan resemble the patterns carved on rocks from the fifth millennium BC onwards along the route of the nearby Karakorum highway. There was once a flourishing sun cult in the region. These patterns are always outlined in white beads and have added buttons, coins and metal discs.*

SWAT

Close by Kohistan in the valley of the river Swat which rises in these mountains the women embroider their black cotton dresses over the entire front, shoulders and cuffs with diamond-shaped rather than circular discs, and with a proliferation of horned motifs. The work is in shocking pink floss silk in darning stitch, mainly arranged in diagonal rows with voiding, and is outlined in yellow double running, with touches of green and white.

SIND

The greatest of the rivers whose source lies in these mountains is the Indus, home at Harappa and Mohenjo-daro of one of mankind's earliest civilizations. In its lower reaches in the province of

Sind are to be found groups of tombs built from the fifteenth century on, the major ones sited in the desert at Chaukhandi. The tombs are ornately carved in sections, some with geometric motifs and some with rosettes symbolizing the sun, sometimes cut in half as though rising or setting. The men's tombs are often capped with a carved turban, a custom also of Turkey where a man's turban is placed on an indoor tomb and preserved as an effigy. The women's are decorated with the pattern of their necklace and earrings.

Left The desert tombs of Sind are carved with rosette patterns symbolizing the sun and closely resembling the mirrorwork blouses of Sindhi women. Offerings to the spirits, in the form of bits of rag, hairs, or dead animals or their skins, are hung on the tombs or tied to the nearest bush.

Left Woman's skirt, Bansali caste, Kutch, India. The Bansalis, a Hindu farming caste, believe themselves descended from the sun god Surya and the women wear yellow or orange skirts embroidered with sun discs.

The people of Sind have retained many of their ancient animistic beliefs and the patterns on these tombs are still worked on the women's embroidery, especially that of the Lohana merchant class and the Jats, herders who are believed to have originated in the region of Iran/Iraq. The fronts of their backless blouses, *choli*, are worked in sections with rosettes, some halved, interspersed with geometric pattern. The whole bodice is dominated by mirrorwork which forms the centres of the rosettes and defines the remaining pattern areas.

GUJARAT

Many of the same peoples, Hindu and Muslim herders and farmers, straddle the political border of Pakistan and India. Those in Gujarat retain from the ancient Indian belief in the sun god Surya the symbol of a circle or swastika on their embroideries. In particular the Kanebi Hindu farmers embroider sun discs together with swastikas, dancing women and peacocks on their skirts and on the borders of their *sadlo*, a draped shawl given to women at the end of their first year of marriage. The Kanebi combine interlacing stitch in white cotton with open chain in yellow, green and pink.

The Bansalis, another Hindu farming group from the Kutch area of Gujarat, believe they are descended from Surya and the women wear skirts covered with sun circles embroidered in running stitch on yellow or orange cotton fabric.

RELIGION AND ITS PATTERNS

OPPOSITE *Hanging, Hong Kong. The attributes of the Eight Taoist Immortals are among the most popular of all Chinese motifs. On this hanging are Zhang Guo-lao with bamboo tube and rods and Lü Dong-bin with sword.*

ABOVE *Prayer cloth, Hazara, Afghanistan. The Shi'ite Hazara embroider small mats to wrap their prayer stones. The cloths were considered holy objects and should never be sold or used in a household where there are menstruating or pregnant women.*

3 TAOISM

The world's major religions were all established in the thousand-year period between 500 BC and AD 500, with the exception of Islam which followed Muhammad's flight from Mecca to Medina in AD 622. Within these structured world religions the purpose of most embroidered textiles is to decorate churches, temples, mosques and synagogues. Such specifically ecclesiastical embroidery is not the concern of this book, but rather the patterns and influences that established religions have introduced into secular embroidery.

Of all secular embroidery, by far the strongest influence of religious philosophy is on that of China, where Confucianism, Taoism and Buddhism existed together. Taoist beliefs in particular, and other symbols associated with Chinese religious thought, feature on most embroideries, even those made for export where such patterns are meaningless to the recipient. The Taoists, originally alchemists, loosely followed the teachings of Lao-Tse, a philosopher believed to have lived in about the fifth century BC.

Attributes of the Eight Taoist Immortals:

LEFT (CLOCKWISE):
*castanets (*ts'ao kuo-ch'iu*);*
*fan (*chung-li chüan*);*
*double gourd and crutch (*li t'ieh-kuai*);*
*lotus pod (*ho hsien ku*);*

RIGHT (TOP TO BOTTOM):
*sword (*lü tung-pin*);*
*bamboo tube and rods (*chang kuo lao*);*
*flute (*han hsiang-tzu*);*
*basket of peaches (*lan ts'ai-ho*).*

TAOIST EMBROIDERED TEXTILES

Taoist priests' robes are richly embroidered with motifs which include the *yin/yang* (female/male) principle of the universe, surrounded by the eight trigrams, the mystic complex of three broken and unbroken lines which is also a motif on secular costume.

The eight holy men of Taoism are known as 'Immortals' as they had the right to feast on the fruit of immortality at the peach festival of Hsi Wang Mu,

the goddess who ruled over a fairy realm in Western Paradise. Each is associated with an attribute which commonly stands alone, especially on clothing. The most popular is the gourd – also one of the essential accoutrements of the Taoist magicians – belonging to Li T'ieh-kuai. He is believed to have been a shaman who returned to the world to inhabit the body of a cripple and is thus normally depicted with a crutch as well. His face is often

blue. Another favourite is the fan of Chung-Li Chüan, patron of the military, perhaps because his fan resembles the banners under which the Manchu military were organized.

The other Taoist Immortals and their attributes are Lü Dong-bin with sword, He Xian-gu with lotus pod, Lan Xiang-zi with flute, Zhang Guo-lao with bamboo tube and rods, Cao Guo-jiu with castanets and Lan Cai-he with basket of peaches or flowers.

THE INFLUENCE OF THE CHINESE LANGUAGE AND SOCIETY

Because of the tonal aspect of Chinese languages two words can be phonetically alike but their meaning distinguished by a different tone of voice. This affords ample opportunity for the symbolic representation of two otherwise unconnected things. Examples in embroidery are legion: 'bat' is the same word, *fu*, phonetically as 'good fortune', and is one of the most common symbols. On exactly the same basis the fish symbolizes abundance and wealth, the carp advantage, the butterfly and chrysanthemum long life, and the vase peace.

Symbols of all kinds permeate Chinese life and thought. Veneration of ancestors, believed to afford access to the next world, and the desire for long life and many sons are expressed by auspicious symbols of longevity and good luck. The dead are believed to enjoy everlasting bliss amidst pine trees with cranes flying above, so that the pine and crane are particularly popular as symbols of long life. Clouds, either banked or as ribbons, provide transport through the heavens for the immortals and thus also symbolize longevity. They can also be interpreted as magic fungus, *lingzhi*.

The attributes of various animals were assigned to the wearer of the embroidery. Mandarin ducks represent connubial bliss. The peacock, a protected bird, is sacred and symbolizes beauty and dignity, as do pheasants and kingfishers. Cocks are honoured as they are believed, as in solar mythology, to drive off the evil spirits of the night. Quails denote bravery. The *ch'i-lin*, a mythical horned animal based on the deer but with dragon-like skin, is a creature of good omen.

The seasons are represented by flowers, and are particularly popular on informal robes. Winter is figured in the Three Friends – the bamboo, pine and plum

blossom, spring the iris or magnolia, summer the peony or lotus, and autumn the chrysanthemum.

The official court robe, the *ch'i-fu* popularly known as the dragon robe, is a symbol in itself. Its decoration is a magnificent portrayal of the universe. At the hem are wavy lines depicting the cosmic ocean, topped by a bank of mist. At the centre front, back and sides, representing the four cardinal points, rises a triple-peaked mountain, symbolizing the primordial world. Over the rest of the gown, surrounded by clouds and good luck motifs, writhe nine dragons, ancient symbol of imperial power. Eight (the number associated with Taoism and Buddhism) are visible and the ninth, representing man, is hidden on the inner flap. Man inside the robe forms the axis of the universe.

The dragon is an essentially Chinese animal and first appears as a rather

ABOVE *Child's bodice, China. Symbolism permeates Chinese life: the dead are believed to enjoy everlasting bliss amidst pine trees and cranes, so that both denote longevity.*

snakelike creature on bronze ritual vessels of about 1400 BC. The animals of the hunt of nomadic Central Asia with half-turned head seem later to have been incorporated into this dragon form, as do stags, horses and especially tigers. This writhing dragon, part snake part tiger, originally belonged to an ancient Chinese belief which classified the universe into five elements, each grouped with a colour, animal and cardinal point. The green dragon dwelt in the east, the white tiger in the west, the red bird in the south and the tortoise and snake together comprised the black warrior of the north. They were part of an even older concept, first found

ABOVE *Dragon robe, ch'i-fu, China. The official Chinese court robe, it is a symbol in itself. Nine dragons, ancient symbol of imperial power, are accompanied by the Taoist gourd and basket of peaches, the crane and the flaming pearl.*

depicted on a mirror of the seventh century BC, that divided the cosmos into four directions.

By the Tang era of the seventh century, the dragon and the red bird had become the most auspicious of the animals, featuring on architecture, clothing and decorative arts. The red bird gradually became confused with another mythical bird with exotic tail plumage, the *fenghuang*, also depicted on early ritual bronze vessels of around 1000 BC. This composite bird is commonly referred to as the phoenix, though it is not the same Western legendary phoenix rising from the ashes. Its association with the empress and the female counterbalances the dragon which had come to symbolize imperial power and the male. Both creatures are embroidered on women's and men's clothing.

ABOVE *Hanging, China. The Chinese believed in many gods: of wealth, longevity and of the kitchen – a family deity who apportioned the length of days, wealth of the household and noted the inhabitants' vices and virtues. Another was Kuan Ti, god of war.*

RIGHT *Woman's jacket, China. The phoenix is associated with the empress and is often worked on women's clothes. The Taoist attributes are woven into the damask fabric.*

3 BUDDHISM

The teaching of Buddha, born in India in about the sixth century BC, is based on the renunciation of desire and the achievement through nirvana of a release from the relentless cycle of birth, suffering, death and rebirth.

BUDDHIST EMBROIDERED TEXTILES

Buddhism was disseminated by wandering, begging monks and in the first century AD reached China along the ancient routes whereby silk, ivory, glass and horses were traded between East and West. Here its earliest association with embroidery is to be found.

The region of Central Asia traversed by these trade routes is now mainly desert but was not always so. As mountain glaciers retreated oases dried, burying towns and monasteries under sand, where they lay hidden until the beginning of the twentieth century. Tales of cities lost in these desert sands then began to attract the attention of Western archaeologists. Sir Aurel Stein was the first to reach the oasis of Dunhuang in the Gobi desert where thousands of cliff-hewn temples protected the traveller along the ancient silk road. In one of these caves, guarded by an old Buddhist priest, was a small library walled up since the eleventh century. Stein persuaded him to open it and 'in the dim light of the priest's flickering lamp' he discerned piles of rolled-up manuscripts and paintings on silk.

Among the textiles preserved there by the arid climate since the eighth century were a few embroideries. The major work was a large hanging of Buddha preaching, solidly worked in lines of long straight and chain stitch in thick dull floss silk on a hemp cloth lined with silk. The colours are soft shades of beige and orange, with highlights in blue.

The Buddhist faith of the transit routes to the north of India remained strong in the Tibetan area when Muslims destroyed the monasteries of northern India, and those in Tibet became a repository for Buddhist religious texts. On ceremonial

BELOW *Cloth, Mongolia. Buddha decorates cloths for the house altar.*

occasions these huge monasteries were covered by enormous embroideries, *thang-ka*, draped over the entire facade, depicting fierce demons or goddesses worked in appliquéd fabric and gilded cardboard, outlined with piping or with yak or horsehair. For ritual dances the lamas wear aprons decorated with the same patterns and techniques.

Depictions of the Buddha himself are one of the subjects of the Burmese embroideries known as *kalagas*, on which he may appear in one of his incarnations. These embroideries decorated temples during festivals or were hung on bullock carts taking people to religious feasts. The work is in appliqué, the figure usually padded and enlivened with ric-rac and sequins.

Actual representations of Buddha were still recently embroidered in Mongolia to decorate the part of the home used for worship. The ritual involved in embroidering a likeness of Buddha required fasting beforehand, washing the hands and burning incense in a quiet room reserved for working. The image of Buddha follows accepted lines but accompanying motifs are freely chosen and drawn with burnt incense sticks.

Buddhism is more often represented in embroidery by its symbols, the most important of which is the lotus. Though pre-eminently Buddhist the lotus is also a potent and complex universal symbol associated with the sun. With its roots in mud, its stem in water and its flower in the air and sun, it symbolizes creative force. As its petals open with sunrise and close with sunset it also represents renaissance and immortality.

With trade goods and people this pattern migrated across Central Asia and was depicted in Buddhist architecture there as an adapted Western acanthus and half-palmette. Lotus patterns, especially of the half-opened flower, are therefore not always instantly recognizable. The petals of the fully opened lotus form a rosette and often resemble a solar symbol.

ABOVE Ashon, *Bengal. The lotus is the central motif of* kanthas. *This* ashon *shows the Hindu goddess Lakshmi and the* rath.

BELOW *A lotus pattern of* AD *700–800 decorates the ceiling of a Buddhist cave temple of the Dunhuang oasis in the Gobi desert.*

3 BUDDHISM

LEFT *The Eight Buddhist Precious Things: canopy; sacred vase; lotus; state umbrella; pair of fish; endless knot; conch shell; wheel of the law/karma.*

This fully opened lotus pattern is the central motif on the ceilings of the Buddhist cave temples of Dunhuang. It is also the central motif on cloths used by brides to wrap their dowry, and on marriage canopies from Saurashtra, surrounded by stars and patterns of possible solar origin. On the *kanthas* of Bengal it is almost without exception the central motif. The *kantha* is a quilted cloth, made from old saris and thus incorporating the Buddhist theme of recycling, used to cover beds or wrap precious objects, or for guests to sit on at weddings. The central lotus is often complemented by the tree of life in each corner, several decorative borders and the field filled with symbolic motifs, often solar or Hindu, and with objects from everyday life, such as combs and mirrors.

It is on Chinese embroidery that the symbols of Buddha's enlightenment, known as the Eight Precious Things, are to be found, though considerably less frequently than the attributes of the Eight Taoist Immortals. The lotus, the endless knot and the sacred vase are the most popular.

The vase is again one of the Hundred Antiques, which include books, brushes and other calligraphic materials and also comprise the Eight Secular Precious Things. These also relate largely to scholarly purposes and some are specifically Confucian. Most common on embroidery are the tripod, the two-cash (copper coins with a square hole in the middle), pairs of books, lozenges and horn cups, and a jewel or pearl.

Some confusion exists in the Buddhist symbolism of Chinese embroidery. Buddha's disciples, the Lohans, sometimes appear as the Taoist holy

men, and Buddha's dogs, the dogs of Fo, were originally lions. The lion, symbol of power and guardian of sacred buildings in the Middle East, was brought to China from the West, having been used with the same symbolism by the Mughal ruler Ashoka in the third century BC, when he converted to Buddhism and promoted its dissemination eastward. Guardian lions were then depicted at the foot of figures of Buddha, as on the eighth-century embroidery found at Dunhuang. They then gradually evolved into cuddly dogs with frilly ruffs in place of manes. They are often portrayed as a pair chasing each other around a flaming pearl.

The motif of the flaming pearl or jewel sits often at the tip of the dragon's tongue, symbol of imperial treasure. The pearl also symbolizes the Buddhist jewels, of which there are three: Buddha himself, his teaching (*dharma*) and the order of monks and nuns who continued his work (*sangha*).

Three such jewels, with trailing lines or ribbons that were originally bands of clouds, became an important decorative motif adopted by Timur, the fourteenth-century Turkic ruler of a vast Asian empire governed from Samarkand. Depicted as three balls and known as *çintemani* (Buddha's eyes) this pattern came with the Turkic peoples to Turkey where it was a frequent device on Ottoman decorative arts from the sixteenth century. In textiles and embroidery it seems to be connected mainly with the imperial court. Contemporary paintings show sultans wearing gowns with this motif, while their officers and courtiers wear more complex patterning. It came to be known as 'leopard spots' and 'tiger stripes', and denoted power. Each ball capped by a smaller ball inside creates a crescent, a suitable device for the Islamic peoples of Turkey.

A popular motif on Turkish domestic embroideries is a small building and tree known as the 'mosque and cypress'. The absence of a minaret and the juxtaposition of trees indicate that this is not a mosque but the Buddhist cosmological device of a celestial kiosk, *harmika*, set in a park by water. The kiosk captures the five directions, that is the four cardinal points leading to the four cosmic oceans and the canopied centre which is Buddha himself under the cupola of heaven. Eighth- and ninth-century paintings of the Uygur Turks of Central Asia show a mountain rising from the cosmic ocean topped by this celestial cupola under which the saints meditate. Uygur art and literature represent paradise as a group of such kiosks set in a garden where saints contemplate beside the cosmic western ocean.

BELOW *Sleeve cuff of robe, China. The sacred vase is a Buddhist symbol and is also one of the Chinese Hundred Antiques. The bat symbolizes happiness.*

The religious significance of the kiosk was lost in the Islamization of Turkey but remained as an architectural concept. The Ottomans, instead of emulating Byzantine architecture, built kiosks in parks by water, as the Topkapi palace complex and the buildings along the Bosphorus which became popular in the nineteenth century as embroidery motifs.

The secular significance of the cupola as the centre of power remained in the domed tents that were an essential part of Ottoman rule. The Seljuks, first of the Turkic tribes to enter Anatolia and who laid the foundations for the later Ottoman civilization, originated as armed nomadic shepherds living in round felt tents known as *yurts*. The Ottomans continued to live in tents and even after the establishment of Bursa as their capital the sultans spent part of each year on the move; and when the prince moved his tent, because of its symbolism, his seat of power moved with him. Turkish miniatures show the sultans in embroidered tents receiving gifts, or on military campaigns in luxuriously decorated encampments. Their sumptuously embroidered tents amazed western Europeans when Vizir Kara Ustapha was obliged to abandon his on his retreat from Vienna in 1683. The domed tent with trees survives as another important motif of Turkish embroidery.

Above left Art and literature of the Uygur Turkish kingdom of Koço in eastern Turkestan (AD 850–1212) and of Dunhuang (AD 911–1016) depict paradise as an assembly of celestial kiosks beside the cosmic Western ocean where fruit trees bear gems and pearls and saints meditate.

Above The Buddhist kiosk with trees and water and the domed tent as the secular seat of power were popular motifs on nineteenth-century Turkish napkins and towels.

Above Variations of the Buddhist çintemani motif on Turkish embroideries of the sixteenth and seventeenth centuries.

Below Towel, Turkey. The Buddhist cosmological device of a celestial kiosk, or harmîka, set in a park by water was a theme of the arts of the Uygur Turks of Central Asia and is frequent in Turkish embroidery.

3 HINDUISM

The small wayside shrines and intimate domestic altars of India, strewn with offerings of marigolds, glass bangles and misshapen stones, mark the daily immediacy of the panoply of Hindu gods in the local people's lives.

HINDU EMBROIDERED TEXTILES

The Hindu religion grew from the world of gods and animal deities of the Dravidian Indus valley civilization, absorbing some of the mythology of these early peoples – Indra the sky god, Surya the sun god, Agni the fire god. The Dravidian society was overrun in about 1500 BC by invading Aryans, speaking the Indo-European language of Sanskrit and originating probably from southern Russia. Like all Indo-European groups they were divided into a social hierarchy of three: the priests (*brahmins*), the warriors and the artisans. To these the conquered peoples were added as a fourth group and later a fifth group of tribal poor were denoted as 'untouchables'. From these beginnings developed the Hindu caste system still tenaciously fundamental to Indian society.

Hinduism then developed from the sacred Vedic hymns, from innovations of the brahmins, from the concept of rebirth which gained favour in about 500 BC, from the idea of the all-pervading, universal spirit of god manifest in every living thing, and also from the epic tales of the *Mahabharata* of about 300 BC. These epics recount the legends of hundreds of gods, of whom Vishnu the benevolent (incarnated in Krishna the lover), Siva the malevolent and the goddess in various forms are the principal trio. The goddess always derives from the primitive mother but can take the form of Vishnu's partner Lakshmi, Siva's consort Parvati, Krishna's lover Radha, or the destructive goddess Kali.

In embroidery it is the legend of Krishna that features most widely on articles that are narrative. Krishna's face is often blue, a holy aspect of Dravidian origin. In his life as a young cowherd Krishna danced with a group of cowgirls (*gopis*) using his divine power to make each believe she was dancing alone with him. The seals of the Indus valley civilization also depict goddesses in a dancing pose from which the *gopis* may derive. On clothing Krishna and his dancing *gopis* are often abstracted into five interlacing squares representing the dancers holding hands.

Temple hangings, Hindu and Jain, commissioned specifically by patrons for their particular sect, emulate painted ones in their mythological storytelling. Otherwise in the immensely varied range

LEFT *Door hanging, toran, Gujarat, India. Ganesh, the elephant-headed son of Siva, promises fertility and happiness and is worshipped before any important undertaking. His image is therefore often the central motif of the cloths hung across the door at festivities.*

of Indian embroidery only two types are narrative. These are the wall friezes, the *pachhitpati* of the Saurashtra peninsula of Gujarat, and the small ceremonial cloths called *rumals* which were made in Chamba in the Punjab.

The *rumals*, embroidered through the eighteenth and nineteenth centuries by the ladies of the court, depict scenes from Hindu epics, probably inspired from the palace wall-paintings, especially from the legends relating to Krishna. They were used to cover gifts to the deities or at weddings and are usually squares of fine bleached cotton, embroidered in muted colours in double darning.

Saurashtra homes comprised two rooms, one for living and the other for storing and displaying textiles. For this room friezes recounting stories of the gods, especially those relating to Krishna as legendary ruler of a Saurashtra kingdom, were embroidered by the women to line the top beam of the wall. Episodes from his life mingle with images of the sun god, of the countryside, animals and other Hindu gods. When made by Kathi women the embroidery is usually in herringbone stitch on cotton with added mirror discs. Friezes commissioned from the professional Mochi, originally cobblers whose fine embroidery was praised by Marco Polo, are worked in chain stitch using a hook known as an *ari*.

The domestic embroideries of Gujarat are made almost entirely for the dowry, and the women delight especially in picturing those gods that promise fertility and happiness: Krishna still, but also Ganesh the elephant-headed son of Siva. Ganesh is worshipped before any important undertaking, especially marriage, so is frequently embroidered at the centre of the *toran*, the hanging stretched across the top of a doorway as a sign of welcome. Small embroidered or

beadworked shrines to Ganesh are also hung in the house on special occasions. The god is stylized to a hardly recognizable form and is flanked by his consorts Siddhi and Buddhi. These hangings are five-sided in shape to recall the actual shrines dedicated to Ganesh.

Other Hindu motifs that are used are the attributes of the gods: the trident of Siva, and the peacock – vehicle of Sarasvati, goddess of wisdom, music and the arts, and a symbol of happiness, love and fertility. The animals of the ancient Indus culture have been retained in Hindu iconography: Ganesh rides on or is accompanied by a rat, Siva's attribute is a bull. Animals as a source of holy power and as a cleanser of the soul are exemplified by the sacred cow, that gentle creature that holds up the Indian traffic while it munches its way through roadside market-stall displays.

The *Mahabharata* recounts the legend of the gods churning the milky cosmic ocean, an image which finds its everyday counterpart in the women's regular chore of churning curd. This is a motif often embroidered on the decorative edge of the Kanebi *sadlo*.

ABOVE *Temple hanging, pichhavai, Mochi caste, Gujarat, India. The Hindu legend of Krishna dancing with the cowgirls,* gopis, *is one of the most popular embroidery themes.*

Perhaps the greatest influence of Hinduism on embroidery is the caste system. People were forbidden to marry or eat with those outside the *jati*, or subdivision, of their caste and were obliged to follow the trade of their forbears, customs that still have a tenacious hold. Skills and patterns are therefore transferred through generations over hundreds of years and the distinctive styles of domestic embroidery thus vary from caste to caste rather than from village to village. Such continuation through generations shaped the hands of Indian artisans, for example, and prevented them from converting to power looms. Many starved as a result. In the same way, *chikan* embroidery gave the workers' hands an inherited flexibility, impossible to acquire.

3 ISLAM

Islam is the newest of the world's great religions and within a century of Muhammad's migration its proselytizing had established it with amazing rapidity northward into Palestine, Syria, Iran, Iraq and Central Asia and westward through North Africa to Spain and Portugal, and eventually to France where Muslim forces were defeated at Poitiers in AD 732. Subsequent conquests assured it a symbolic crescent of power in the world from South-East Asia to West Africa. Throughout this vast area there is a certain uniformity in artistic and architectural style.

ISLAMIC EMBROIDERED TEXTILES

Calligraphy, geometry, interlacing, the arabesque, all that subjugates free-flowing art into a disciplined surface-covering decoration are the hallmarks of the Islamic decorative arts. Though the Koran itself does not actually forbid representation of human and animal forms, usage generally does.

Embroidery of the Islamic world has little in the way of style or motifs that come specifically from the Islamic religion, though the deliberate touch of the wrong colour, an unfinished pattern, a fault of stitch encapsulate the belief that only Allah is perfect.

The earliest example of Islamic calligraphy in embroidery is the work known as *tiraz*, decorative bands inserted at the armhole seam of the robes of rulers and persons of note throughout most of the Islamic world. Woven or embroidered, they were made in workshops in Egypt and at Sana'a in Yemen during the Abbasid dynasty of Baghdad (AD 749–1258) and the Fatamid of Egypt, North Africa and Syria (AD

909–1170). Inscriptions are embroidered in red, black or silver thread and comprise the name of the caliph, a religious invocation, the name of the weaving workshop and the date. In the later Fatamid period such comprehensive information yielded to large geometric pattern, plant and animal motifs and the expression of some simple pious hope.

Intricate Islamic patterning in embroidery is best exemplified by the Hispano-Mauresque embroideries of Spain which were made, probably in the provinces of Granada and Toledo, while the Arabs were still in possession of much of the Iberian peninsula. These handmade linen cloths are almost or entirely covered with floss silk stitchery in salmon, yellow, brown, red and shades of blue. The strict geometric patterning, which closely resembles Islamic tiles, was marked out by professional artists. The embroiderer then outlined the design with linen thread in stem stitch and filled the spaces with long-armed cross stitch. This stitch was probably introduced to the Iberian peninsula by the Moors.

Embroideries with a specifically Islamic purpose include the small cloths made by the Shi'ite Hazara of Afghanistan to wrap their *mohr* (prayer stones). These are of terracotta and should come from Karbela,

LEFT *The fish and hand of Fatima are Islamic amulets against the evil eye and are ubiquitous motifs in Tunisian embroidery and jewelry.*

ABOVE *The fish as protective device – like hands, horns, the cross and the solar rosette – frequently decorates the threshold of a house.*

a place of pilgrimage. The *mohr* is kept wrapped in the cloth which for prayer is laid on a prayer mat. The design – worked most commonly in long satin stitch in multicoloured silk and either of radiating geometric pattern or pictorial with mosques, minarets and hands – indicates where the *mohr* should be placed so that the forehead of the prostrate worshipper touches it. The cloth is considered a holy object and should never be sold or used for any other purpose. It must also never be used in a household where there are menstruating or pregnant women.

In north-western India, in the isolated region of Kutch along the border with Pakistan where Muslim and Hindu live side by side, many traditions, even as basic to Hinduism as caste or to Islam as purdah, are shared. Dress styles can also be interchanged, but in general the Muslim women distinguish themselves by the cut of their dress and particularly by the fineness of their embroidery. The Dhanetah women may take anything up to three years to work the front bodice panel on their *churi*, the long dress that is the most important item of their dowry. If the woman has herself made the pilgrimage to Mecca, she will not include mirrorwork in this embroidery.

Here and across the Pakistani border in Sind Islamic women embroider masks for their wedding and small bags to hold the Koran; in Bangladesh it is wrapping cloths that fulfil this purpose. The Koran, the teaching and laws of God divulged to Muhammad in Arabic, plays a supreme role in the Islamic world. More than just a book it is God incarnate. Excerpts from it are deemed to have the power to ward off evil and are often encased in silver jewelry. They can also be inserted into amulets appliquéd on to costume.

The talismanic role of pattern is of immense importance in the Islamic world where motifs such as the fish, and the hand of Fatima (*khomsa*), as well as amulets of crescents, triangles and squares are believed to deflect evil spirits. Painted hands and fish protect houses from India to Egypt and embroidered versions dominate the costume of Tunisia.

ABOVE *Fragment, Hispano-Mauresque, Spain. Intricate Islamic patterning in embroidery is best exemplified by the Hispano-Mauresque cloths of Spain made while the Arabs were still in possession of the peninsula. The designs closely resemble those of Islamic tiles and were marked out by professional artists.*

RIGHT *Woman's skirt, Aleppo, Syria. Though the Koran does not expressly forbid the portrayal of human forms usage generally does and anthropomorphic motifs are rare in Islamic embroidery. The figure is combined with the fertility symbol of the carnation, which in the embroidery of northern Syria is stylized into a hexagon.*

ZOROASTRIANISM

Zoroastrianism is a Persian religion established by Zarathustra. a figure of whom little is known for sure but who is accepted as having lived in eastern Iran around the seventh/sixth century BC. The religion he founded was monotheistic with theological concepts of good and evil, spirit and flesh, light and dark, heaven and hell, which strongly influenced other world faiths. In its later phases it accepted minor deities including Mithra the sun god. It is probably best known for its fire temples, its practice of hanging the dead on Towers of Silence to be picked apart by vultures and most of all for its priests, the Magi, to whom the three wise men who came from the East bringing gifts to the infant Jesus belonged.

BELOW *Marriage shawl, Persia. Zoroastrian embroidery is distinctive with its small animals worked in thick twist silk both on the dresses of the women, which are of counterbalanced red and green silk, and on their dark indigo silk marriage shawls.*

ZOROASTRIAN EMBROIDERED TEXTILES

Under the Sassanid dynasty (AD 226–650) Zoroastrianism spread westward to the Persian gulf and eastward to Afghanistan and the Indus valley. From about the eighth century onwards, after persecution by the Muslims, some Zoroastrians settled on the west coast of India where they are known as Parsees, a corruption of Persians.

Zoroastrians in Iran form a minority group settled in the province of Kerman and around Yazd on the edge of the great salt desert. The women used to wear a distinctive shift of counterbalanced red and green silk embroidered with countless little animals, fish and plants in heavy multicoloured twist silk. The same animals were worked on the baggy trousers made of brightly coloured strips of fabric with tie-dye circles. With these was worn a red tie-dye shawl or, for marriage, a black or dark indigo silk one with the same animals and a large sun motif or circle of animals in the centre. A peacock often features on the shawl, closely resembling those on the satin skirts of Gujarat, where many Parsees settled. The Zoroastrians also wore white garments worked with small cross-stitch motifs of animals and trees.

CHRISTIANITY

Christianity is centered on the life and teachings of Jesus of Nazareth, whom Christians believe to be the Son of God and the Messiah prophesied in the Old Testament. This monotheistic religion began in Palestine in the first century AD.

BELOW Casket, England. Biblical stories were the theme of English stumpwork of the seventeenth century, on pictures, caskets and mirror frames. The tale of David and Bathsheba was a favourite: here David is seated under a canopy while Bathsheba bathes in a pool.

CHRISTIAN EMBROIDERED TEXTILES

The decorative arts of the early Middle Ages in western Europe were a hymn to the glory of God, recounting and praising the lives of Christ and the saints. Most of the embroidery surviving from this period is also ecclesiastical, a tradition which through a series of lapses and revivals such as the Reformation and Counter Reformation, is still thriving today. In secular embroidery the contribution of the Christian church is particularly evident in the sixteenth and seventeenth centuries. Linen cloths and canvaswork furnishings were in the same narrative style as other decorative arts: just as stained-glass windows instructed the illiterate, so did embroidery.

Sources of biblical designs were the pattern books first printed in Germany in the early sixteenth century. The Bible woodcuts published by Bernard Saloman and Jean de la Tournes in Lyon in 1553 were copied all over Europe, while in England it was those of Gerard de Jode published in Antwerp in 1585 that proved most popular. As woodcuts and engravings of classical mythology and allegories were copied equally assiduously

it seems evident that by the time these themes came into the hands of the amateur needlewoman they were chosen merely for their decorative qualities, rather than from deep-rooted religious faith.

A blend of tableaux from the Old Testament, Greek and Roman mythology and hunting scenes worked in wild yellow silk in chain or back stitch, feature on quilts made mainly around Hughli in Bengal in the time of Portuguese patronage from the late sixteenth century to the collapse of their power in India in 1632.

INDIVIDUAL MOTIFS

Individual motifs of Christian origin, as opposed to biblical narrative, are found in secular embroidery, particularly in white household linen and in lacis or filet work, and were also disseminated by pattern books. The pelican in her piety, symbol of Christ's sacrifice, is one of the designs in Vinciolo's pattern book published in Venice in 1587. From Sibmacher comes the Agnus Dei in his *Schön Neues Modelbuch* published in Nürnberg in 1597, and St Michael and the dragon, Christian image of the folkloric victory of good over evil, in his *Neues Modelbuch in Kupffer gemacht* of 1601. In Catholic countries the holy monograms of IHS and M were believed to hold power over evil and were also frequently chosen.

As floral designs came to dominate European embroidery from the mid-seventeenth century, so the Christian motifs survived in children's samplers, especially those of continental Europe. A great range of biblical motifs occur: the crucifix with the instruments of the passion and the sun and moon, recalling Luke's description of the darkening of the sky at Christ's death, Adam and Eve, Jacob fighting the angel, the spies from Canaan. Some of these survive as occasional motifs on such linen items as display towels, particularly Adam and Eve.

ABOVE *Hanging, Portugal. The pelican in her piety, symbol of Christ's sacrifice, is one of the designs in Vinciolo's pattern book published in Venice in 1587. It became, with the Agnus Dei and Adam and Eve, a popular Christian motif in secular embroidery.*

LEFT *Sampler, Nürnberg, Germany (1728). The instruments of Christ's passion feature on many continental samplers, propagated by pattern books such as Jean le Clerc's 1613 reprint of Vinciolo. The format of Nürnberg samplers of the seventeenth and early eighteenth century was always a central two-handled vase of flowers with upholstery patterns and scattered motifs mainly from Sibmacher's pattern book of 1597, such as the seated stag and the peacock.*

THE CROSS

The cross is a universal symbol of such antiquity that it cannot always be ascribed to a purely Christian source, but in certain instances one can be quite sure of its origin: in the case of the embroidered cross on a child's knitted sock of the Coptic Christians of Egypt, and the staggered cross motif of Romanian shirt sleeves that is also the design stamped on consecrated bread for the Orthodox church, for example. There are also two outstanding examples of a cross used on costume as a declaration of affiliation to the Christian church in the midst of a society of Islamic faith. These are found on the festive shawls of the women of Qaracoche in Iraq and the shifts of the women of the villages around the mountain town of Livno in Herzegovina.

Qaracoche is a Christian village of around 6,000 people in a region of northern Iraq where most communities are of mixed faith. Over their caftan the women wear a draped shawl tied on the shoulder, of which the festive version – *châl* – is richly, if crudely, embroidered. A cross always forms the centre motif and further crosses are scattered around, for a large number is thought to bring luck. Here and there is a scene depicting priests officiating at an altar, a ritual fascinating to the women who, though Christian, are seated a long way from the altar as they are thought to be unclean. Other motifs include a flower enclosed in a serrated leaf, very reminiscent of the Turkish *saz* motif, and a crescent moon shape, both believed to offer magic protection and avert evil spirits. Birds and dancing women fill the rest of the shawl. The embroidery is in bright floss silks on black or check wool of red and black, and is worked with stem-stitch outlines filled with rough satin stitch. It is done by women specialized in the task, with the client choosing the designs from the traditional repertoire. The woman is buried in her *châl*.

Half a dozen villages around Livno in Herzegovina have retained their Orthodox faith in a region that is strongly Islamic. The women of these villages are distinguished by their shifts known as 'cross shifts'. Made of homegrown handspun linen embroidered in red and blue goats-hair they have a large red cotton cross appliquéd on each sleeve. The shift was worn for the first time for the wedding ceremony, together with the large white cotton headscarf similarly appliquéd with red cotton which the woman had been allowed to wear as a young girl as soon as she was considered marriageable. A heavy sleeveless woollen jacket and tapestry-woven apron, with motifs that varied according to the woman's age, completed the outfit. After the wedding the shift would be kept for festive occasions during the first year of the woman's married life or until her first child was born, after which it was carefully folded away to be handed on to her daughter.

ABOVE *The seal in the form of a staggered cross, used to stamp consecrated bread, serves as an embroidery motif on Romanian blouse sleeves.*

BELOW *The festive shawl of the women of Qaracoche is embroidered in bright rough stitchery with motifs declaring their Christian faith in a Muslim society: the cross in particular but also scenes of an Orthodox altar with priests officiating.*

RIGHT *Woman's bag, Sweden. The peasant tradition of Europe associates red particularly with young women and with marriage. It is the dominant colour in all costume.*

OPPOSITE *Dress cuff, Bethlehem-style sleeve on Beit Dajan dress, Palestine. Embroidery is strategically positioned on garments to protect the body from evil spirits. Edgings and seams are particularly important and a common device in many parts of the world is to decorate them with threads of alternate colouring.*

THE MAGICAL SOURCE OF PROTECTION

THE MAGIC OF EMBROIDERY

It is sometimes hard for us to realize that within living memory people inhabited – and indeed some still do – a world they believed controlled by supernatural beings both good and evil. Every spinney, every copse, every crossroads, every stream, every stone held its own spirit; every culture had its own hobgoblins.

The modern Japanese businessman travels with ticket and insurance; the Slav requiring medical treatment has doctors, drugs and hospitals at his disposal. In the early years of the twentieth century both relied on magic for their well-being, which involved, for the sick man, having a black cat slit open, laid across his stomach and left to rot; for the traveller, carrying on his person an inscription bearing the character *tsuchi*, 'earth', preferably written in vermilion ink as red was thought to be particularly distasteful to spirits.

EMBROIDERY AGAINST EVIL SPIRITS

The traveller left his home, which was known to be protected by guardian spirits, to set forth along roads that were infested with evil beings and haunted by wandering souls. Animals lay in wait ready to transform themselves into spirits to do him harm, demons tarried at crossroads and beside muddy tracks. To confront these dangers he used, as embroideries do, both pattern and material. Earth from his home was essential for his survival in strange regions even in the form of a written character, for characters were considered not only to represent the object, as a word or pattern does, but also to hold the spirit of that object: the character was as potent as the earth itself.

In Islamic belief there were not only men and angels but also a third class of beings made of fire, *jinns*. The Indians believed in witches and liver-eaters – *jiggerkhars* – who just by looking at a person could steal their liver and kill them.

Magical powers were not confined to supernatural beings, but were held also by women. Human conception was not understood and when in the eighteenth century it was first established that it was

the result of sexual intercourse the claim was greeted with derision. Women's ability to produce children was therefore regarded as miraculous and their fertility was protected by decoration.

Women could also be feared and reviled as witches. Among the Ghiliak and Néghidales, peoples who live around the basin of the Amour river in eastern Siberia, embroiderers are the worst witches of all. In the loops made by their threads they can ensnare the souls of people in their presence. The Ghiliak verb *tcagcott* has two meanings: to embroider patterns and to cast spells. Men do not embroider nor would they approach a woman doing so for fear that watching the threads being twisted around would cause them to become disorientated when hunting.

Women could also house the evil eye – the most feared of all spirits, for the eye is the mirror of the soul. In the Siwa oasis of the western desert of Egypt widows were believed to possess the evil eye and were clothed in white and imprisoned for four months until considered clean. In the late 1980s Reuters reported that a synagogue in Israel had stopped admitting women because of a series of disasters in the area for which it was believed women with their evil eye were responsible.

The evil eye is envious and wishes to destroy perfection: brides and babies are particularly vulnerable. It, and evil spirits in general, can attack the body and cause illness or even death. Against them three aspects of embroidered decoration are considered effective – the position in which the embroidery is placed, patterns that hold a mystic power, and assertive materials. The evil eye especially can be overpowered by anything that dazzles and makes it blink, such as shiny objects, pieces of metal, coins, buttons, mirror that reflects and holds its image; by anything that tinkles and distracts it; by objects that can pierce it, particularly triangular ones holding the power of the trinity and the feminine mystique; by gaudy bright colours; by alternating colours along edges; and by anything that confuses it through asymmetrical pattern where it loses its way.

The evil eye and *jinns* are still greatly feared in the Islamic world and there the protective devices of embroidery are usually consciously employed. Often, however, the choice of pieces of mirror, alternating colours and the like have become almost subconscious, as has superstition in the West. A black cat brings good luck in some Western countries, bad luck in others and is still in our children's books the familiar of every witch though we never pause to wonder why. Viruses attack our computers on Friday the 13th, we cross our fingers walking under ladders, perform pagan topping-out ceremonies on our new airport buildings, and decorate our Easter buns with a cross to keep away evil spirits that might prevent the dough from rising – a protective pattern also found in embroidery worldwide.

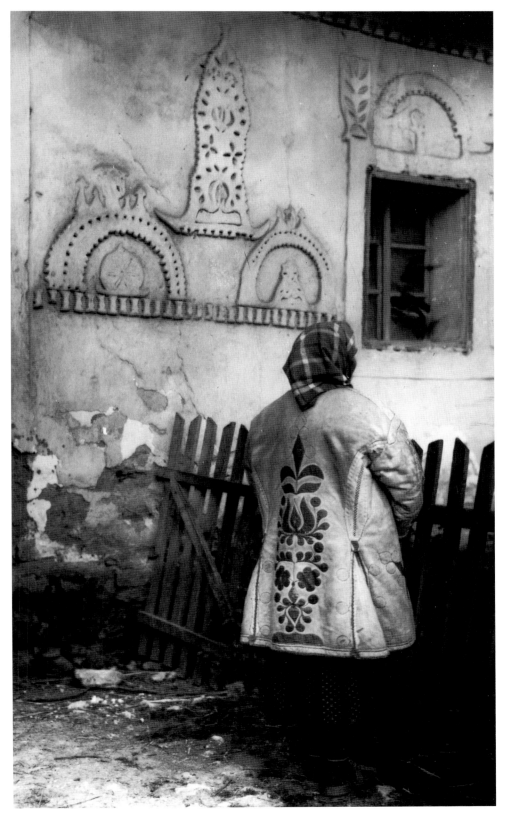

LEFT *The patterns decorating houses with the purpose of protecting their inhabitants from evil are also used on clothing.*

PROTECTIVE EMBROIDERY

Costume in general and embroidery in particular play a protective role both physical and spiritual. Those evil spirits likely to attack the body are kept out by decorative devices at every edge and opening. From Asia to western Europe embroidery is commonly placed encircling the neck, along hem and cuff, around pockets and also at buttonholes. Seams are closed with decorative stitchery and certain vulnerable places carry heavy embroidery. These are the front bodice, the shoulders and sleeves and often also the sexual area and the centre back. Even when they cover much of the garment these areas of embroidery never intermingle but are always clearly defined. In each case such embroidery was destined to protect these specific and significant parts of the body. Most heavily embroidered – and the last item of western European costume to disappear – was the coif: as can be seen in any village of eastern Europe the headscarf and apron still linger as everyday wear, though they serve no practical purpose.

ABOVE *The bride's hair is prepared for the marriage headdress, never to be uncovered in public again.*

THE HEAD

Embroidered headgear is breathtaking in its variety: white and gold coifs of Europe, tribal caps of Central Asia, skull caps of the Jewish and Islamic worlds, pixie-hoods of North Africa, coin caps of the Finno-Ugric and Turkic peoples, beaded and feathered headdresses of the Native North American, head and face veils of the Middle East covered in talismanic materials such as tassels, shells, buttons and blue beads. In many societies headgear accentuated an unnatural shape, as the head was not only protected by coverings but also deliberately deformed for magical as well as social reasons – the coifs of France serve as one example, where distorting the head by binding was practised until the end of the nineteenth century.

Hair was universally regarded as magical, a concentration of the life force of the person, and was particularly potent in the Judaeo-Christian and Native American

LEFT *Child's cap, Sana'a, Yemen. The head is protected by the potent amulet of a triangle.*

traditions. In the Paracas culture snakes shared the supernatural powers of hair, and burial turbans were decorated with serpentine patterning.

Hair was also, like nails, a part of the body from which pieces could be cut and then, retaining its spiritual strength, fall into the hands of witches. Women's hair especially was believed to possess magical force in its power of seduction. In Russia women were considered impure and only their hair was clean, and girls' tresses were plaited with totem animals in tin. In almost every society girls' hair was highly decorated and then at marriage covered with great ceremony by a headdress. After this the woman never again uncovered it, even hiding it from her husband and wearing a bonnet in bed. She was especially careful never to show the nape, and scarves or headdresses with embroidered flaps are common wear for married women. Embroidery could be placed on the actual head section or on the extension. Long flaps decorated with stitchery or with materials that flashed or dazzled were common in much of the costume of Europe. The bridal dress of Lindnorst in Germany, for example, has the back of the head entirely hung with ribbons holding mirrors to avert the evil eye.

An extended version of the hanging headcovering was the *chyrpy* of the Tekke Turkmen women, a cloak worn draped over a high headdress, the main motif of which was the fertility symbol of the tulip. The skull caps of their children, ornately embroidered in the same style, were often hung with coins and amulets. Similar caps worn by the men, children and unmarried girls of the Uzbek, another people of Central Asia, clearly had a symbolic meaning, for a new mother would ask another woman who had brought up a healthy child to make her baby's cap for her.

In many places the source of life was believed to lie in the ear and special protection was provided by heavy embroidery or by strategically placed pattern or material. A triangular amulet of fabric or an embroidered cross was positioned over the ear on children's caps. But often – particularly in Europe – it was with embroidery on the shoulder of the linen shift or shirt that the ear was afforded protection from ill.

THE BREASTS

Though seldom as blatantly as in the 'Viking breastplate' style of the embroidered blouses of Kutch, women's breasts – as the source of life for the newborn baby – are frequently covered by heavy embroidery. In Europe they were protected by the detached stomacher, ornate with stitchery: in gold on those of peasant France, for instance, and with an unchanging tree of life motif on those of Pilsen in Bohemia.

Heavy metal breast clasps were typical of the Finno-Ugric peoples and much of the most emphatic decoration over breasts is to be found among their descendants living in central Russia and western Siberia. The Tcheremiss of the Kazan region on the Volga river east of Moscow embroider the front of their rough hemp shifts with a V-shaped pattern they call 'guardian of the breasts'. The Chuvash, descendants of the Volga Bulgars who live in the same region, appliqué red fabric in a diamond shape over the breasts, leaving a gap over the nipple. Here they embroider a small, plant-derived motif in blue and beige silk, or sometimes in red. Alternatively they embroider a solid geometric motif with an 8-pointed star at its centre and hooked

motifs at the edges, in red with touches of beige and green. The neck edges and underarm gussets of these shifts are commonly of blue, blue/red or blue/white fabric and red cotton is appliquéd along most other edges and seams.

The women of the Evank-Tungus, hunters of the forests of eastern Siberia who are highly tattooed, have embroidery on the breast area of their shifts that shows their origin and clan. The

Mordvinians, a larger group who live in the Volga region, wear breast ornaments of leather embroidered with red cloth, shells, glass beads and brass ornaments. In Bahriyah, one of the oases of the western desert of Egypt – now linked to Cairo by road where previously it was nine to ten days' camel ride away – the women's traditional dress is a wide black cotton shift with breasts and pockets accentuated by contrasting colour and stitch. The linear embroidery over the front of the dress is in raspberry-red floss silk in double herringbone – with the shoulders and top sleeve surface further emphasized with extra stitching or metal discs – while the embroidery over the breasts and pockets is sharply divergent with its green and orange cross stitch.

ABOVE *The stomachers of Pilsen are always embroidered with a version of the tree of life as a heart.*

BELOW *The shifts of the Tcheremiss and Chuvash women of Siberia protect the breasts with symbolic embroidered patterns.*

SHOULDERS AND SLEEVES

On the linen shifts and shirts of Europe the disposition of embroidery on shoulders and sleeves is specific and relative to the construction of the garment. Its density is often linked to the seam which with a straight cut will fall across the upper arm. Heavy shoulder embroidery follows this seam or lies above it. Decoration in this position can be seen on a Russian figurine of the eleventh to twelfth century.

Significantly, while the traditional *huipil* of Central American costume is normally brocaded with motifs from local iconography, the imported item of the blouse is embroidered following its sleeve construction with European motifs of flowers and animals.

In the distinctive and rigid disposition of the shift sleeves of Bucovina in north-east Romania the shoulder area, *altita*, is thickly embroidered, while below it the horizontal band, *incret*, of fine pulledwork, brocading or pastel-coloured embroidery separates it from the narrow vertical or diagonal lines of small embroidered patterns that continue to the cuff. These are known as *râuri*, or rivers: the swift rivers which flow through the villages were always believed to have magic powers.

On many linen shifts of eastern Europe the embroidery extends in a panel from the shoulder over the entire upper arm surface but is always separated from the cuff, which remains an edging decoration. It is easy to recognize the protective power of the arm raised across the body, or even at rest at the sides, and the consequent relevance of this part of costume.

LEFT AND ABOVE *Heavy shoulder ornamentation features on a figurine of 3000 BC from Turkestan and on a Russian stone statue of the eleventh to twelfth century.*

The straight-cut narrow sleeves of most dresses and blouses of north-west India and Pakistan are also embroidered down their whole length ending with a distinct cuff edging. There is frequently a separate and dominant motif on the shoulder that is solar in origin.

Where decorative bands descend from the shoulder to the chest, rather than down the arm, shoulder embroidery can also recall the cut of the shift known as the *tunica manicata* or *tunica dalmatica*, worn at the decline of the Roman empire. Shoulders can also be worked as epaulettes of almost military importance, as in the jackets of Albania and Tunisia.

Sleeves as a separate item in themselves were a ritual object, their importance perhaps deriving, as so much in peasant costume, from the dress of aristocrats and bourgeois of earlier periods. The heavy silk sleeves of medieval upper-class costume may find a counterpart in the ballooning sleeves of so many villagers, intricately pleated or embroidered in a distinctly local style. Such sleeves, often of a finer fabric than the rest of the garment, formed part of the dowry for both bride and groom. In Hungary a grandmother would start embroidering sleeves for her granddaughter as soon as the child was born, devoting most of her time to this task until the girl was married. The girl herself made sleeves for her groom, sewing them to a shirt only after the engagement when she was sure of his size.

Embroidery on the sleeves of Chinese costume, unless part of the overall design, is concentrated on the cuff and plays no particular protective role. The cut of clothing stems from earlier clothing of animal skin or of cloth. The sleeve derived from the skin clothing of the nomadic Manchu, designed for riding horses over steppelands, is long and narrow with a

horsehoof cuff covering and protecting the hand. On court costume the body of this sleeve is plain or ribbed and pushed back to facilitate arm and hand movements, and the cuff is embroidered with motifs conforming to Chinese symbolism and aesthetics. The sleeve of clothing derived from the cloth tradition is enormously long and wide, designed as a display of wealth in its yards of silk and as a modest cover for hands considered unseemly to display in public. The cuff is embroidered in a straight band in a style unrelated to the patterning on the main body of the garment. The Chinese man, bowing slightly with clasped hands, thus shields the front of his body with a silken muff depicting delicate landscapes of figures, pagodas, bridges and butterflies and those floral tributes to the seasons – peonies, chrysanthemums or narcissus.

ABOVE *Romanian blouse from the region of Olt. The eastern European tradition of heavily embroidered sleeves on linen shifts is particularly strong in Romania.*

ABOVE *Woman's blouse, Piešťany, Slovakia.*
The sleeves of European peasant costume were
frequently a ritual object associated with marriage.
They were usually of fine fabric or were intricately
pleated or heavily embroidered.

THE SEXUAL AREA

The purpose of the ubiquitous apron of most European peasant costume, and particularly that of eastern Europe, is symbolically protective and not practical. Varying in style with each village but normally heavily embroidered, intricately pleated or finely woven in striped patterning, it covered a dress or petticoat that almost always was deliberately left plain where the apron would be worn. It is the antithesis of an apron worn to protect precious clothing. Instead it protects the body.

The ritual associations of the apron are many. In Transylvania it was worn inside-out for mourning; in Hungary it formed part of the costume of unmarried men and the bridegroom; an illegitimate child in Romania was said to be 'from the apron'; but mainly it was everywhere associated with marriage. This was the moment at which the bride, as well as taking a new hairstyle and headdress, changed the type of apron she had worn

as a young girl to another that declared her status as a married woman. Sometimes, as in Romania, the materials used to decorate it were a gift from the bridegroom and the apron, often of red fabric, would be used in the marriage ritual or carried through the streets in the wedding procession, hung from a pole like a flag for all to see. Women of the nomadic Sarakatsani, now living mainly in Greece, embroidered twenty to forty aprons (*panoules*) during their youth, each with different symbolism – such as the cross, the serpent, or the moon – that showed the woman's social status or was thought suitable for various occasions and moods. She would then choose each day the appropriate one to wear. The apron – the *podia* – of all Greek costume was imbued with magical properties: in Thrace, for example, it is thrown over the stomach of a woman in labour to facilitate the birth.

Throughout Europe styles of apron differed not only from village to village or with the marital status of the woman, but also with everyday or festive wear. Festive ones were obviously more ornate. For everyday use, the upper half of the two-part apron of Russia, for example, was embroidered and the bottom fringed, while the festive version has brass chains, beads and shells added to the embroidery. In Blata in Bohemia festive aprons were covered in beadwork and sequins, negating any possible practical role, while those of Croatia and Bosnia were covered in coins and edged with red triangles. They were often hung from the neck. Almost everywhere the usual edgings of bobbin lace, crochet or

LEFT A feature of the costume of the newly-wed Erza Mordvinian bride of the Volga region was the back apron, common also in eastern European dress. The wimple hat was worn by the bride only for a short while after the wedding. It went out of fashion about the time of the First World War.

embroidery were deeper, and insertions – such as the central vertical bands of bobbin lace, needleweaving, embroidery in alternating colours or floral ribbons of the aprons of Slovakia – were more decorative. When embroidered, both everyday and festive aprons featured mainly flower designs or symbols of fertility such as the pomegranate.

In many areas of eastern Europe a back apron was also worn, or the back was often hung with brocaded floral ribbons. Among more primitive peoples it is also often the buttocks that are decorated. An example is the Mru tribe of the Chittagong Hill Tracts in Bangladesh. Their simple skirts made of a band of cloth edged with small beads have a central panel of patterned weaving supplemented by light embroidery.

Dresses which carry embroidery specifically over the sexual region are a feature of the costume of some of the Muslim peoples of north-west India and Pakistan. Women of the Khatrie clan, dyers of Kutch, wear a shift, an *aba*, which is decorated in a deep panel over the chest with a pendant pattern of exceptional fineness worked below the waist. Even when the dress is decorated with couched metal braiding or in the tie-dye technique the same disposition of pattern is adhered to. When embroidered the work is of tiny pieces of mirror with open chain and extremely fine interlacing stitch. A red silk version is worn for marriage and is one of the dowry gifts presented by the groom. The Seyhud farming community wear dresses of the same type.

The silk dresses of the Baluch of Pakistan, in addition to embroidery at the breasts, shoulder and neck, have a deep rectangular pocket called a *pudo* down the centre front of the skirt, embroidered at the top in an upwardly pointed triangle that lies over the pudendum.

Protective embroidery on a dress is often placed slightly higher than the sexual region so that it lies over a pregnant stomach, as on the sunburst decoration on the dresses of the Siwa oasis, where the most densely embroidered squares with buttons lie over the breasts and stomach. In the costume of many countries embroidery edging the neck slit ends in extensive patterning over the stomach.

Belts carry immensely important sexual symbolism but this is more concerned with how or when they are worn than with the embroidery on them. In North Africa on 'the day of the belt' the bride resumes her normal life; in Oltenia, Romania, a metal belt which must have been made by a naked gypsy in one night, was worn before childbirth to protect the foetus from evil spirits and to relieve childbirth pains. This belt was hung with amulets, which included in particular keys to facilitate the passage of the baby, and axes and knives to encourage the birth of a boy. These amulets were suspended across the apron, which thus carried no embroidery.

The embroidery on a belt occasionally held some meaning: men of Alpine regions, for example, wore wide belts covered in quillwork that was meant to pinpoint the source of their courage and virility. It could also denote a trade: boatmen on the canals of England wore wide canvas belts embroidered in multicoloured wools with spiderweb patterns in squares, made for them by their womenfolk.

LEFT *Apron, Bosača, Slovakia. The European apron was symbolic and not practical: it protected the body rather than the garment below, which was normally left plain where the apron would cover it. Ritual associations of the apron are legion.*

SUPPLEMENTARY EMBROIDERY

While decorative stitchery on edges and seams is believed to afford magical protection, it also physically strengthens.

EDGINGS

In man's earliest clothing a decorative effect must already have been achieved by stitching skins together with sinew. Such thonging leaves gaps which could then be filled with ornament. A similar opportunity for embellishment can occur with appliqué, where a piece of fabric may first be applied to cover a hole, then repeated to make a pattern and then suggested by outline stitchery alone, as on the patched raffia cloths of the Kuba of the Democratic Republic of the Congo. On the sheepskin coats of Hungary such patches are known as 'witch patches'.

The strengthening action of stitchery is apparent in the vocabulary used to describe Palestinian costume, where edgings are of extreme importance, the back hem being the most significant. Zigzag appliqués are known as *tishrifeh*,

meaning 'to make good', and form a row of triangles considered a protective amulet, a *hejab*. Bands of fishbone stitch in striped colours, when edging necks and cuffs, are called *habkeh*, 'to make stronger'. On village dresses hems are finished with a band of appliquéd fabric on the inside and decorative stitching on the outside. On Bedouin dresses hems are deeper, with several rows of satin stitch, giving the strong finish needed for walking in the desert.

The strengthening role of embroidery is also apparent in other desert clothes – trouser cuffs are thickly stitched, those of Yemen to afford protection against thorns, and those of the Qutayfé area of Syria to protect against prickly straw and thistles.

ABOVE AND BELOW *Precious front neck placket, collar and cuffs from Moravia, worked in intricate Slav knot stitch, are cut off the man's shirt to be used again when it is worn out.*

BELOW *Kirghiz man's waist sash. These triangular sashes of bright silk flowers in Bokharan couching were tied round the waist. Tasselled needleweaving forms a magnificent edging.*

RIGHT *Skirt wrap for a man or woman of the Wodaabe people of Niger. Symbols of life in an encampment decorate the edges visible in wear.*

SEAMS

The most frequent decoration for seams is colour alternation, commonly of a stitch that straddles the two pieces of fabric, such as fishbone, buttonholing or faggoting. This device is to be found from Asia through the Middle East to eastern Europe. Red is frequently alternated with white or with green, and colours can be paired or in multiples. Even where the women are predominantly weavers and their clothes carry almost no embroidery, as in Jordan or Djerba, the seams joining the handwoven loom widths will be accentuated with striped stitchery.

In the Turkmen embroidery of Central Asia and in eastern Europe, the selvedge of the fabric when coloured is left visible as a supplementary decoration to the seam embroidery. The shifts of the Dinaric mountains of Croatia, for example, though always embroidered in copper, blue and green, will have visible red selvedges at the seams.

In Romania the word for ornamental stitchery on seams is *cheite*, meaning 'little key', the word also used for the house and courtyard key. Keys, invented by the bronzesmith Theodore of Samos in the sixth century BC, always had quasi-magical powers. Travellers in medieval France, for instance, branded them on their horse or donkey for safety on the road.

THE NECK

The edging to which the main attention is directed varies with different countries. In most it is the neck that bears the finest work: Baluchi dresses have rows of exquisitely fine stitchery; the Tcheremiss of Siberia border the necks of their dresses with shells, with the specific purpose of protecting from the evil eye; in Norway the coloured edging at the neck identified the district the wearer came from.

Though in most countries it is usually the front of the neck opening that is especially highly decorated, sometimes the nape is of greater significance. The wedding dresses of Thano Bula Khan in Pakistan have a neck slit flanked by small pockets of sand from the girl's home village, permeated with strong-smelling spices to protect her in her new surroundings, in the same way as his home earth protected the Japanese traveller. The dress is worn for marriage with these pockets at the nape, after which it is turned and worn with the slit to the front. Frequently decoration of the nape was not in fact on the dress itself but on a hanging headdress. An old marriage coif

ABOVE *Man's robe, Nigeria. Whereas the front neck placket is usually one of the most decorated parts of a garment, the back neck, particularly of men's clothing, often carries a strong ornamental motif. This is common, not only in West Africa but also in India.*

of Madhia in Tunisia bears as its only ornamentation an inscription at the nape of the neck worked in flat silver thread which has tarnished with time but on which 'that protection may last' is still just legible, expressing a hope of some magical safeguard.

RIGHT *Dress, Baluch, Pakistan. Patterning is concentrated at the neck and shoulder, over the breasts and sexual area, and on all edges and seams. Even when protective ornamentation almost covers the entire garment, the areas of embroidery never intermingle but are always clearly defined.*

POCKETS

Pockets are nearly always strengthened and protected by embroidered patterning. The eighteenth-century dandy of most of Europe wore a silk waistcoat or jacket with floral embroidery at the edges and around the pockets; the pockets of the Englishwoman of the same period – two pear-shaped bags hung from a tape round her waist – were delicately embroidered, usually with trailing floral designs or with canvaswork, though they were buried unseen beneath her petticoats.

In peasant costume the asymmetrical aspect of protective embroidery is often linked with pockets. They are placed out of alignment or are false, to distract the evil eye. The men's jackets of Brittany, *chupenn*, are embroidered round the pockets with zigzags, strips of colour and shiny buttons. The outside jacket pockets are false and placed asymmetrically to confuse evil spirits, whilst those of the waistcoat, though not seen, are embroidered and appliquéd with protective devices.

Men's trouser pockets are also highlighted with distracting pattern.

In most of the Carpathians – Poland, Romania, Slovakia – and also in Alpine regions, the pocket slits from front waist are decorated with floral patterning or couched braiding. In Romania they are known as *feresti* – 'windows' – and are embroidered with the same patterns as those which surround house windows to protect the occupants against demons and illness with their magic powers.

In northern Syria women made wedding trousers for their husbands in heavy indigo cotton, embroidering zigzag patterning round the side pockets and also on the cuffs. Their own coats of indigo have one side pocket ornately decorated with embroidery and appliqué, while the other side of the skirt is left plain.

Most dramatic of all embroidery around pockets is that of the enormously wide cotton robes made and worn by the Hausa men of northern Nigeria. A large rectangular pocket is covered with embroidery and then applied on the left side of the chest, the patterns being continued across to the right and up around the neck to the centre back. The stitchery is most often of open chain and eyelet, traditionally in cotton thread or wild silk. The designs, drawn by specialist men, combine interlacing patterns of Islamic inspiration, long triangles known as 'knives', criss-crossed squares and the indigenous motifs of spirals, ornate crosses and open angular shapes found on other decorative arts including body scarification.

ABOVE *The openings of pockets are frequently almost concealed in a splendour of protective embroidery, as on the shift of a manservant of one of the beys of Tunis.*

LEFT *Woman's dress. Uzbek, Afghanistan. Pockets were strengthened and decorated with embroidery. They were often placed asymmetrically to confuse the evil eye.*

THE HEM

In Turkey, in Syria and in many parts of the Ottoman empire, and also as far west as Moravia, an intricate and colourful piece of appliquéd fabric in a complex or jagged shape is worked inside the hem at the openings of a garment. In Syria the fabric is usually silk ikat and the outline of its shape is stitched in red on the outside of the garment; in Moravia the appliqué is in red wool. With movement a dazzling effect is achieved. Similar patterns are occasionally hidden inside sleeves, as with the sheepskin coats of Hungary.

LEFT *The insertion of a dazzling piece of appliqué inside the hem of a garment became a device of costume in much of the Ottoman empire. An early example is on a kaftan belonging to the Turkish sultan Şehzade Korkut (1470–1513).*

BELOW *Woman's robe, Sana'a, Yemen. A frequent protective device is some intricate pattern worked inside the hem of a garment so that with movement a dazzling effect is achieved. Sequins that sparkle and triangular amulets increase the power of this design hidden under the back hem.*

PATTERNS

Embroidered patterns deemed effective against evil spirits are those also chosen for amulets and jewelry, for tattooing, for felts, and as decorative devices on buildings, particularly at thresholds. Many are geometric whose origin lies in ancient mythology: the triangle, zigzag, rhomb, labyrinth, crescent, circle, 8-pointed star and cross. From the animal world fish, hands, eyes and horns have tremendous power. Birds, especially cocks, are often associated with horns as protective clan symbols. They are usually paired: in Bulgaria they are placed across the front neck in order to form the pattern of a cross.

The force of a pattern is strengthened by doubling or repeating it, by positioning it strategically and by adding protective materials such as tassels or shells. On shifts of eastern European countries formerly under Ottoman rule a small single unfinished pattern, set asymmetrically or alone, is especially powerful. Symbolizing the continuity of life, it is of more ancient origin than the Islamic desire to leave something imperfect. Patterns forming a border are also frequently left with a gap.

THE TRIANGLE, ZIGZAG AND RHOMB

The triangle has many associations. It defines the female sexual region and thus evokes fertility, its sharp corners have the power to blind the evil eye and it symbolizes the power of the trinity in many religions both established (as in Christianity) and pagan (as in ancient Slav mythology with its three-headed deities). It is still an amulet for people and animals alike, from India to Morocco. In a row it forms zigzags or chevrons, symbols of water and of the snake, frequently depicted on prehistoric pottery; doubled it forms a diamond or a rhomb (an oblique-angled parallelogram), another fertility symbol and a common protective brickwork pattern on the houses of northern Europe. One of the meanings of the Greek word *rhombus* is 'magic circle'. In embroidery the triangle is a ubiquitous pattern, used especially as a zigzag row along the edge of a garment, often in appliquéd material

with added stitchery. Such edgings are common on the clothing of the Lapps, on Palestinian dresses and on the headgear of many countries, such as that of the men of the mountain villages of Galicia in northern Spain, whose black wool hoods topped with three red tassels have red zigzag felt edgings and red and green zigzags embroidered across the forehead.

The triangle is the leitmotif of the embroidered costume of the Akha hill tribes of northern Thailand and Myanmar. Their villages are guarded by sacred gates and wooden posts supporting huge triangles of wood and painted zigzags, against 'hawks and wildcats, leopards and tigers, illness and plague, leprosy and epilepsy, vampires and weretigers, and all other bad and wicked things'. Their ritual triangular swings tower above their villages.

LEFT *The most common motifs of neolithic and Bronze Age pottery of Europe are the geometric patterns associated with pagan cults: the 'running dog', scrolls, triangles, chevrons and zigzags, as on this Bronze Age pot of 1300 BC from Videlles, Essonne, in France.*

OPPOSITE *Egyptian bridal shawl from Azute, silver plate on blue net, figurative motifs stylized into geometric patterns set in diamonds. Some shawls are purely geometric, others depict rural life.*

RIGHT *Tourist dress from Aswan. The crude patterns on this dress are debased motifs from Egyptian mythology. They include, for example, the eye of Horus, the crescent moon as an attribute of Isis, the solar symbol of the double axe and the ankh, symbol of life.*

BELOW *Patterns deemed effective against the evil eye often originated in ancient cults: the ram's horn motif from palaeolithic hunting societies is one. This jacket has a powerful red edging to the neck, and, on the front, a small isolated asymmetric pattern embroidered in dazzling silks.*

CIRCLES AND THEIR DERIVATIONS

The circle and spiral – potent symbols of the cosmic force of the sun and moon and of the motion and rejuvenation of the wheel – also offer protection from evil spirits, as do their derivations, such as the crescent, 8-pointed star, swastika, cross within a circle and the labyrinth.

A circle within a circle often has the appearance of an eye. On the bodice fronts of the dresses of Bethlehem and Jerusalem four such circles known as 'angels' eyes' are embroidered around a medallion, surrounded by as many as eighteen borders forming a frame. The circles are reputed to protect from the evil eye. The frame, ostensibly to prevent them escaping, consists of a complex series of wavy lines, often enclosing small flower heads and rows of black, white and pink fishbone and tiny satin stitch. Above the panel are two small sinuous birds, believed to bring good luck.

The evil eye as a pattern in itself forms a dramatic back to the hooded brown woollen cloaks of the Berbers of the High Atlas in Morocco. It is inserted as a woven section of red wool above the hem, stretching right across the back of the garment, and diamond, triangular and zigzag patterns are added in supplementary weft weaving and embroidery, with loose threads left hanging to create movement.

Variations of the circle have protective powers. The spiral – a pattern that was trodden on to ancient ground to sanctify it before a city was built, and is still marked on thresholds and floors from Bangladesh to the Czech Republic – is a distinct motif of felt carpets and is frequent in embroidery. It features, with horns and swastikas, on the embroidered clothing of the region of Zadar in Croatia.

The 8-pointed star is one of the most common motifs of all but does not always have protective powers. It was, however, embroidered on the lappets of *beniqa*, Algerian pixie-hoods mentioned by Haedo

in the seventeenth century as being worn by all Muslim women in Algiers, specifically to repel evil spirits. These bonnets had two long lappets which were wound round plaits, with the embroidery at the bottom or massed on the part covering the head.

The square was considered a magical source of protection by the Chinese, Indians, Arabs and Persians. The rectangular and latticed labyrinth patterns embroidered in sober monochrome on the front of women's blouses in the village of Navalcan in Spain were, too, considered to have magical properties.

Associated with the circle as symbol of the sun is the *boteh*, *kairi* or paisley shape that held the soul bird as the sun held the soul and was believed to have powers against witchcraft. It developed in Mughal India from Persian sources, and then passed into European textiles, but with no lingering supernatural associations.

The circle enclosing a cross is one of the patterns of the embroidered *shabraks*

of Pazyryk and is a powerful symbol. It appears on the costume of the Chuvash and also on that of Bulgaria, where many patterns are shared with medieval monuments and with runic script.

The motif of the cross itself is used with the power of Christianity but also with its more ancient pagan associations as a pattern against evil. Tracing a cross on an object cuts it and sacrifices it; crossing oneself asks for protection; crossing another takes away their influence; crossroads disperse evil as the spirits are disorientated; and the cross is also a talisman and a chest pendant favoured above all others.

NUMBERS

Numbers are also effective against witchcraft. In the peasant costume of Europe rhythms can be discerned in patterns, which can be simply single or double; in threes and sevens, or multiples thereof; or in twelves, and these repetitions appear persistently on coifs, costume and jewelry. Three is interpreted as the Trinity and seven the gifts of the Holy Spirit, but they undoubtedly stem from earlier sources. The bonnets of Sarthe in France, for example, have seven flowers embroidered on the crown as a protective device.

OPPOSITE *Woman's scarf, Gabès, southern Tunisia. Circular sundiscs and cocks, themselves a solar symbol believed to drive away the evil spirits of the night, are here combined with the Islamic world's most potent talismanic patterns, the hand and fish.*

HAND AND FISH

Both hand and fish feature in palaeolithic art, the one symbolizing the female pudendum, the other the phallus. Though their symbolic meaning is now lost, their potency against the evil eye remains. The fish shape as amuletic jewelry is popular from eastern Asia to Europe, protecting and bringing good luck. The hand is chosen as a motif in Islamic countries, the five fingers being associated with the five tenets of Islam. The hand can be raised palm outwards, where it opposes evil spirits with the reproductive power of the female, or palm inwards where it constitutes an obstacle deflecting the evil eye downwards. Raised hands on scarecrows in many lands kept not only birds but also harmful spirits away from fields.

ABOVE *Woman's jacket, Le Kef, Tunisia. The fish, an ancient phallic symbol, is a major amulet in Tunisian life. It features on embroideries, usually together with the hand, hangs from rearview mirrors of taxis and is painted over thresholds and at the bottom of soup bowls.*

In embroidery it is particularly in the costume of Tunisia that the pattern of hand and fish predominate, especially on marriage robes. The hand is often stylized into an almost floral pattern, or has an eye in the palm, a design which would originally have more closely resembled the female genitalia. The fish is sometimes embroidered with a horn shape in its mouth, intended to pierce the evil eye. Both hand and fish often merge into a general overall pattern and are hardly discernible.

MATERIALS

Embroidery and jewelry almost merge in the materials associated with stitchery in its protective and magical role. The earliest jewelry – holding talismanic powers and denoting kinship and social standing – stemmed from the natural world: teeth, claws, bones, hair, feathers, shells, stones. Linen and felt, indigo and incense, even the act of spinning, have similar magical associations. Still today the materials whose own potency against spirits enhances that of embroidery come often from ecological sources: cowrie shells are the supreme example. These, with scraps of felt, tassels of hair or wool, pompoms, mirrors, coins, beads, objects that tinkle or flutter and gaudy colours, put evil spirits to rout. Often the choice depends on what is available – a local shell or beetle wing – but sometimes goods are traded over great distances. By their very nature many of these materials do not strictly constitute embroidery but are so frequently found associated with it that their role cannot be ignored. The juxtaposition goes far back in time.

Opposite Woman's blouse with Job's tear seeds. These tropical grass seed shells are frequently used as a decorative device in the clothing of the Akha and Sgaw Karen women of Indo-China.

EMBROIDERY WITH PROPHYLACTIC MATERIALS

When Howard Carter first shone his torch into the inner chamber of Tutankhamun's tomb in 1922 and gazed on fabulous treasures of gold and lapis he may scarcely have noticed a small linen headkerchief. Dating from about 1350 BC it combines embroidery with prophylactic materials. It is decorated with chain stitch and covered with appliquéd circles, strips, small rectangles and snakes, with added metal discs, flat circular beads and tassels.

A later example is a Chinese silk embroidery of pheasants on branches, found among the Pazyryk textiles. Probably taken to Siberia by a Chinese princess given in marriage, it had been made into a saddle lining by the semi-nomadic 'barbarians' of the Altai, who had added around its edge a primitive decoration of inlaid gold and tinfoil with a fringe of large tassels of hair and wool and little hanging bags.

COWRIES AND OTHER SHELLS

Most powerful of all talismanic additions to embroidery is the cowrie. The shell of the mollusc *Cypraea moneta* found in the Indian Ocean around the archipelago of the Maldives – a string of atolls south of India – the cowrie, resembling as it does the female vulva, is universally appreciated for its magical powers. It was also widely accepted as currency: it functioned as coinage in ancient China, where cowries have been found in Stone Age graves, and still served as money in the early twentieth century in West Africa.

In Ceylon and Bengal, cowries were traded for rice, from whence Arab merchants took them to the Red Sea and the Mediterranean, and by camel across to West Africa – a camel could carry up to 150,000 shells. In 1887 a French officer named Caron visited Mali and noted that two and a half kilos of rice were worth one hundred cowries, and a sheep five thousand. Cowries accompany embroidery on much royal regalia of Africa and also on masks and musical instruments. Arabs and Persians also traded cowries up the Volga river to

Siberia, where they feature on the embroidered costume of the Finno-Ugric people. Here they are known as *vzhova* (adder) as they resemble a snake's head, and were as valuable as silver.

Other examples of their value are given by Ibn Battúta, the Moroccan traveller who toured the Islamic world in the fourteenth century. When he called at the Maldives, the Wazir presented him with a hundred thousand cowries for his expenses. He was later given two slave girls, some pieces of silk and a casket of jewels. He sold some of the jewels for cowries with which he hired a vessel to take him to Bengal.

Cowries feature particularly on accessories and are widely used on embroidered headdresses and animal trappings from India to the Middle East. They are generally stitched in mass or in lines, but sometimes form a symbolic design such as in the ritual textiles of the Naga and the peoples of western Sumatra.

Various shells and seeds are often substituted for cowries. The belts of the Akha women of Thailand, for example, are decorated with solid rows of cowries, but if the woman is poor they are replaced by Job's tear seeds. These seeds are the outside shells of the tropical grass *Coix lachryma jobi*, which are left in the embers of a fire for two weeks so that they turn the desired shade of white. The only other hill tribe who use them are the Sgaw Karen whose married women embroider their blouses with the seeds, and with stitchery in geometric pattern.

Du Halde, who travelled to China in the early eighteenth century, noted that the Miao people of the south-west wore jackets with the seams loaded with the smallest shells they could find in the seas around Yunnan and the local lakes. In Mexico shells and feathers were used both as jewelry and on garments of pre-Hispanic design, such as the Aztec men's cloaks (*tilmatli*).

LEFT *Woman's cap, Chitral, northern Pakistan. Materials added to embroidery increase its potency against evil spirits. One of the most widely appreciated, as it resembles the female vulva, is the cowrie. On this cap an old coke bottle top, buttons, the tree of life and red further enhance protection.*

COINS

There has always been a persistent belief in the power of coins to heal and to avert evil, so they have often been pierced to make jewelry and to stitch on to clothing. They are used in conjunction with embroidery in many parts of the world.

Coins feature particularly on headdresses. Skullcaps decorated with coins were part of the Iron Age dress of the Finno-Ugric and Turkic peoples of central Russia and a distinction is still made between areas of Russia where

headgear is a coin cap and hanging scarf and others where the stiffened beaded headdress known generally as *kakoshnik* is worn. In Ottoman countries headscarves, caps and face masks are edged with coins.

The custom of a woman wearing her dowry wealth as jewelry has led to coins also being frequently incorporated with embroidery on the fronts of dresses, one special coin often being strategically placed at the base of the neck opening. The Lahu, Akha and Lisu hill tribes of Thailand also use coins, together

with silver discs and dangles, on their headgear and festive jackets. The Akha women wear sashes so heavily weighted at the ends with embroidery, coins, buttons, beads and tassels that as they squat the ends fall between their legs, affording protective covering.

There are many substitutes for coins, including silver discs, old bottle tops, bits of zips and lead shot. Buttons are especially common, mother of pearl or white shirt buttons being favourites.

ABOVE *Child's jacket, Kohistan, northern Pakistan. Coins, believed to heal and avert evil, were often replaced by buttons. Old zips form an effective, though non-functional, metallic edging.*

LEFT *Man's robe, Ethiopia. Metal discs and pendants are sewn over the ears and back neck of this robe and decorate the edges, which have appliquéd triangles of fabric as additional ornamentation.*

BEADS

Beads were also used as currency – the *wampum* beads of Native North American peoples are but one example. As jewelry they decorated the mummies of ancient Egypt, and as rosaries they figure in the Catholic, Buddhist, Hindu and Islamic religions.

When used in a prophylactic manner combined with embroidery – as opposed to comprising articles made entirely of beads – they are arranged in much the same way as shells and coins, edging an article or pattern or else placed individually in a strategic position. They are usually of white, blue, red or yellow glass. The cloths used to cover precious textiles by the nomadic peoples of Central Asia, such as the Uzbek, are usually edged in beads of white – also chosen by the tribal peoples of Kohistan to outline the patterns on their clothing.

Blue beads are associated with the power of the eye: a modern Turkish shawl will have just one blue bead hidden in the fringe at the precise centre of the back. They are chosen by the Pashtun of Afghanistan to edge purses and tobacco pouches. Many headdresses, and also amulets and charms, contain blue and coral beads.

Throughout the Mediterranean world coral is believed to ensure an abundant milk supply in women and therefore frequently decorates infants' clothing, or perhaps babies' rattles in the form of a red or coral-coloured bead or a piece of coral itself, whose shape symbolizes the power of the horn, with phallic overtones. Because of this association, coral is frequently allied with the fish in Tunisian embroidery.

The Ugrian people, hunters and fishermen of western Siberia, sacrifice beads to their gods and bury their dead womenfolk in their finest embroidered clothes, leaving on them the coins and the yellow, blue and white beads but removing the shells.

BELOW *Woman's cap, Yemen. Blue beads are associated with the power of the evil eye and one is sufficient to protect the wearer.*

MIRROR

Mirror in the Islamic world is believed to trap the evil eye, holding its reflection for ever. In Morocco women ensure their husband's fidelity by opening in front of him a lidded box lined with mirrors. As they close it again the marriage is sealed with his soul held captive. Mirror also refracts, dispersing the power of the evil eye. In 1880 Sawai Madho Singh lined his entire apartment in the city palace of Jaipur with mirrors to frighten away evil spirits. Mirror also dazzles and thus is believed to cause the evil eye to blink or even to blind it.

It is in countries that have been at some time under Islamic influence that pieces of mirror are used in embroidery. They dominate most especially in the domestic embroidery of the geographical area of north-west India into Afghanistan, and also feature on the leather and woollen garments of central and eastern Europe. Rows of reflective mica also figure on the ceremonial cloths of western Sumatra.

That mirrors are now merely a decorative element in Indian embroidery is indisputable; that they may not always have been so is indicated by the position in which they are placed. They form the centre of flowers and eyes for animals and birds; they divide pattern into areas and provide a focal point; they are placed strategically in a geometric design, or are isolated and accentuated by the surrounding stitches. In the festive hangings of Saurashtra they are used pictorially to depict, amongst other things, the ears of Surya the sun god, or the breasts of Radha, Krishna's consort. Mirrors almost never appear just scattered around the background, except in modern commercial embroidery.

The original material was mica which is still sometimes used. For mirrorglass large globes of blown glass are silvered on the inside and then broken into small pieces. These are still widely marketed in the villages of north-western India. The mirrors are attached by crossed stitches which are then worked over by buttonholing; otherwise a ring of thread over the mirror is fixed to the fabric by interlacing stitch.

The style of mirrorwork of each Muslim clan or Hindu sub-caste is individual. The Rajput and Ahir farming castes combine square mirrors with yellow and white interlacing in heavy cotton in strong geometric patterns, while the Rabaris mix mirrors of varied shapes in bold motifs accentuating the breasts. These castes are very religious, the earth goddess being one of their deities. They decorate their bodies with tattooing and their houses with mudwork which incorporates mirrors.

In Asia mirror was normally combined only with stitchery and not with other added decorative devices. In Hungary and in Croatia, however, woollen and leather garments, that by their cut and their vestigial sleeves betray their steppe origin, began in the nineteenth century to be decorated with pieces of mirror, along with leather discs, rosettes and tassels. The *cifraszür*, the coat owned by every young man of marriageable age in Hungary, became so overloaded with such ornaments that legal action was taken to curb excess. In Croatia it was the jackets of white or bright felted wool and the leather waistcoats that were decorated by mirror and appliquéd scraps of leather or felted wool.

In Spain the village of Montehermoso is famous for its women's high straw hats thickly covered with every protective device possible: mirrors, buttons, red cloth, bright pompoms, tassels and even horns. In Spain too small hanging purses were made for both men and women, decorated with mirror, tassels, buttons, sequins and bells.

LEFT *Blouse, choli, Rajput caste, Kutch, India. A source of life for the newborn baby, breasts are protected by heavy embroidery on the women's clothing of many cultures (in Europe a separate embroidered stomacher fulfilled the same purpose). Here the breasts are additionally protected by mirrors.*

BELOW *Child's jacket, Rajput caste, Kutch, India. Mirror was believed to dazzle the evil eye and even blind it. Just one, strategically placed at the centre back waist, would ensure the child's safety.*

SEQUINS

The sequins of Western embroidery, like gold thread and jewels, were chosen only for their expensive aura and their sparkle under the lights of church or evening ball. In peasant embroidery the shine of gold was associated with kings and gods, with dragons and serpents, and with wealth and festivity. The sparkle of sequins, however, had much in common with mirror in its protection from evil spirits.

The sequins used on the embroidered indigo dresses of Yemen, for example, are known as *lamma*, and the same word in Arabic with a long vowel means the evil eye. These sequins were made until the late 1980s in the market, the *suk*, of the capital Sana'a. An eighteenth-century report states that they were copper but on most dresses now they are brass. Punched out of the metal plate they have a distinctive central indentation. The dress front is covered to a greater or lesser degree with rows of them attached with two stitches of red cotton thread, combined with lines of white stitchery, small pieces of mother-of-pearl from the Red Sea, and triangles made of loops of brass chain.

RIGHT *Woman's face mask, Yemen. Sequins have much in common with mirror in their protective role. Here the combination of small triangles in brass chain and mother-of-pearl, and the colour red, increases their power.*

ELEMENTS TO CONFUSE EVIL SPIRITS

Tinkling sounds, gaudy and alternated colours, tassels and pompoms confuse the evil eye, while they also attract attention. Silver discs, bells, and even thimbles edging clothing vibrate with movement that distracts and creates a sound that in hot countries is cooling. Du Halde mentions the women of western Manchuria who wore long garments of skin with a red or green border and pieces of copper or little bells at the back hem, which gave notice of their approach. Siberian women aroused the attention of suitors with the jingling of metal sewn on to their clothes.

Edges are very frequently of fluttering tassels, often of rags, or of fringes which are a natural outcome of the weaving technique. Tassels may in some parts of the world be substitutes for feathers: the cloaks of Maori chiefs are sometimes edged with feathers and sometimes with tufts or tassels clearly in imitation. For Native American tribes feathered headdresses and skin garments that were deeply fringed and beaded denoted social standing. In Hawaii, for example, feathers were deemed a vehicle of divine power when red or yellow, and in Central America were an integral part of pre-Conquest festive clothing.

A tassel or pompom will often be placed in precisely the same manner as a cowrie or coin at the base of the neck opening of a dress or at an embroidered pocket or other vulnerable spot. The linen trousers and shirts that the women of Lagartera in Spain made for their bridegroom are densely embroidered on shoulders, cuffs and all around a deep neck placket in bands of white and honey needleweaving with drawn threadwork. The base of the neck and of the trouser flies are adorned with tassels.

Gaudy colours, especially when alternated or when applied in little pieces of fabric, are powerful deterrents against evil. The most potent colour by far is red.

ABOVE *Pouch, Plains tribes, North America. Fringes and tassels – and in this case feathers – around the edge of an embroidery were already a feature of the Pazyryk textiles. Their movement distracts and confuses evil spirits and they are a ubiquitous device on textiles.*

THE POWER OF RED

The symbolism of colour is complex and associations can be totally opposed: in another culture, at another point in time, the widow wears white and the bride black. The colours of the liturgy, those of joy or of jealousy, those of the clothes of kings or of chimneysweeps are imposed by society. In contrast three colours are basic to the human state: these are red, white and black. Though interpretations of their symbolism may vary, white traditionally denotes purity and the celestial, and recalls the potency of human milk and semen, while black, associated with excreta and earth, denotes decay. Though both black and white are used symbolically in costume they play no similar role in embroidery.

Red is the most powerful, the most vibrant, the most exhilarating of colours: it is the blood of life and of death. As such it is also ambiguous: life, fire, the sun and power are counterbalanced by sacrifice and death. Red threads and fabrics are associated with spirit worship and demons, with youth and marriage, with talismanic charms and secret powers. It is the predominant colour in all tribal and peasant embroidery, but is used in two entirely different ways – to protect and to mark.

OPPOSITE *Woman's hood, Micmac tribe, North America. Red is the most powerful and vibrant of colours, associated with blood and thus with life and death. It is often used protectively in the form of appliquéd red fabric.*

BELOW *Ritual cloth, Naga, north-eastern India. This cloth could only be worn by a man whose father and grandfather, and he himself, had sacrificed mithan buffalo and completed the whole cycle of necessary ceremonies. Red dog's hair, cowries, stripes and patterns on Naga textiles all had ritual meaning.*

RED FOR PROTECTION

In its protective role red is most commonly deployed as fabric appliquéd on vulnerable areas such as seams, edges and over the breasts. The material will generally be more expensive than that of the garment and often imported: red flannel, silk and, in linen-producing areas, fine cotton. It will often be superimposed with decorative embroidery and strengthened by cowries, bells, tassels and mirror. Patterns will be the symbolic ones of the cross, zigzags, triangles, circles, diamonds and squares.

Early examples are the linen shift found at Pazyryk, dating from about the fourth century BC, with red thread couched on all its seams, widening at the neck and wrists into a braid; the mummy wrappings of Paracas from about the same period with borders of red embroidery; and the clothes discovered in the Coppergate diggings at York, dating from the tenth or eleventh century when Jorvik was a Viking capital, which appear to have been edged with red silk ribbons, emphasizing the neck and cuffs.

burial cloths of red are displayed on the roof of a hut where an eminent man has died, while in Madagascar burial cloths are known as *mena* (red) even when that colour no longer predominates but is replaced by an embroidered edge.

In the Far East the Ainu of Japan notch the hems of their gowns, binding the slit with red, as they do the base of the neck opening. The Dyak of Borneo appliqué red flannel on men's ornamental jackets, as people do in Sumatra where figurines of the dead are also wrapped in red cloth. Babies in Hong Kong were swaddled in embroidered red cloths with mirror stuck on their forehead to protect them: in the 1920s only seventy-two out of a thousand lived beyond a year. Married women of the Sgaw Karen tribe of northern Thailand and Myanmar embroider their blouses with red and with Job's tear seeds, inserting a deep band of red fabric along the bottom. With these blouses they wear tie-dye skirts, which they make by tying the cloth with red threads. As they associate these with spirit worship they dye the cloth in the forest where they cannot be seen. The Blue Hmong appliqué red on to clothing and baby carriers; the White Hmong place a red fabric cross at the back of a woman's jacket after the curing ceremony when a shaman has evicted from her body the offending spirits that made her ill.

In India vermilion is a sacred colour, decorating animistic shrines. It is considered auspicious and marriage textiles are predominantly of red fabric or decorated in red. The protective qualities of red are strong: account books begin

with a red swastika, red thread around the wrist makes demons impotent, sweets wrapped in red cloth are placed at crossroads to thwart evil spirits.

In Russia costume is decorated overwhelmingly in red – the word 'red' in early Russian is synonymous with beauty. The shifts of the Tcheremiss and Mordu of Siberia have every seam and edge and the eye-motifs over the breast appliquéd in red, with beads and sequins added. The ritual towels of the Ukraine have a plain red band, considered sacred in pagan belief.

In eastern Europe red dominates all embroidered costume and is believed to have magic properties, effective against witches. In the Balkans red felted wool is embroidered and appliquéd on to the woollen sleeveless coats, called *zubun*, of Serbia and the jackets of Bosnia. In the Dinaric mountains it is the linen shifts that have red cotton appliquéd on edges, and at the base of the officer collar a snippet of red fabric or a tassel is placed. In Hungary red leather appliqué was the earliest decoration of skin garments; the red ribbon encircling a couple at a Romanian marriage was then used by the bride to tie her apron on Sundays; and in Bulgaria small red tassels on linen shifts or else an asymmetric pattern in red cross stitch

Geographically, red decoration on clothing is common to many societies though interpretation of the power of red and the right to wear it vary; among the Naga, for example, only a man who has killed is entitled to red.

In Africa the Benin chiefs of Nigeria wear red cloth as ceremonial court dress to protect themselves and their king from evil spirits, while other tribes associate red with achievement. The Ful of Senegal stitch a small piece of red fabric at the nape and centre forehead of their caps. It is also the prerogative of young girls – a cloth with a red stripe is worn in Nigeria for betrothal rites, and the Masai of Kenya decorate young girls' skin skirts with red ochre. Red also relates to death: in Nigeria

LEFT Fertility doll, Ghana. The relationship of red to blood and fertility is expressed in the simple red cord of this doll, used by a woman when she wants a child.

separate from the rest of the design are deemed to have magic powers.

In western Europe cottages in Wales were painted red to keep demons away; in the isolated Pyrenean valley of Bethmale men's jackets were embroidered with red feather stitching around all edges, along seams, pockets and over the shoulders, with appliquéd bands of black velvet decorated with red zigzags and crosses to afford protection. Italians wrap newborn babies in vests of red silk, believing it will bring luck; in Germany evil spirits were thought likely to attack newborn children before there was time to baptize them, so christening robes and covers spread over the child while it was being taken to church are heavily embroidered in red with appliquéd bands and facings that are mainly red. In 1526 Luther declared that white was not essential for christening robes, whereupon the people of Småland in southern Sweden returned to more pagan clothing and wrapped their babies in bags with red triangular edges, red fringing and appliquéd silk ribbons. These they hired from church, together with caps, for one silver krone.

RIGHT *Man's cap, Sierra Leone. Symbolic motifs of crosses over arches and a lizard are embroidered on this cap which has a small, powerful piece of red applique at the forehead and nape.*

RED FOR MARKING

Primitive man's sealing of contracts with blood, his marking of possessions, and the decorating of graves with red ochre finds an echo in the extraordinary power of red in western European embroidery. While costume and embroideries for the home slavishly follow fashions, linen articles for the trousseau remain resolutely monogrammed and numbered in red cross stitch. This custom of marking ritual textiles in red is almost inextricably bound to the life-consuming production of home-grown, handspun, handwoven linen. Replaced by purchased cotton the bottom-drawer linen of continental Europe is still marked in red.

In Spain and Portugal linen shirts, made by the bride for her groom, are marked in red cross stitch below the neck placket, which is heavily embroidered in white. Red tassels were almost always added. Those of Caceres and Salamanca have the man's name or initials, those of Segovia the couple's names and marriage date and those of Guimarães in Portugal a sentimental word like *amizade* or *amor*. Sometimes the lettering has no meaning as the women embroiderers were of course illiterate. Such marking by red cross-stitch initials is common on the women's linen chemises of Abruzzo in Italy and of Switzerland. In the Black Forest region of Germany married men's shirts were worked with symbols such as hearts, stars and zigzags in red, and the bachelors' in white. Their braces, similarly embroidered, were reversed in colour – red for bachelors and white for married men. A newborn Bulgarian baby's shift, ritualistically made and symbolizing the child's skin, is always marked with red stitches around the neck as a first statement of the child's passage into the human race.

Western European household linens for the trousseau are marked with red cross stitch, usually by a monogram, and are frequently also numbered. As laundry was a social activity at river bank or village washhouse such marking served in addition a practical purpose, in the same way that bread baked in a communal oven was stamped with distinctive symbols to identify its owner. The marking of linen was the motivation for the myriad red alphabet samplers of the schoolgirls of Europe.

LEFT *Sampler, Italy. Trousseau linens are often also numbered in red cross stitch as laundry was a communal activity. The marking and repairing of linen was the motivation for the red alphabet and plain sewing samplers of the schoolgirls of Europe.*

BELOW *Trousseau aprons, France. The linen of western Europe is marked in red cross stitch, reflecting primitive man's marking of objects in blood. This pile of aprons, made by 'DJ' for her trousseau, remains neatly folded and unused as her hand was never sought in marriage.*

HIGH DAYS AND HOLY PLACES

Textiles have always played a significant ritual role, even in the earliest societies, being offered or exchanged as gifts, or else burned or buried at the major events in life, whether religious, military or social.

HIGH DAYS

The high days for embroidered textiles in the human life-cycle – when the magical power of decoration on dress is invoked to protect from evil spirits – are the rites of passage: birth, marriage, death. In most societies, a period – either of vulnerability, as for the newborn or the spirit of the recently deceased, or of uncleanliness, as for the new mother – was set at forty days, after which some ceremony involving embroidered clothing was held to signal the return to normal life. In the astrological religion of Babylon forty, together with three and seven, was considered a perfect number, linked to the completion of the lunar cycle.

The role of embroidered clothing in celebrating the passage from one human condition to another is exemplified by the linen shirt or shift of Europe. Representing the human skin in an analogy of the regeneration of the scales of mythological creatures, it acts as a marker through life. It is a ritual and sacred object, its decoration the transference of the tribal signs of tattooing into embroidery, its cut the simple joining of loom widths with nothing wasted. In Romania the small piece cut out for the neck is thrown with incantations into a fast-flowing river; in Bulgaria the linen for the new baby's first shirt is not cut but torn out by beating with stones. In almost every society from the stitching round the neck of the baby's shirt – in Bulgaria always in red thread – the embroidery reaches its richest and heaviest for the young and most particularly for marriage, to become more subdued and end as a simple neck border in old age. In most parts of the world people were buried in their marriage shirt or entire costume, ostensibly so that their partner could recognize them in the next world, but on a magico-religious plane to identify them as a human being.

BIRTH

Until the birth of her first child the mother was considered vulnerable to evil, belonging neither to her own family, nor yet to her husband's, and in many countries she kept on for everyday wear her marriage costume and amuletic jewelry. On giving birth she was normally considered unclean, and new baby and mother were protected by embroidery and other devices against illness and the mother's own uncleanliness. In Bulgaria she was known as *lehusa* and her shirt was decorated with a needle threaded with red, pieces of garlic and blue beads around the neck to keep her own evil spirits within her and prevent others from entering. On the fortieth day these decorations were left on a tree and she was taken to church.

In Slovakia, where as many as twenty or thirty people lived in one room and concepts of hygiene were not understood, an embroidered bedcurtain known as a *kutnice* protected the mother, separating her from the room, a magical separation that was enhanced by objects placed around the curtain: herbs, garlic, strips of red and green cloth, needles and knives. The patterns embroidered on the curtain were symbolic, deriving from both ancient cult and Christianity, and often included open drawn threadwork, enabling the mother to see into the room. For six weeks mother and baby were totally confined

ABOVE *In Germany, a child was prepared for baptism by being wrapped in a cloth decorated in red; in Grisons, Switzerland, the protection was afforded by the symbolic tree of life with the fertility motifs of carnation and tulip.*

and then attended a cleansing ceremony in church, the 'Churching of Women' of the Christian faith. In some villages the mother went shrouded in the *kutnice*, in others she wore her marriage stole or else a special cloth was embroidered.

Similar purification ceremonies were performed at the hammam, the public baths of Ottoman countries, also involving embroidered cloths both for the mother and for the ritual washing of the baby. In Turkey the groom's mother would rent the hammam for forty days and the bride would be bathed and her hair unplaited, with towels embroidered for the occasion.

Symbolic embroideries also assisted labour. In the Ukraine the cloth used the previous year to bless the *packa* (Easter bread) was tied to a beam above the mother's bed for her to pull on; in Tunisia it was the marriage belt that was so used. In Thrace her apron was thrown over her stomach.

At the birth it was often the grandmother's role to begin embroideries to which she would devote most of her time until the child married, as in Hungary. In the Punjab at the birth of a boy the paternal grandmother began the *bagh*, the embroidered cloth that he would give his bride.

In China, about forty days after the birth of a male child, the first ceremonial hair-cutting takes place, at which the mother is entitled to wear the embroidered jacket she was given as a bride by her parents. The baby's first hair-cutting had magical significance in many other countries, as the hair was believed to retain the spiritual strength of the person.

ABOVE *The protective role of the bedcurtain confining mother and baby for forty days after childbirth is often augmented by devices such as garlic and knives or, in the case of this curtain from Poprad, Slovakia, a display of trousseau linen shifts.*

BELOW *Bedcurtain,* kutnice, *Moravia. The curtain protecting mother and newborn child depicted the tulip, pomegranate and carnation of fertility, the stag and heart of hunting mythology, or the Christian IHS.*

MARRIAGE

Almost everywhere the event at which embroidery plays its major ritual role is marriage. Customs are immensely varied, but universal themes are common to most countries: the preparation by the girl throughout her childhood of items for her trousseau; the significance of her ability as an embroideress in gaining a husband; the public display of the embroidered trousseau to demonstrate her skill and the textile wealth she is bringing to the marriage; the use of embroidery on costume to mark the change in status, particularly of the bride; the ritual offering of embroidered gifts by both parties; the use of embroidered cloths in the wedding ceremonies and, above all, the quasi-sacred status of the marriage shirt or dress.

RIGHT *Betel bag, Banjara caste, India. The exchange of embroidered gifts is part of marriage ritual. Brides of the nomadic Banjara traditionally worked a betel bag for their groom. In Europe the gift was usually a linen shirt.*

Trousseau embroideries mainly consist of a lifetime's supply of clothing for the bride and gifts (such as the embroidered betel bag given by the Banjara bride to her husband, the linen shirts made for him by European girls, the tobacco pouches, purses and caps made by the Syrian bride for the men of her family to lessen their grief when she leaves home, or covers such as the one the Korean groom ties round a small wooden goose to give the bride's mother as a token of his fidelity). Embroideries that feature in the wedding ceremonies, such as cloths for the couple to sit on, to decorate the bridal room, or to cover ritual articles – the coconuts and water used in some Indian marriages for example – are also included, together with one of the most important items, linen for the marriage bed.

In eastern Europe sets of linen were embroidered by the girl for the symbolic bed, set in the corner of the 'best' room and never actually slept in. Embroideries stacked up to the ceiling were normally seen only by the family but when the girl was of marriageable age, they were shown to others, even displayed outside the home. On marriage they were carried through the village to the bridegroom's house. The linen was changed for childbirth, and at time of death, when it was put on the funeral bier and again carried for all to

see. Trousseau linen remained the property of the woman and was handed down through the female line. If a woman had no daughter it was buried with her or reclaimed by her family.

Embroidery was also significant in the lives of young men. In Hungary every young man of marriageable age owned a *szür*, a coat of fulled wool with floral embroidery on its large square collar and edges, often acquired as his first wages. He would wear it all through courtship, at his marriage and afterwards for festive

LEFT *Marriage undershift, El Jem, Tunisia. In many countries, after consummation of the marriage the embroidered shift with its blood stains was shown by the bride's mother to the village women to prove her daughter's virginity.*

occasions. The bridegrooms of Mezőkövesd wore floral aprons and shirts with immensely wide embroidered sleeves made for them by their bride. In Montenegro young men were only allowed to wear embroidered clothes after marriage when they were considered fit to go fighting. The young men of Minho in Portugal would buy at fairs sweetheart hankies embroidered in red with some sentimental device, to bestow on the girl they loved. These had the same significance as a ring, ending the engagement if they were returned. Among the hill tribes of Thailand young men, especially the Lisu, carried elaborate 'courting' bags decorated with beads, stitchery, tassels, strips of cloth and silver ornaments.

The consummation of marriage brings its own customs involving embroideries. In many countries the shift or a cloth

stained with blood on the wedding night is displayed by the mother to prove her daughter's virginity. In North Africa on the third or seventh day the ceremony of the belt marks the transition of the bride from a goddess-like creature shrouded in embroidered robes to a domesticated woman. Her wide marriage clothing hid her body from evil spirits who might make her sterile before the marriage was consummated. When this danger is past she puts on a heavy woollen shawl – in eastern Tunisia dyed half indigo and half henna – with a densely embroidered centre strip, clasping it round the waist with a belt. This is done in the presence of a small boy to ensure that the bride will have sons. The shawl is later worn over the head without a belt.

ABOVE LEFT *Throughout eastern Europe the bride, however poor, would have an immense store of embroidered linen for her trousseau. Some she would have spent most of her childhood making and some would have been inherited from or made by her mother.*

ABOVE *The bridegroom's shirt was an important element of embroidered trousseau linen. Most spectacular are those of Mezőkövesd where a boy was given his shirt on becoming a young man. At death his shroud was made from the sleeves of the shirt he had worn as a bridegroom.*

BURIAL

In many societies textiles – not necessarily embroidered – were buried with the dead as provision for the afterlife or as ritual gifts. Though embroidery was occasionally done specifically for burial clothes, more frequently the marriage shirt or entire costume becomes the shroud at death. Often each partner is buried with half the cloth that tied them at marriage and was then torn in two.

It was a tradition among Turkic peoples for a man who died in battle to be buried in his clothes; otherwise, as they symbolize the man, they were tied to a pole on the burial mound or replaced by a piece of crudely embroidered felt. In many societies it was customary too for offerings of embroideries, or bits of rag or animal skin, to be tied to a bush near the tomb.

In Indonesia most ornamental textiles are buried with the dead, but few are embroidered. Only in the women's sarongs of Lampung in southern Sumatra is embroidery the dominant technique, and in those of the east of Sumba island where decoration is appliquéd. Both these areas are wealthy, the first trading in pepper and the second in horses.

Sumba chiefs were required to bury fifty to a hundred textiles with the corpse and to donate others to guests. Such decorated textiles were once the prerogative of the nobility and the women's skirts, known as *lau hada*, decorated with beads and imported nassa shells were both an important part of the dowry and also served as grave gifts, buried with their owner. The design is always an upright figure with arms raised in worship and with exaggerated sexual parts. Between the legs is a lizard, symbol of fecundity, and around the figure are fish or crustaceans such as crabs and lobsters – denoting rebirth as they regenerate their limbs – and crocodiles whom several Sumba clans believe to be their ancestors. Cotton tufting separates the motifs.

ABOVE *Woman's sarong,* lau hada, *Sumba, Indonesia. Crustaceans and lizards are symbols of rebirth. Sarongs were part of the dowry and were also grave gifts. Sumba chiefs were required to bury hundreds of textiles with their dead.*

The most famous textiles of the Lampung area of southern Sumatra are the ritual weavings known as 'ship of the dead' cloths. Similar patterns are worked on one type of the women's embroidered sarongs, the *tapis* that come from the mountainous region. They consist of bands of ikat alternated with embroidered bands of ships bearing trees and people, worked in satin stitch in cream, brown and blue silk with the patterns outlined. Another type has embroidery of weird shapes resembling cells under a microscope. Those of the Abung of the south and south-east are worked in couched gold thread

with geometric patterns or motifs of people and animals. Those of the Kauer on the far west coast bear hundreds of small mirrors or pieces of mica, and were worn with jackets embroidered with mirror and shells. A girl could only marry once she had completed her *tapis* and they were worn at all rites of passage.

FUNERAL

In many European countries embroideries were made specifically for the funeral, or for the religious ceremony forty days after death: in the village of Csokoly in Hungary girls would start to embroider sheets and pillows in red for their own funeral bed, and at about forty years of age they would begin a new set in yellow; in many parts of Sweden and Norway it was customary for the coffin to be displayed in the home before the procession set out and richly embroidered cloths would be laid over it; it was a Spanish custom to place funeral mats with Christian symbols worked in dark wool over the coffin, and on All Souls Day cloths embroidered with funereal motifs were spread on the church floor and candles stood on them; in the Ukraine ritual cloths were tied to crosses; and in Romania cloths in red and black cross stitch were offered to the family and priests and worn by the pall bearers over their shoulder. They were deemed to have magic powers to protect the deceased's spirit and when hearses carried the body instead, the cloths were not abandoned but were tied to the car door handle.

At funerals of the Pwo Karen in Myanmar and Thailand girls carry singing shawls made from the woven red blankets that normally cover the sleeping with the fringe at the foot, but are placed with it at the head for the dead. One half of the blanket is covered with white beads in groups of three or five and a fringe of beetles' wings and bells is hung from the bottom.

MOURNING

Mourning generally involves sober colouring and often the reversal of garments. The custom of turning clothing inside out for mourning is recorded by Ibn Battúta who describes mourners, on the death of the son of a sultan in about 1330, wearing rough, badly stitched garments inside out for forty days. Wearing clothing inside out or reversed at funerals was a recent custom in Europe and was believed to denote the disarray of the soul at death and its need of protection from magic forces. The women's jackets of Pont-Aven in Brittany are embroidered specifically for such use, their orange and yellow patterning being richly worked on the right side and more soberly on the left, the side they are fastened when the wearer is in mourning.

BELOW Tab, probably from skirt hem, Paracas, Peru. Textiles of the Paracas mummy bundles, dating from 400 to 250 BC, included embroideries depicting trophy heads, part of the mythology concerned with the role of death in sustaining life.

HEADHUNTING

Decapitation was at the root of Paracas mythology, symbolizing the role of death in sustaining life. Embroideries depict mythical feline figures, raptorial birds and round-eyed figures known as oculate beings, bearing trophy heads in baskets or as appendages to their body.

Almost three thousand years later, to the warlike Naga tribe headhunting was a deeply symbolic practice, which even the British administration in India had difficulty in stamping out. The magical power residing in the head made it imperative to present that of a human victim at the funeral of a chief, though heads were also taken merely as a result of simple feuding or because of a more complex belief. A woman's head with abundant hair encouraged fertility and even a child's was considered a trophy. The hunters wore shawls of striped brown and black cotton with circles of cowries denoting the moon and small brocaded red squares. They were not allowed red until they had killed nor

ABOVE Shawl, Manipur, north-eastern India. The Naga erected monolithic stones in honour of their dead. When a man had arranged this Herculean task, had offered feasting to his people and had lived apart from his family for one year, he was entitled to wear a shawl embroidered with animals.

cowries until they had slain two men, when the shells were often applied in the form of a human figure, added to a circle or as a separate motif.

The same people erected monolithic stones in honour of their dead, which entailed hundreds of people dragging the stone uphill, an event for which the women would sew masses of coins on the back of their sarongs. This Herculean task was followed by feasting, after which the young men who had participated, now known as *lung-chingba*, had to live apart from their family for a year. They were then entitled to wear a shawl of dark blue cloth woven in Manipur and embroidered with quaint figures of animals, mainly in red.

The Naga would also give a series of feasts of merit, when a man would provide food for all the village. Once this had been achieved and a *mithan* (buffalo) had been slaughtered, the hunter responsible was entitled to wear cloths decorated with cowries, as were his womenfolk.

FESTIVITIES

In European peasant life 'best' or marriage clothes were worn for festivities that were mainly concerned with the seasons and the production of food and linen. Ceremonies to greet the spring often involved young girls ripe for marriage treading fields and collecting eggs, dressed in their best embroidered costume. The proportion of peasant income spent on embroideries is astounding: a poor girl, living in a shack in Hungary simple enough to take only a day to erect, could have as many as thirty or forty embroidered dresses and several hundred pieces of linen.

Richly embroidered costume was worn on any occasion that was considered social. This included churchgoing, communal work in the fields and visits to market – eastern European women can still be seen wearing elements of

BELOW *After haymaking, girls of Dobra Niva in Slovakia put on their best embroidered costume and present a cake to the landowner.*

embroidered costume at market. Even mundane agricultural tasks, once they were performed by a large group of peasants together, were treated as an opportunity for 'best' wear. Martha Wilmot, travelling around Russia in the early nineteenth century, comments on an occasion when several hundred peasants had gathered together to cart manure, and even for this the women wore their shifts embroidered with red and their horned headdresses.

Churchgoing was at the heart of every community and the prime occasion for dressing up. Pagan rites of spring had been successfully incorporated into Easter, but cloths were still embroidered to cover baskets of eggs, fruit and bread, to be taken to church. Easter eggs in Moravia are still painted with the same patterns as those on embroidered clothing. In the early twentieth century in Mezőkövesd clothing was becoming more and more overloaded with sequins to the detriment of the embroidery, sequins which cost the peasants dear – one apron could have the value of a calf stitched on it in baubles. To save the peasants from ruin the Church stepped in and on Ash Wednesday in 1925 banned all sequins. At the Easter service the six thousand girls and young people of the town turned up at church in new embroidered clothes with patterns imitating the banned sequins. There was no question of individual choice but only of belonging to the community and establishing status by embroidery.

Religious processions are also high days for embroidered clothing in Catholic countries, including those of Central and South America. In Spain banners are hung from balconies, in other countries effigy bearers wear embroidered cloths on their shoulders.

In Jewish homes special cloths for the Sabbath table and plaited bread (*challah*) are usually embroidered with biblical quotations and religious symbols such

as candles and the bread itself. At the festival of Passover, commemorating the exodus from Egypt, services are held in the home. For these, cushion covers are embroidered and also bags in which three symbolic slices of the unleavened bread (*matzah*) could be kept. Jewish embroidery is normally in the style of the country in which the people live.

Surpassing all other festive activities – its roots in the animal instincts of the human psyche – is dance. Native North American war dances, dances for fulfilling dreams and curing illness, Bushmen's primeval dances of the moon, and many more similar dances throughout the world, required decorated costume, be it only special beads or feathers. The dance festivals of Europe are the last repository of embroidered dress. In most a hybrid 'national costume' has been cobbled together from diverse regional styles, but gradually care is beginning to be taken to use or copy genuine old costumes, with the correct style of embroidery of the region from which each particular dance comes.

ABOVE *Women wearing their best dress for market day in Urgut, Uzbekistan.*

HOLY PLACES

The modest town of Banske Bystrica in Slovakia straggles along the flank of a hill, its streets a jumble of the shabby baroque of an outpost of the Ottoman empire and the bleak concrete of Communist rule. The front door of a typical house leads directly into a kitchen/dining/living area furnished in 1950s style, a bizarre note struck by a radio shrouded in embroidery. The second room is what used to be called in Britain until very recent years the 'front' room. Here visitors are received. The room has chests full of textiles, the housewife's heritage from her mother's trousseau and her own. A television stands on a table by the wall, with plates displayed behind. Embroidered cloths cover the TV set and are draped around the plates. This is the holy corner of the ancient Eurasian hunting societies.

The holy corner marked the entry point for spirits coming into the earthly world, and the resting place of the souls of the departed who, it was believed, returned to their homes on festive occasions. The corner is usually sited by the family dining table on the opposite side of the room from the stove. The simplest have an icon and a lamp hung across them, as in Russia. More commonly a triangular shelf fills the space, on which bread is often placed, or an egg at Easter. A newer version is a religious picture hung on the wall. There were traditionally five elements: a holy picture or statue, an embroidered linen cloth symbolizing the bands that swaddled Christ at his birth and death, something green for the tree of life, a bird linking the soul to earth, and a light denoting the presence of God. In Catholic homes the picture or statue is of the Madonna; in Orthodox households, it is an icon; amongst Muslims, where a prayer mat is unrolled on the floor for daily prayers, it is a *mihrab* or a Koran on a shelf draped with embroidery; for Jewish peoples it is the *menorah* (the seven-branched candelabrum used in the Temple and an emblem of Judaism), the *Torah*, a painted amulet or, on the eastern

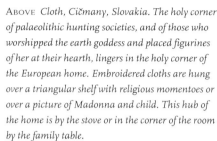

ABOVE *Cloth, Cičmany, Slovakia. The holy corner of palaeolithic hunting societies, and of those who worshipped the earth goddess and placed figurines of her at their hearth, lingers in the holy corner of the European home. Embroidered cloths are hung over a triangular shelf with religious momentoes or over a picture of Madonna and child. This hub of the home is by the stove or in the corner of the room by the family table.*

wall of the house, the *mizrach*, a picture that may be embroidered.

Gradually the five elements of the holy corner have largely been replaced in many homes by records of family rites of passage – photos of communion and marriage, diplomas, certificates of military service – and above all, by the television set. All are still draped with embroidered cloths like those hung on birch trees or in sacrificial groves. They are almost always long and narrow with embroidery at each end, usually in red cross stitch and with motifs derived from ancient cult, although north European motifs are those commonly worked on samplers: initials, dates, the tree of life and confronting birds. Similar cloths are also hung by the stove, where often the family's clothing is displayed, and in northern Europe more frequently on posts by the door, or by washbasins which, like wells, merit decoration because of the power of water. Everywhere painted plates are similarly draped, as are sources of light such as windows, candlesticks and mirrors.

LEFT *Cloth, Banske Bystrica, Slovakia. The icons and religious pictures of the ancient holy corner have in the modern world gradually been replaced by records of family rites of passage; wedding photos, certificates of military service and the television set. They are still draped with an embroidered cloth.*

MIRRORS

Mirrors are hung with embroidered cloths in countries from China to eastern Europe. The blue and white embroideries of the peasants of south-west China include hangings for mirrors; in Syria *mikhala*, small shield-like panels designed to hang over mirrors to avert the evil eye are embroidered in small zigzag patterns devised to dazzle, with the usual addition of tassels, blue beads, coins and sometimes patchwork; in eastern Europe mirrors are covered at death. In Tetouan, Morocco, a mirror hung opposite the marital bed is draped with an embroidered cloth for forty days after the wedding, bearing a design of a pyramid of pomegranates at each end.

ALTARS

Many homes have temporary altars: at Easter in Minho, Portugal, the priest would go round all the houses blessing them, and in each a small altar would be made of a table draped with a cloth embroidered in red cross stitch with Christian symbols and even declarations of fidelity to the king. The nomadic Banjara of India make an altar by placing a small embroidered cloth edged with cowries on a table or chest and laying on it five balls of dough, one in each corner and one in the centre. The *rumals* of Chamba, embroidered with mythological scenes, were hung behind a cult picture to form an altar.

THRESHOLDS

The threshold of house or tent is sacred, the place whose decoration safeguards the home and its inhabitants. In ancient Egypt a winged globe with snakes either side was placed above the lintel as a protection from evil; Friar William of Rubruck, travelling to Central Asia in 1253 commented on the hangings depicting vines, trees, birds and beasts over doorways, and Carpini, ambassador to the Mongol Great Khan in 1246, mentioned

LEFT *The threshold of a home is a sacred place. Those of Bengal are decorated with symbols in rice flour that are also embroidered on* kanthas.

ABOVE *The Calcutta pavement dweller hangs at the hub of 'home' an embroidered cloth.*

felt images of men on each side of tent doorways; O'Donovan cites the Scythian practice of sewing near doorways a square piece of linen making a pocket to receive the bounties of wandering spirits. Today in many countries sacred symbols – swastikas, fish, solar circles, crosses – are common above doors; the Bedouin tent has red rags tied at the entrance, the Mongolian *yurt* a criss-cross pattern of red fabric; in Bengal the threshold floor is decorated with the same symbols in rice flour (as thanksgiving for the safety of the house) that are embroidered on *kanthas*; in the streets of Luxembourg doors carved with the tree of life, sun discs, crosses and the arrows of Saint Sebastian are still to be seen.

Embroideries are commonly hung around doorways in a geographical swathe starting with those of China, through the *suzanis* of Central Asia to the appliquéd portières of Egypt. In Jewish homes the *mezuzah*, a parchment inscribed with a

prayer from Deuteronomy to be recited daily, is placed on the doorpost: in North Africa it hangs in an embroidered case.

In many countries, however, it is the spot right opposite the threshold that forms the living core of the house and it is here that embroideries are displayed. This is often where the family altar or the best bed, used only for marriage or occasionally guests, will be sited. This bed almost everywhere carries the finest embroideries of the household – covers, valances, pillows, curtains. Other embroideries might be hung on a beam opposite the threshold or perhaps the household's wealth in textiles might be piled here and covered with an embroidery, as the *dharkala* quilts of Gujarat. Even a Calcutta pavement dweller hangs an embroidery at the hub of 'home'.

On the Dodecanese islands it is on bedcurtains or on the doorways of bed-tents, rather than of the house, that embroidery is concentrated, with figurative motifs on the gable, particularly birds but also the goddess, stags, boats and two-headed eagles.

PRECIOUS OBJECTS

Precious objects afforded protection by embroidery range from babies and camels to guns and spoons. Each society has its own priorities.

In sixteenth- and seventeenth-century Turkey, for example, the turban, worn as a public declaration of adherence to Islam, was a symbolic garment placed on a carved wooden shelf when it was not being worn, where specially embroidered cloths, *kavur örtüsü*, covered it. These were of pale linen worked in double darning stitch with tulips and artichokes, palmettes, or *çintemani*. When the fez, a simple hat without symbolic meaning, replaced the turban, covers were no longer embroidered.

BELOW *Spoon bag, Baluch, Pakistan. For the nomadic Baluch, among their valuable possessions to be protected by embroidery are their spoons. Mirrors in metal surrounds, tassels and a tree of life, reminiscent of horn patterns and applied with cowries, will deter passing evil spirits.*

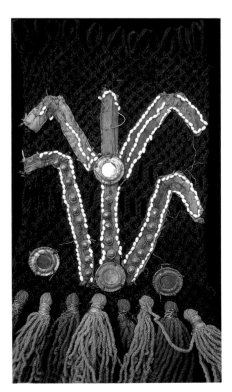

Once a turban was wound it was never undone and on the death of an important person it was placed on his tomb. The sultans' caftans were also wrapped in similar embroidered cloths called *bohça* when not worn, and on their death were stored in the treasury inside a number of such cloths.

The custom of wrapping precious articles or clothing in decorated cloths is of nomadic origin, but is practised in other societies. The *kanthas* of Bengal protect all manner of precious things, such as books, the Koran, musical instruments, money, betel nuts, mirrors, combs and toilet articles. Their making is a ritual activity: for Muslim women Friday is an auspicious day to begin, while for Hindus it is a Tuesday. Patterns vary with district and purpose but are conventionally a central lotus with a tree of life in each corner, with motifs of everyday household articles – rice huskers, betel cutters or earrings, which are a symbol of the married state – scattered over the rest of the cloth. The long narrow *kanthas* for the women's personal toiletries, known as *arshilata*, have floral or linear patterning, often with red edges and a red tassel at each corner.

ABOVE *Bullock's horn cover, Lammani caste, India. Animals were protected from harm by being branded with magical symbols and hung with amulets. For special occasions they were decorated with embroidered regalia increasing that protection and also displaying their owner's wealth. Cowries and mirror were favoured talismanic additions.*

Afghan women embroider covers for almost everything, especially guns, which enable their menfolk to show others the needlework skills of their bride. The Baluch embroider bags for their spoons; the Chinese, purses and cases for spectacles and fans to hang from a belt; and Jewish people, bags for the men's embroidered prayer shawls (*tallit*).

Almost every society embroiders bags for money in the form of purses or hanging pockets. These are worked in the different styles and techniques of each people but, unless subjected to commerce and fashion, always include protective motifs and materials.

Babies are, of course, among the most precious of all possessions and

ABOVE *Cloth, bostani, Bengal. Embroidered cloths,* kanthas, *wrapped and protected precious objects. Making them was a ritual activity and the motifs chosen were symbolic: the central lotus, a tree of life in each corner, solar whorls and a gateway. Small objects from the women's daily lives – earrings, mirror, comb, betel cutters – fill the spaces.*

everywhere cradles are decorated with amulets and talismanic embroidery, almost always with something red. In the territory of Daghestan on the Caspian Sea babies are still swaddled and covered with red. Children of south-west China are dressed in hats with animal faces to fool evil spirits, and wear night and day jerkins with highly decorated fronts, while in South-East Asia babies are toted around in richly embroidered carriers with tassels, pompoms and patterns of red.

Animals, too, are protected by amulets, by branding with symbols, and by embroidered regalia. Horses as animals of combat were protected physically by quilted covers, and in medieval Europe the decoration on their trappings and the rider's banner and shield served as identification at any passage of arms. The regalia of animals also displayed the owner's wealth and still sometimes in India and the Middle East on ceremonial occasions, particularly marriage, the domestic beasts of the family will be decked out in embroidered accoutrements: for bullocks horn covers, headdresses and hump cloths with rag birds; for camels, donkeys and horses' saddle covers, necklaces, kneebands and headcloths worked in the local style of embroidery or weaving. The Indian bridegroom traditionally arrived on a painted and caparisoned elephant and maharajahs rode in ceremonial processions swaying on howdahs strapped to elephants that shimmered with gold and silver embroidery, sequins, mirrors and rock crystal. The cars of today often betray the heritage of the past by the embroidered and sequined fish or triangle – or Saint Christopher – dangling from the rear view mirror.

ABOVE *Child's headband, south-western China. Children are the most precious of all objects to be protected by embroidery. In China boys, in particular, are dressed in hats embroidered with animal faces to fool evil spirits. To the horned bull are added other protective devices: bells, beads, tassels and pieces of red fabric.*

RIGHT *The Ch'ing Miao of southern China are among the many peoples who carry their babies in embroidered cloths. Many boys also wear hats that are hung with talismanic devices or that disguise the child as an animal so that evil spirits will leave him alone.*

TRANSITIONAL EMBROIDERY

The aesthetic beauty of embroidery made by the poorest of people stems from its inherent truth – truth of purpose, truth of material. Once this has gone – once the social context no longer exists and the beliefs and fears that embroidery promoted or deflected no longer torment, once linen is no longer painfully cultivated, spun and woven, sheep are no longer the mainstay of life and exotic silks from other lands a precious luxury – then traditional embroidery is doomed. It has become commercial: the tourist is an undiscerning purchaser, the trader accepts the crude and gaudy.

Slowly since the Industrial Revolution, gradually since the First World War and precipitately since the Second, technology, communications, changed values and lifestyles have disrupted all but a few pockets of human society. Even politics have played a role: the Communist rulers of Hungary with some pride replaced the old family marriage with mass weddings – 'splendid festivities at which the entire community happily participates, with the factory, plant and city workers who have given unselfish assistance throughout the year to the village in question being invited as guests'. It is hard to imagine the bride embroidering the traditional fine white handkerchief for them all. Nor, with the defeat of Communism and the return to Nationalism, are the old customs likely to be revived.

In embroidery the greatest motivation for change has been the education of girls: the Turkish girl can no longer only assure her future by embroidering exquisitely to gain a husband but is better equipped with perhaps a degree in civil engineering. Hope even glimmers for nomadic women such as the Baluch who lead a life of drudgery – erecting and dismantling tents, grinding corn, hauling water, cooking, raising children, weaving, embroidering and making carpets and felts, while their men tend the horses.

Attempts to revive traditional work by copying old patterns – by schools of embroidery, as in Istanbul and Salamanca, for example – are bound to fail when the social infrastructure has gone. The future lies with the individual embroideries of the West and possibly with those which have new-found social purpose such as the embroidered dresses of Palestinian women, worn throughout the Middle East as a political statement of affiliation to the Palestinian cause.

The ritual and social purpose of peasant and tribal embroidery, the symbolism of motifs that have lingered from the prehistoric era, are doomed to disappear within our lifetime. Clearly, it is already too late to be certain of the meaning and origin of many patterns and the purpose of much embellishment, but the juxtaposition of archaic embroideries from many parts of the world highlights a common theme: faith in the power of decoration to tame the gods and control the destiny of man.

OPPOSITE *Marriage headcloth, Patzún, Guatemala. Trees were linked to the magic power of crossroads and the cross is one aspect of the tree at the centre of the universe. Flanking birds and animals betray this Guatemalan motif as an import from another culture.*

GLOSSARY

acanthus Foliage design based on the Mediterranean plant *Acanthus spinosus*, widely used in European arts.

appliqué Needlework technique where pieces of fabric are sewn on to the ground material to make a design.

arabesque Stylized interlaced foliage pattern which reached European arts from the Middle East in the sixteenth century.

ashon A *kantha* for guests to sit on at weddings.

batik Technique of decorating textiles by the application of wax to retain undyed areas in the design.

betel Leaf of the *Piper betle* which Indians chew together with lime and the nut of the *Areca catechu*.

bey A Turkish governor.

boteh Curvilinear shape with curled top derived from Persian flower spray pattern and perfected during the Mughal period in India. Popularly associated with shawls.

bouclé A yarn or fabric of bulky loops.

brocading The addition during weaving of supplementary weft threads to give a raised pattern.

broderie anglaise White cotton eyelet embroidery which developed in England in the mid-nineteenth century.

caftan Long loose robe with full sleeves, worn especially in North Africa and the Middle East.

caliph Ruler of Muslim empire.

canvaswork Embroidery worked on evenweave canvas fabric by counting threads.

couching Technique where a thread is laid on fabric and attached by stitching with another thread, usually finer.

crêpe Crinkly fabric of tightly spun yarn.

damask Fabric with woven design that is reversible, generally shiny to matt.

drawn threadwork Openwork technique where threads are removed from the ground fabric.

etamine Fine loosely woven fabric, usually cotton.

eyelet Embroidery of holes strengthened by stitchery.

fichu Large wraparound collar, usually of delicate fabric.

filet Handmade net darned with like thread (*see also* lacis).

floss silk Very shiny untwisted raw silk.

fulling Process for shrinking woven cloth and thus thickening it.

gauze Very fine open fabric with twisted warp threads, usually silk.

godet Triangular piece of fabric inserted into a garment for fullness.

griffin An imaginary creature with the body of a lion and the head and talons of an eagle.

icon In Orthodox religion a sacred painting or mosaic representing Christ or a saint.

ikat Technique in which the warp threads, and occasionally both warp and weft, are dyed with the design of the fabric before weaving commences.

kantha Traditional quilted cloth of Bengal.

kit Embroidery with the design already prepared, supplied with instructions and the requisite threads.

lacis Handmade net darned with like thread (*see also* filet).

lappet Long piece of fabric hanging from the side of a cap.

menorah Seven-branched candlestick of the Jewish liturgy associated, when stylized, with the tree of life.

mihrab Arched niche in a mosque marking the direction of Mecca.

needlepoint In England lace made with a needle, in America canvaswork.

paisley *Boteh* pattern commonly used on European shawls of the nineteenth century, many of which were made in Paisley, imitating Kashmiri shawls.

palmette Stylized palm leaf of classical decoration.

pattern books Books of designs for artisans, published from the early sixteenth century, mainly in Germany and Italy.

portière Curtain hung around or over a doorway.

pulledwork Openwork technique in which threads of the ground fabric are teased apart rather than withdrawn.

purdah Indian system of screening women from public gaze.

purl Coiled hollow gold wire for embroidery.

rath A wheeled carriage transporting the idol of Vishnu.

resist dye Technique where a dye-resistant paste is used to retain undyed areas in the design.

runic Ancient Germanic alphabet.

saz Ottoman design of round stemless blossom encircled by curling leaf, named from 'reed pen' drawing.

stele Standing stone, usually carved.

stencil dye Technique where stencils are used to retain undyed areas in the design.

stupa A Buddhist dome-shaped memorial shrine.

tambouring Chain stitch worked with a hook instead of a needle.

tie-dye Technique of tying small bunches in fabric before dyeing so that these areas remain undyed.

wazir Muslim minister of state.

DICTIONARY OF STITCHES

Embroidery stitches are based on two principles. The first is their suitability to working freely drawn designs and the second is the use of a background fabric where the threads can be counted.

Some stitches are commonly found almost throughout the world. Examples of these in the first category are stem and chain and in the second cross and herringbone. Others are used particularly in goldwork, such as couching and bullion, while still others are important in drawn and pulled threadwork, such as eyelet and satin.

In some places, one particular stitch dominates, such as Holbein in Fez and couching in Bukhara, or is unique to one place, such as Slav knot in Moravia, *kesdi* in Turkmenistan and radiating in Sind.

Occasionally, a geographical link will mean an unusual stitch is found in very diverse places. An example is the *chenuk* interlacing of the Baluch people, which was the *marash* of Armenia, introduced there by traders.

blanket

chain

chenuk 4

diagonal tent

brick

chenuk (*marash*) 1

couching

double running

bullion knot

chenuk 2

cross

eyelet

buttonhole edging

chenuk 3

darning

eyelet hole/broderie anglaise

faggot filling/single faggot

horizontal tent

mirrorwork

satin

fishbone

interlacing

open/square chain

Slav knot

fly

kesdi (double chain)

pattern darning

split

French knot

long and short

Pekin knot

stem

herringbone

long-armed cross

radiating

tambour

Holbein (stepped running)

loop

FURTHER READING

ASIA

Mis, Zaira, and Marcel Mis, *Asian Costumes and Textiles*, Milan, 2001
Young Yang Chung, *Silken Threads: A History of Embroidery in China, Korea, Japan and Vietnam*, New York, 2005

China

Baker, Muriel, and Margaret Lunt, *Blue and White: The Cotton Embroideries of Rural China*, London, 1978
Corrigan, Gina, *Miao Textiles from China*, London, 2001
Costume and Accessories of Chinese Minorities, National Museum of History, Taipei, 2000
Garrett, Valery M., *Traditional Chinese Clothing*, Oxford, 1987
Hua Mei, *Chinese Clothing*, Shanghai, 2004
Vollmer, John E., *In the Presence of the Dragon Throne*, Canada, 1977
Wang Yarong, *Chinese Folk Embroidery*, London, 1987
Wilson, Verity, *Chinese Dress*, London, 1986
——, *Chinese Textiles*, London, 2005

Korea

Classical Korean Embroideries, exh. cat., V&A, London, 1984
Traditional Korean Wrapping Cloths, exh. cat., Fitzwilliam, Cambridge/Ashmolean, Oxford, 1990

Japan

Allen, Jeanne, *The Designer's Guide to Japanese Patterns*, London, 1988
Buisson, S. and D., *Kimono*, Lausanne, 1983
Gray, Julia D., *Beginners' Guide to Traditional Japanese Embroidery*, London, 2001
Ita Motoko and Inove Aiko, *Kimono*, Osaka, 1982
Jackson, Anna, *Japanese Country Textiles*, London, 1997
——, *Japanese Textiles*, London, 2000
Kiyoko Ogikubo, *Kogin and Sashiko Stitch*, Kyoto, 1993
Kyoto Shoin's Art Library of Japanese Textiles, *Japanese Embroidery*, 1993
Moes, Robert, *Mingei: Japanese Folk Art*, New York, 1985
Rathbun, William Jay, ed., *Traditional Japanese Embroidery*, London, 1993
Shuji Tamara, *The Techniques of Japanese Embroidery*, London, 1998

Indo-China

Cultural Palace of Nationalities, *Clothing and Ornaments of China's Miao People*, Beijing, 1985
Innes, R. A., *Costumes of Upper Burma and the Shan States*, Bankfield Museum, Halifax, 1957
Lewis, Paul, and Elaine Lewis, *Peoples of the Golden Triangle*, London, 1984
Musée des Tissus, *Costumes Traditionnels de la Chine du Sud-Ouest*, Lyon, 2002

Prangwatthanakun, Songsak, and Patricia Naenna, *Lan Na Textiles*, Chiang Mai, 1987

Oceania

Haddon, A. C., and L. E. Start, *Iban or Sea Dayak Fabrics and their Patterns*, reprint Cambridge, 1982
Hitchcock, Michael, *Indonesian Textile Techniques*, Shire Ethnography, Bucks, 1985

The Indian Subcontinent

Askari, Nasreen, and Rosemary Crill, *Colours of the Indus*, London, 1997
Bhattacharyya, A. K., *Chamba Rumal*, Calcutta, 1968
Crill, Rosemary, *Indian Embroidery*, London, 1999
Elson, Vickie, *Dowries from Kutch*, Los Angeles, 1979
Gillow, John, *Traditional Indian Textiles*, London, 1991
Jacobs, Julian, *The Nagas*, London, 1990
Kalter, Johannes, *The Arts and Crafts of the Swat Valley*, London and New York, 1991
Kumar, Ritu, *Costumes and Textiles of Royal India*, London, 1999
Morrell, Anne, *The Techniques of Indian Embroidery*, Colorado, 1995
Paine, Sheila, *Chikan Embroidery*, Shire Ethnography, Bucks, 1989
——, *Embroidery from India and Pakistan*, London, 2001
Whitechapel Art Gallery, *Woven Air*, London, 1988
Zaman, Niaz, *The Art of Kantha Embroidery*, Dhaka, 1993

Central Asia

Dupaigne, Bernard, transl. Sheila Paine, *Afghan Embroidery*, Lahore, 1993
Fitzgibbon, Kate, and Andy Hale, *Ikats: The Rau Collection*, Oxford, 1988
——, *Ikat: The Guido Goldman Collection*, London, 1997
Harvey, Janet, *Traditional Textiles of Central Asia*, London, 1996
Kalter, Johannes, *The Arts and Crafts of Turkestan*, London, 1984
Kalter, Johannes, and Margareta Pavaloi, *Uzbekistan*, London, 1997
Medjitova, Elmira, *Turkmen Folk Arts*, Ashkabad, 1990
Paine, Sheila, *Embroidery from Afghanistan*, London, 2006
Rudenko, Sergei I., *Frozen Tombs of Siberia*, London, 1970
Wutt, Karl, *Pashai*, Graz, 1981

THE MIDDLE EAST

Baker, Patricia, *Islamic Textiles*, London, 1995
Black, David, *Embroidered Flowers from Thrace to Tartary*, London, 1981

Kawar, Widad, *Costumes Dyed by the Sun*, Tokyo, 1982
Scarce, Jennifer, *Domestic Culture in the Middle East*, Edinburgh, 1996

Gulf States

Topham, John, *Traditional Crafts of Saudi Arabia*, London, 1981
US Committee for Saudi Arabian Cultural Heritage, *Palms and Pomegranates: Traditional Dress of Saudi Arabia*, exh. cat., Washington, 1987

Palestine

El Jisr, Bassem, *Mémoire de Soie, Costumes et Parures de Palestine et de Jordanie, coll. Widad Kamel Kawar*, Paris, 1988
Rajab, Jehan S., *Palestinian Costume*, London, 1989
Weir, Shelagh, *Palestinian Embroidery*, London, 1970
——, *Palestinian Costume*, London, 1989
Weir, Shelagh, and Serene Shahid, *Palestinian Embroidery*, London, 1988

Syria

Kalter, Johannes, *The Arts and Crafts of Syria*, London, 1992

Turkey

Black, David, and Clive Loveless, *Islemeler: Ottoman Domestic Embroideries*, London, 1978
Ellis, Marianne, and Jennifer Wearden, *Ottoman Embroidery*, London, 2001
Johnstone, Pauline, *Turkish Embroidery*, London, 1985
Taylor, Roderick, *Ottoman Embroidery*, New York, 1993

AFRICA

Adler, P., and N. Barnard, *African Majesty*, London, 1992
——, *Asafo!*, London, 1992
Gardi, Bernhard, *Le Boubou – c'est chic*, Museum der Kulturen Basel, 2000
Gillow, John, *African Textiles*, London, 2003
Menzel, Brigitte, *Textilien aus Westafrika*, Berlin, 1972
Meurant, G., *Abstractions aux Royaumes des Kuba*, Paris, 1987
Picton, John, and John Mack, *African Textiles*, London, 1979

North Africa

Denamur, Isabelle, *Moroccan Textile Embroidery*, Paris, 2003
El-Habib, Béatrice Riottot, and Marie-France Vivier, *Algérie: Mémoire de Femmes au fil des doigts*, Paris, 2003
Jereb, James F., *Arts and Crafts of Morocco*, London, 1995
Lemaistre, Joëlle, and Marie-France Vivier, *De Soie et d'Or*, exh. cat., IMA, Paris, 1996

Musée des Arts d'Afrique et d'Océanie, *Noces tissées, noces brodées*, Paris, 1995
Spring, Christopher, and Julie Hudson, *North African Textiles*, London, 1995
Stone, Caroline, *The Embroideries of North Africa*, Harlow, 1985
Tazi, Tamy, and Lucien Viola, *Points et Entrelacs: broderies et tissages du Maroc*, exh. cat., Marrakech, 1999
Vivier, Marie-France, *Broderies marocaines*, Paris, 1991

EUROPE

SOUTHEAST EUROPE

Mainland Greece

Hatzimichali, Angeliki, *The Greek Folk Costume*, Athens, 1979
Papantoniou, Ioanna, ed., *Greek Women's Dress and Jewellery Past and Present*, Nafplion, 1985
Welters, Linda, *Women's Traditional Costume in Attica*, Greece, Nafplion, 1988
Zora, Popi, *Embroideries and Jewellery of Greek National Costumes*, Athens, 1981

The Greek Islands

Benaki Museum, *Epirus and Ionian Islands Embroideries*, Athens, 1965
——, *Skyros Embroideries*, Athens, 1965
——, *Crete, Dodecanese, Cyclades*, Athens, 1966
——, *Greek Embroideries*, Athens, 1980
Johnstone, Pauline, *Greek Island Embroidery*, London, 1961
Kelly, Mary B., *Embroidering the Goddess of the Greek Islands*, Denver, 1977
MacMillan, Susan L., *Greek Island Embroideries*, Boston, n.d.
Taylor, Roderick, *Embroideries of the Greek Islands*, London, 1998

The Balkans

Gervers, Veronika, *The Influence of Ottoman Turkish Textiles and Costume in Eastern Europe*, Toronto, 1982
Horniman Museum, *Folk Art of Montenegro*, exh. cat., London, 1983
Kasparian, Alice Odian, *Armenian Needlelace and Embroidery*, Virginia, 1983
Papantoniou, Ioanna, *Macedonian Costumes*, Nafplion, 1992
Welters, Linda, ed., *Folk Dress in Europe and Anatolia*, Oxford, 1999
Zdunic, Drago, *Costumi Poplari della Croazia*, Zagreb, 1975

Albania

Gjergji, Andromaqi, *Albanian Folk Costumes*, Tirana, 1999
Start, Laura E., *The Durham Collection*, Halifax, 1977

EASTERN EUROPE

Bulgaria

Koev, Ivan, *Embroidery Motifs*, Sofia, 1982

Komitska, Anita, and Veska Borissova, *Bulgarian Folk Costumes*, Sofia, 2005

Kwasnik, Elizabeth, ed., *British and Bulgarian Ethnography*, Liverpool, 1989

——, *Tradition and Beauty*, Liverpool, 1989

Pountev, Penko, *Bulgarian Folk Embroidery Designs*, Sofia, 1980

Valeva, Maria, and S. Dancheva, *Bulgarian Folk Dresses and Jewellery*, Sofia, 1983

Romania

Batca, Maria, *The Romanian National Costume*, Bucharest, 1996

Graur, Tiberiu, and Maria Bosce, *Cojoace Sasesti* (Saxon leather costume), Cluj-Napoca, 1998

Netcu, Maria, *Wedding Ornaments and Head Adornment*, Bucharest and New York, 1998

Petruscu, Paul, et al., *Arta Populara din Mehedinti* (Romanian folk art), Bucharest, 1983

Pop-Câmpeanu, Denise, *Se Vêtir*, Freiburg, 1984

Secosan, Elena, and Paul Petrescu, *Portul Popular de Sarbatoare din Romania* (Romanian costume), Bucharest, 1984

Ukraine

The Changeless Carpathians (various authors), New York, 1995

Grabowicz, Oksana, and Maria Shust, *Traditional Designs in Ukrainian Textiles*, exh. cat., New York, 1977

Grabowicz, Oksana, and L. Wolynetz, *Rushnyky: Ukrainian Ritual Cloths*, New York, 1981

History of Ukrainian Costume (various authors), Melbourne, 1986

Kara-Vasyleva, Tatyana, *Ukrainska Vishivka* (Ukrainian embroidery), Kiev, 1993

——, *Ukrainska Sorochka* (Ukrainian blouses), Kiev, 1994

Kmit, Ann, *Ukrainian Embroidery*, New York, 1978

Nukolaeva, T. A., *Ukrainskaya Narodnaya Odeshda* (Ukrainian folk costume), Kiev, 1987

Wolynetz, Lubow (curator), *Ukrainian Folk Art*, exh. cat., New York, 1984

Russia

Chuvash Arts Museum, *Chuvash Folk Embroidery*, Cheboksary, 1991

Kalashnikova, N., *National Costumes of the Soviet Peoples*, Moscow, 1990

Maiassova, N., *Russian Ecclesiastical Embroidery*, Moscow, 1989

Molotova, N. H., *Folk Art of the Russian Federation*, Leningrad, 1981

Nikolaev, V. V., G. N. Ivanov-Orkov, and V. P. Ivanov, *The Chuvash Costume: From Ancient to Modern Times*, Cheboksary, 2002

Peterburgsky, I. M., et al, *Crafts of Mordovia*, Saransk, 1985

Yefimova, L., and R. Berlogorskaya, *Russian Embroidery and Lace*, New York, 1987

Caucasus

Chenincer, Robert, *Kaitag: Textile Art from Daghestan*, London, 1993

Kasparian, Alice Odian, *Armenian Needlelace and Embroidery*, Virginia, 1983

Tashjian, Nouvart, *Armenian Lace*, Berkeley, Calif. n. d.

THE BALTIC STATES
Poland

Bazielich, Barbara, *Stroj Ludowy w Polsce* (Folk costumes in Poland), Warsaw, c. 1998

Majka, Christopher, and Sheilagh Hunt, *Polish Folk Costumes*, Halifax, Canada, 1991

Piskorz-Branekova, Elzbieta, *Polskie Stroje Ludowe* (Polish folk costumes), Warsaw, 2003

Rostworowska, Magdalena, *Slaski Stroj Ludowy* (Silesian folk costumes), Wroclaw, 2001

Turska, Jadwiga, *Polish Folk Embroidery*, New York, 1997

Lithuania

Tamosaitis, Anatas and Anastasia, *Lithuanian National Costume*, Toronto, 1979

Latvia

Rozenberga, Velta, *Latvian National Costumes*, Riga, 1995

SCANDINAVIA

Berg, Inga Arnö, and Gunnel Hazelius Berg, *Folk Costumes of Sweden*, Västeras, 1975

Fossnes, Heidi, *Les Costumes Régionaux de Norvège*, Oslo, 1995

Grenander Nyberg, Gertrud, *Lanthemmens Prydnadssöm*, Stockholm, 1983

Gudjónsson, Elsa E., *Traditional Icelandic Embroidery*, Reykjavik, 1982

Lehtinen, Ildikó, *The Finno-Ugric Collections at the National Museum of Finland*, Helsinki, 1990

——, *Pirkko Sihvo: Rahwaan Puku* (Folk costume), Helsinki, 2005

Vilppula, Hilkka, and Toini-Inkeri Kaukonen, *Folk Costumes and Textiles at the National Museum of Finland*, Helsinki, 1982

CENTRAL EUROPE
Hungary

Csiba, Eva, *Bormuvesseg* (Leatherwork), Budapest, 1975

Fél, Edit, *Peasant Embroidery*, Budapest, 1976

Hofer, Tamás, and Edit Fél, *Hungarian Folk Art*, Oxford, 1979

Kresz, Maria, *The Art of the Hungarian Furriers*, Budapest, 1979

——, *Virag es nepmuveszet* (Embroidery patterns), Budapest, n.d.

Musée de l'Homme, *Fiers Magyars*, Paris, 2001

Nepviseletek, I., *A Szür* (Embroidered woollen coats), Budapest, 1977

Undi, Maria, *Hungarian Fancy Needlework and Weaving*, Budapest, n.d.

Whitworth Art Gallery, *Historic Hungarian Costume from Budapest*, exh. cat., Manchester, 1979

Slovakia

Abelova, Viera, *L'Udovy Odev* (Embroidered costume), Trencin, 1986

Brassington, Linda, *Indigo Country Cloths and Artifacts from Czechoslovakia*, Farnham, 1987

Chlupova, Anna, *Slovenska l'Udova Vysivka* (Slovak embroidery), Bratislava, 1985

Markov, Jozef, *The Slovak National Dress through the Centuries*, Prague, 1956

Nixdorff, Heide, *Europäische Volkstrachten: Tschechoslowakei*, Berlin, 1977

Nosalova, Viera, *Nase Kroje* (Regional costume and patterns), Bratislava, 1988

Czech Republic

Ludvikova, Miroslava, *Moravska lidova vysivka* (Moravian embroidery), Brno, 1986

WESTERN EUROPE
Germany and Alpine Lands

Pettigrew, D. W., *Peasant Costume of the Black Forest*, London, 1937

Rapp, Anna, *Neue Sammlung von Schweizertrachten aus der XII Cantonen*, Zurich, 1980

Schneider, Jenny, *Schweizerische Leinenstickerei*, Bern, 1972

Schürch, Lotti, and Louise Witzig, *Trachten der Schweiz*, Bern, 1978

Tracht in Österreich, Vienna, 1984

The Netherlands

Cammel, Hilde, *Op maat gesneden*, Zuiderzee Museum, Enkhuizen, 2005

Nieuwhoff, Constance, *Onze Kleder-Drachten*, Wageningen, 1975

——, *Klederdrachten*, Amsterdam, 1976

France

Creston, René-Yves, *Le Costume Breton*, Paris, 1993

L'Elégance et la Nécéssité: Costumes de Lorraine (various authors), Metz, 2001

Tricaud, Anne, *La Constitution des collections de Costumes du Musée National des Arts et Traditions Populaires*, Paris, 1994

Spain

González, Mena Angeles, *Catálogo de Bordados*, Madrid, 1974

Portugal

Museu de Arte Antiga, Lisbon, *Embroidered Quilts*, London, 1978

Museu de Etnologia, *Traje Popular*, Lisbon, 1977

Pereira, Benjamim, *Têxteis: Tecnologia e simbolismo*, Lisbon, 1985

Ribeiro, Cardoso, *O Bordado*, Castelo Branco, 1980

Taxhina, Maria José, and Natalia Correia Guedes, *O Bordado no Trajo Civil em Portugal*, Lisbon, 1975

AMERICA
NORTH AMERICA

Dubin, Lois Sherr, *North American Indian Jewelry and Adornment*, New York, 1999

Horse Capture, Joseph D., and George P. Horse Capture, *Beauty, Honor and Tradition: The Legacy of Plains Indian Shirts*, Minneapolis, 2001

Turner, Geoffrey, *Hair Embroidery in Siberia and North America*, Oxford, 1976

CENTRAL AMERICA
Mexico

Sayer, Chloë, *Mexican Costume*, London, 1985

——, *Arts and Crafts of Mexico*, London, 1990

——, *Textiles from Mexico*, London, 2002

Guatemala

Deuss, Krystyna, *Indian Costumes from Guatemala*, Manchester, 1981

Hecht, Ann, *Textiles from Guatemala*, British Museum Press, London, 2001

Panama

Kapp, Capt. Kit S., *Mola Art*, Ohio, 1972

Puls, Herta, *Textiles of the Kuna Indians of Panama*, Shire Ethnography, Bucks, 1988

Salvador, Mari Lyn, ed., *The Art of Being Kuna*, Los Angeles, 1997

SOUTH AMERICA

Sawyer, Alan R., *Early Nasca Needlework*, London, 1997

Wasserman, Tamara E., and Jonathan S. Hill, *Bolivian Indian Textiles*, New York, 1981.

COLLECTIONS AND COLLECTING

COLLECTIONS

Collections of peasant and tribal embroidery are mainly to be found in ethnology, folk and local museums rather than in major museums of textile history or of decorative arts. A handful of individual museums are world-famous for their collections, which include such material. They are:

Victoria & Albert Museum, London
Royal Scottish Museum, Edinburgh
Royal Ontario Museum, Toronto

Ethnology and archaeology museums
holding international collections of which embroideries are a part (particular specialities are bracketed):
Musée du Quai Branly, Paris
Museum für Völkerkunde, Vienna
Völkerkundemuseum der Universität Zürich
Museum für Völkerkunde, Berlin
Rautenstrauch-Joest Museum für Völkerkunde, Cologne
British Museum, London
Pitt-Rivers Museum, Oxford (hair embroidery, Naga)
Cambridge University Museum of Archaeology and Anthropology, Cambridge, England (Paracas)
Smithsonian National Museum of Natural History, Washington
Peabody Museum of Archaeology and Ethnology, Cambridge, Mass.
Field Museum of Natural History, Chicago (Chinese peasant)
Museum of Natural History, Newark (Tibetan)
Museum of New Mexico, Santa Fe (Palestinian)
Horniman Museum, London

Ethnology museums *holding national, regional or ethnic collections:*
National Museum of the American Indian, New York
Museu Nacional de Etnologia, Lisbon
Ethnology Museum, Moscow
Ethnology Museum, St Petersburg
Ethnology Museum, Martin (Slovakian)
Ethnology Museum, Brno (Moravian)
Ethnology Museum, Ljubljana (Slovenian)
Ethnology Museum, Zagreb (Croatian)

National museums *holding significant embroidery collections:*
Benaki Museum, Athens
Finnish National Museum, Helsinki
Hungarian National Museum, Budapest
Bulgarian National Museum of History, Sofia
Yugoslav National Museum, Belgrade
Topkapi Museum, Istanbul
Israel Museum, Jerusalem
Yemen National Museum, Sana'a

Folk museums, *most holding the major collections for the countries concerned:*
Museum für Deutsche Volkskunde, Berlin
Altonaer Museum, Hamburg
Arnhem Open Air Museum, Arnhem
Danish Folk Museum, Copenhagen
Nordic Museum, Stockholm
Norwegian Folk Museum, Oslo
Schweizerisches Landesmuseum, Zürich
Musée des Civilisations de l'Europe et de la Méditerranée, Marseilles
Museum of Greek Folk Art, Athens
Jordan Museum of Popular Traditions, Amman
Azem Palace Museum, Damascus

Art museums *whose collections include some peasant embroidery:*
Hermitage Museum, St Petersburg (Pazyryk and Russian material)
Metropolitan Museum, New York
Brooklyn Museum, New York (Russian)
Museum of Fine Arts, Boston (Greek Island and Oriental)
Cleveland Museum of Art
Indianapolis Museum of Art (Balkan and Moroccan)
Detroit Institute of Arts (Czech)
Museu Nacional de Arte Antiga, Lisbon (Indo-Portuguese)
Fitzwilliam Museum, Cambridge, England (Middle Eastern)
Whitworth Art Gallery, Manchester (Mediterranean, Eastern European)
Ashmolean Museum, Oxford (Oriental)
Museum of History and Art, Zagorsk (Russian)
Fowler Museum at UCLA, Los Angeles (Native American)
Instituto Valencia de Don Juan, Madrid (Spanish)

Museums of historical embroidery *with some peasant work:*
Museo Pedagógico Textil, Madrid
Museu Tèxtil i d'Indumentària, Barcelona
Calico Museum of Textiles, Ahmedabad

All major museums have more embroideries in reserve than on display and require appointments to show these. For the casual visitor local museums can be very rewarding as their collections are often easier to see. Particularly good are those in eastern Europe, such as the regional ones of the former Yugoslavia as at Zadar, Sarajevo and Skopje, or those of Portugal, Tunisia and Morocco, where that of Tétouan is of special interest. In Turkey the ethnology museums of Bursa, Kayseri and Konya have embroideries, as does the Sadberk Hanim Museum of Büyükdere, which is a delight. In India the Calico Museum and the Sheyras Folk Museum, both of Ahmedabad, feature costume.

Most local museums cover local costumes but some will have a specialist embroidery collection, as do the Leicestershire Museum (Indian) and the Angoulême Museum in France (Moroccan). Often this will have been donated by a collector, as with part of the Wace collection of Mediterranean and Near Eastern at the Merseyside museums of Liverpool, and the collection of Albanian and Yugoslavian embroideries at the Bankfield, Halifax, donated by the redoubtable Miss Durham, who first went out to Montenegro in 1900 and returned continuously to the Balkans until the First World War, giving medical assistance, collecting embroideries and, it is reported, separating squabbling Albanians with her umbrella.

COLLECTING

The collector has first to realize that embroideries that were an inherent part of social custom and served to identify the wearer were not originally made for sale. They thus appear on the market in a haphazard way. An exception is Chinese embroidery, for which there is a steady and consistent market.

Choice of collection should not be too specialized, as it will prove difficult to achieve a worthwhile grouping. It is best based on a region – say, eastern Europe or the Middle East – rather than being confined to perhaps Hungary or Syria. The basis of a collection could also be a particular technique such as tambouring or smocking, or stitch such as cross.

First a visit to relevant museums is essential so that the collector is aware of the quality and range that should be taken as guidelines. Most museums have far more in reserve than on display, and because of conservation problems appointments to view are not always easy to obtain.

The period at which costume was discarded affects its availability. Items abandoned soon after the First World War are more difficult to find than articles which have only recently been given up in favour of Western dress and may still be kept in cupboards and chests. Often there is great reluctance to sell something that has been in the family for generations and the collector should never bring pressure to bear. There is a growing awareness that historical embroideries belong to a vanishing heritage, and they have therefore become more precious to the society that created them. For this reason they are often more expensive in the country of their origin.

Because of the fickleness of the market it is possible to find embroideries in the most bizarre of places – car boot sales, for instance, or flea markets – but for sustained collecting, textile auctions are the best source, though the major auction houses no longer handle small items. Regular attendance also gives some idea of prices, though these can vary enormously for rather arbitrary reasons.

There are a few specialist dealers, some of whom own premises while others work directly with customers or by staging exhibitions. Some galleries and shops specialize in 'ethnic' articles and these will include embroideries. The textile world is close-knit and once a collection is embarked on, a snowball effect is soon discovered, with other collectors and dealers proving to be friendly and helpful.

Conservation of embroideries is of immense importance. If they are to be hung on walls the windows should be treated with protective film against ultraviolet light. Silk is particularly vulnerable to light and most colours fade. Items should not be folded as the fibres will eventually break at the fold, silk again being especially weak in this respect. Instead they should be rolled and protected by acid-free tissue. Cardboard rolls from packets of aluminium foil, or gleaned from fabric shops, are a useful base. Ideally, dresses should be laid flat rather than hung. Wool, of course, is susceptible to moths and creepy-crawlies, for whom also starch is a good meal. Woollen embroideries should therefore be aired frequently and cotton ones should not be left starched. No steps should ever be taken that are irreversible. Washing especially should hardly ever be attempted by the amateur.

The purpose of a collection may vary. It can be for the satisfaction of rescuing neglected embroideries, for the pleasure of enhancing one's home, as a source of inspiration for one's own embroidery or other craft where ideas of colour and design can be appropriated, or as a tool for teaching others. There is little point in amassing articles simply to keep them hidden away in cupboards and drawers, and their ultimate destination should always be borne in mind when buying.

SOURCES OF ILLUSTRATIONS

The following abbreviations have been used: *a*, above; *b*, below; *c*, centre; *i*, inset; *l*, left; *m*, main picture; *r*, right; *t*, top.

Photographs
2, 5, 8*l*, 10*ar*, 10–11, 11*al*, 12*l*, 13*l*, 13*r*, 24*l*, 27, 44*b*, 46*c*, 55*ar*, 56*bl*, 58*l*, 97*l*, 133*r*, 136*r*, 137, 138*br*, 139*b*, 141, 143*al*, 151*b*, 157*l*, 157*r*, 162*b*, 168, 169*m*, 171, 173*r*, 177*b*, 178, 179, 182, 186, 193, 195, 197*a*, 197*b*, 201*l*, 203, 205, 206*l*, 206*r*, 207, 208–9, 209, 210, 211, 212, 213*l*, 214, 215*a*, 215*b*, 218*l*, 218*r*, 221*r*, 225*r*, 227*a* by Dudley Moss. The remaining photographs are by the author or from the author's collection, with the exception of the following, which are reproduced by courtesy of: Meg Andrews, Hertfordshire, 19*b*; Anthropological Archives, National Museum of Natural History, Smithsonian Institution, Washington, D.C., 119*tr*; Archives of the Museum of Ethnography, Basle, 227*b* (photo Carl Schuster, 1935); Art Institute of Chicago, 126–27 (1956.408); Museu Nacional de Arte Antiga, Lisbon, 143*r* (3465); Benaki Museum, Athens, 70*br* (6389), 129*m* (6262); Krystyna Deuss, London, 229; Willem Diepraam, 108*l*; Garuda Airlines, Indonesia, 12*l*; Joss Graham, London, 34*l*, 166*c*; Martin Hürlimann, 107*br*; Leicester Museums Service, 167*r* (C.260.1983); Matson Collection, Library of Congress, 51*a*; National Board of Antiquities, Helsinki, Finland, 142*m*, 194; Sue Ormerod, London, 6–7 *background*; Margaret Pratt, Berkshire, 221*l*; Private collection, Cičmany, Slovakia, 190*r* (c. 1950); Erich Rinka, 79*ar*; Sarakatsani Folklore Museum, 69*l*; Slovak National Ethnographic Museum, Martin, Slovakia, 99*tl* (XIV 11135), 152 (135060, photo Cičmany, c. 1906), 189 (17930), 217*a* (46255), 219*l* (XIV-3107, photo Velke Krtiš), 222*l* (14895); Peter Stradling, Devon, 162*a*; John Topham, 45*m*; Troyes Musée de Vauluisant, 106*l* (oil painting by Henri Valton, *Un colporteur vendant des châles*, 1837: photo Musées de Troyes); Museum für Völkerkunde, Basle, 220 (8754); Nick Waterhouse, Longevity, London, 91; Whitechapel Art Gallery, London, 175*a*, 226; Karl Wutt, 42*br*.

Embroideries kindly lent by:
Institut National d'Archéologie et d'Art, Tunis, 62 (67.4.6), 131*bl* (66.31.2), 202 (72.6.4); Museo de Artes Decorativas, Madrid, 184*r* (2012); Musée des Arts Africains et Océaniens, Paris, 64 (1967.10.1), 161*r* (66.29.4); Azem Palace Museum, Damascus, 53*t*, 134; Jenny Balfour-Paul, Devon, 50; Bardo Museum, Tunis, 136*t*; Joyce Doel, Hertfordshire, 5, 70*l*, 161*l*; Diana Dolman, Essex, 2; Embroiderers Guild, 97*l* (M913), 113*b*, 136*br* (3560), 151*b* (M56), 162*b*, 183, 186 (1142); Ethnographic Museum, Brno, Moravia, 217*b* (18393); Joss Graham, London 6–7 *background*, 27, 34*l*, 166*r*, 169*m*, 178, 221*r*, 227*a*; Industrie und Gewerbemuseum, St Gallen, Switzerland, 184*l* (J2921); Widad Kawar, Jordan, 187; Museum of Mankind, London, 56*tr* (1979Af.22), 56*bl* (1934.3–7.218), 57*al* (1966Af.1.16), 118*l* (1921 10.14.99), 158*a* (GA222), 159*bl* (1937.6.171), 197*a* (1934.3–7.199), 206*l* (1868 10–1.23), 213*l* (Q82Am298), 214 (2799); Sylvie Pataut, Paris, 24*tr*; Phillips, Auctioneers, London, 174; Pitt Rivers Museum, Oxford, 158*b*, 211 (16.10.1933), 212 (1923.85–294), 213*r* (38.8.1); Private collection, Paris, 86*b*, 131*br*, 138*t*, 139*a*, 140*t*, 144*b*; Private collection, Yorkshire, 145*a*, 173*l*; Fawzia Radman, Sana'a, Yemen, 199*b*; Gordon Reece, Knaresborough, Yorkshire, 29*al*, 68*bl*, 98*ar*, 99*b*, 147*l*, 155*a*, 165, 225*l*; Dorothy Reglar, Gloucestershire, 117*r*; K. Rudersdorf, Stuttgart, Germany, 190*l*; Slovacka Museum, Uherské Hradisté, Moravia, 154*b*; Slovak National Ethnographic Museum, Martin, Slovakia, 100 (1577), 146*l* (34603); Stella Swift, Paris, 124–5, 135*a*; Angela Thompson, Worcester, 128; Trenčín Museum, Slovakia, 101*bl* (5854); Instituto Valencia de Don Juan, Madrid, 181*a*; Museum für Völkerkunde, Berlin, 101*br* (7036). Other embroideries are in the author's collection.

Sources of **line drawings** are indicated by author's name alone, unless the book does not appear in the bibliography, in which case the title, place and date of publication are also quoted.

p. 8 Kuba women's tattoo marks, Democratic Republic of the Congo, from Georges Meurant, *Abstractions aux Royaumes des Kuba*, Paris 1987.

p. 9 Raffia cloth with cut-pile embroidery, Kuba, Democratic Republic of the Congo, from Gordon Reece.

—— Mummified man, Pazyryk, Hermitage Museum, St Petersburg. Rudenko.

—— Woman's blouse, Bukovina, Romania. Institutul Român de Cercetari, Freiburg-im-Breslau, Germany.

p. 10 Detail of Ainu coat, Japan. L.A. County Museum of Art M.71.87.1.

—— Detail of Chilkat ceremonial tunic, Museum of the American Indian, New York 19/7902.

p. 11 Textile, Pazyryk, Hermitage Museum, St Petersburg. Rudenko.

p. 19 Dragon robe, China, author's collection.

p. 23 Kimono, Japan, author's collection.

p. 28 Boy's helmet, Kanebi caste, Kutch, author's collection.

—— Woman's skirt, Mochi caste, Kutch, India, Joss Graham.

p. 32 Marriage dress, Thano Bula Khan, Sind, Pakistan, author's collection.

—— Woman's dress, Baluch, Sind, Pakistan, author's collection.

p. 33 Marriage dress, Kohistan, author's collection.

p. 51 Woman's dress, Hebron, Palestine, author's collection.

p. 53 'Waterwheel' motif, woman's dress from Saraqib, Syria, author's collection.

—— Women's dresses, Syria, author's collection.

p. 55 Cloth *bohça*, Turkey, sixteenth century, Topkapi Museum, Istanbul.

p. 60 Woman's dress, Bedouin, Sinai, Egypt, author's collection.

p. 71 Cushion cover, Skyros, Sporades, Greece. Benaki Museum, Athens, 147/1.

p. 74 Woman's shift, Macedonia, northern Greece, author's collection.

—— Woman's blouse, Bosača, Slovakia, author's collection.

pp. 126–27 Anthropomorphic motif on shirt RT-02401, feline motif on mantle 2-RT-05901, Paracas Necropolis, National Museum of Anthropology & Archaeology, Lima, Peru. Photograph Eduardo Herrán.

p. 130 Jug, Pierides Collection, Larnaca, Cyprus.

—— Plaque, British Museum GR 1872.6–4.

p. 131 Venus of Lespugue, Musée de l'Homme, Paris.

—— Minoan figurine, British Museum GR 1864.2.2.0.32.

p. 132 Perfume bottle, British Museum GR 1860.4.4.30.

—— Towel, Russia, private collection, Paris.

p. 133 Detail from great felt, Pazyryk, Hermitage Museum, St Petersburg.

p. 135 Figurine, Historical Museum of Razgrad, Bulgaria.

p. 136 Figures with outspread legs. François Hébert-Stevens.

—— Minoan seals, British Museum GR 1947 9–26.2, GR 1921 7–11.2.

p. 138 Ritual mounted worshippers on peasant embroidery, Wang Yarong.

—— Terracotta horse and rider, Boetia, Greece, British Museum GR 1949 7–10.1.

—— Cover, Mithila, India, Calico Museum of Textiles, Ahmedabad, 99A.287.

—— Napkin, Turkey, Ethnographic Museum, Ankara.

p. 140 Pomegranate motif, *suzani*, Nurata, author's collection.

—— Carnation motif, woman's coat, Aleppo, Syria, author's collection.

—— Carnation motif, Coptic cloth AC828, Musée du Louvre, Paris.

p. 142 Gold jewelry, Crete, British Museum GR 1892.5–20.17.

—— Woman's dress, Qutayfé, Syria, Azem Palace Museum, Damascus.

p. 144 Burial shift from Martovce, Tamás Hofer, Edit Fél.

p. 146 Plant motifs. Paulina Mitreva.

p. 151 Saddle lining, *shabrack*, Pazyryk, Hermitage Museum. Rudenko.

—— Mantle, Kunsthistorisches Museum, Weltlicher Schatzkammer, Vienna, XIII 14.

—— Valance, from the Carl Schuster collection, Field Museum of Natural History, Chicago, FM 234389.

p. 153 Gold bovine plaque, Historical Museum of Varna, Bulgaria.

—— Headscarf, G. S. Maslova.

p. 155 Pot, Kansu and ritual bronze, China. Carl Hentze.

—— Man's slipper-sock, Bosansko Grahovo, Zemaljski Museum of Bosnia-Herzegovina, Sarajevo.

p. 156 Sassanid and Egyptian headgear, Slovakian hair arrangements, after drawings by Ursula Müller in Heide Nixdorff exhibition 'Festive Folk Costume', leaflet 3, Berlin 1977, Staatliche Museen Preussischer Kulturbesitz Berlin, Museum für Völkerkunde, Abt. Europa.

—— Uygur woman, cave painting, Chotsko, Turfan, China.

—— Stone idol, Minoussinsk, Carl Hentze.

p. 159 Salmon-skin marriage robe, Ghiliak, Musée de l'Homme, Paris 62.11.1.

ACKNOWLEDGMENTS

p. 160 Solar pictographs, Walter Herdeg. Bouriate drawing, Carl Hentze.

p. 163 Woman's jacket, Pont l'Abbé, Brittany. Musée de Bretagne, Rennes D.60.48/51.

—— Serbian woman's jacket, Olga Ostric.

p. 164 Pazyryk textile patterns. Rudenko.

p. 166 Karakorum highway motifs. Karl Jettmar, Volker Thewalt.

p. 167 Desert tombs of Sind. Ethel-Jane W. Bunting.

p. 170 Hanging, Hong Kong, author's collection.

p. 175 Lotus pattern. Jessica Rawson.

p. 176 Eight Buddhist Precious Things. Wolfram Eberhard, *Lexikon chinesischer Symbole*, Cologne 1983.

p. 177 Turban cover, cushion cover, cloth, Topkapi Museum, Istanbul. Nurhayat Berker, *Islemeler*, Istanbul 1981.

—— Celestial kiosk, Dr Emil Esin.

—— Bath towel, napkin 31/1389, Topkapi Museum, Istanbul.

p. 180 Goldwork bolero, Tunisia, author's collection.

p. 185 Staggered cross motifs. Denise Pop-Câmpeanu.

—— Qaracoche shawl motifs. Musée de l'Homme, Paris 67.100.77.

p. 191 Married woman's stomacher, Regional Museum of Pilsen, Bohemia.

—— Motif 'guardian of the breasts', Narodnoe Iskusstvo, *Il'mikra Medzitova: Marijskoe*, Izzatel'stvo 1985.

—— Tchuvash woman's dress, Musée de l'Homme, Paris 46.6.16.

p. 192 Terracotta figurine, Kara-tépé, Turkestan, Hermitage Museum, St Petersburg; copyright Editions Cercle d'Art, L'Art Barbare Scythe.

—— Russian statuette, Mária Kresz.

p. 198 Tunis pockets. Musée National des Arts Africains et Océaniens, Paris MN.AM.1972.7.17.

p. 199 Ottoman kaftan appliqué. Topkapi Museum, Istanbul 13/829.

p. 200 Bronze Age pot motifs. Musées des Antiquités Nationales, St. Germain-en-Laye, France.

p. 216 Cloth to prepare child for baptism, Daniel Baud-Bovy, *Peasant Art in Switzerland*, Studio 1924.

p. 224 Chimanlals, *Rangoli: Floor Patterns Book*, Bombay n.d.

The task of naming individually all those who have contributed in one way or another to this book would be impossible, but the author no less warmly thanks everyone who has been involved in its creation.

The past thirty years have been devoted to searching for the roots of embroidery and attempting to record the old traditions before they vanish for ever. A lone traveller, the author has been invited into the homes of women in many countries. She has sat on mud floors being offered ill-afforded dry bread and hot tea, or has scooped out food with her hands from a large bowl shared with the women and children after the men had had their fill and left. Such hospitality and insight into women's lives so freely given have been invaluable.

The staff of museums and libraries in many countries have been unstinting in their help and interest and, as a professional linguist and master of five languages, the author has also been able to consult foreign sources, both published and in archives.

To all, from ethnographers of world repute to the simple village women who so painstakingly described their lives, the author extends her most grateful thanks.

Quotation on p. 8 taken from J. Newall, in *The Embroideress*, Vol. I, 1924.

Quotation on p. 86 taken from *A History of Jewish Costume*, London 1967, foreword by James Laver.

Quotation on p. 99 taken from Mária Kresz, *The Art of the Hungarian Furriers*, p. 51.

INDEX

Main references are indicated in **bold** type. Figures in *italic* refer to pages on which illustrations appear.